Stories of the Men
of the
80th Infantry Division
World War Two

Compiled by Robert T. Murrell
Company M 318th Regiment

Edited by Andy Adkins

Table of Contents

Introduction

The 80th Infantry Division was first activated 5 August 1917 at Camp Lee, VA and after extensive training, was shipped overseas and fought in the Artois-Picardy Sector, St. Mihiel Offensive, Somme Offensive, Meuse-Argonne Offensive, first, second and third phases, and deactivated 5 June 1919. It was considered the leading National Army Division in a point of combat time and honors earned. It was third in this respect in the entire American Expeditionary Forces, ranking just after the 2nd and 1st Infantry Divisions. It fought from May 1918 until the Armistice.

In World War II, the 80th Infantry Division was re-activated 15 July 1942 at Camp Forrest, TN and it was the Infantry workhorse of Patton's Third Army, amassing 274 days of combat starting from Omaha Beach on 3 August 1944 when the advance party arrived. It met the Canadian Army to close the Falaise Gap in its first major battle. The division fought at St. Avold, Maginot Line, Siegfried Line, Rhine River, Wiesbaden, Kassel, Erfurt, Jena, Nurnberg, and closing out the war with 200,000 of the German Sixth Army surrendering to them at the Inns River in Austria. It was part of the German Occupation Force and was deactivated 10 January 1946 at Camp Kilmer, NJ.

The story of what, when, and where the 80th Infantry Division fought, to my knowledge has never been told by the men who were in the front line foxholes, the men who saw what was happening in the battle with their own eyes. It is my desire that these men be given a chance to tell what happened as they saw it. It has now been 56 years since they were a part of some of the heaviest action in the entire war, stories that should be part of our history.

For many years, I remained silent on my experiences while with the 80th Infantry Division, a division that made a name for itself in both wars. After a conversation with my daughter Gayle, and of my telling how others were remaining silent on where they fought and what they did, I was told, "Dad, you are one of them. How many times did I ask you what you did, only to be told, I don't want to talk about it?"

In 1973, while attending an 80th Division Veterans Association Reunion at Columbus, Ohio and listening to others tell of their experiences and not knowing where I had fought, I became interested in where I had been and began to accumulate the history of the 80th Division during World War II. It is now my desire to have these men tell their experiences in their own words, and what they witnessed before it is too late.

> *I wish to dedicate this book to my buddies of World War Two, and all those who were attached to the 80th Division, and particularly to the men who sent in their stories. To my wife Doris and children who have been so supportive of me while I have spent so many hours at the computer, both in research and typing the stories.*

Preface

The 80th Division trained at Camp Forrest Tennessee from 15 July 1942 to August 1943. While at Camp Forrest, the Division participated in the Second Army Maneuvers against the Ohio National Guard 83rd Division. In September 1943, it moved to Camp Phillips, Kansas and stayed there until moving in November to participate in the California-Arizona maneuvers under the Pacific Defense Command and camped at Camp Laguna, Arizona in the Mojave Dessert. After a short stay, the Division left in March 1944 for Camp Kilmer, New Jersey. Here the Division was trained in ship evacuation and on 28 June 1944, started boarding the Queen Mary for the European Theater Operation (ETO), landing at Firth of Clyde Scotland on 7 July 1944.

After a long train ride, the Division was staged at various locations around Manchester, England to further hone the skills the men had been taught. The end of July 1944 found the Division moving to Southampton to a staging area to board LST and Liberty Ships which embarked from the channel ports of Southampton, Portland, and vicinity to transport the troops across the English Channel to the shores of France. The advance party landed on 3 August 1944, and the first troops landing at Omaha and Utah Beaches on 5 August 1944. The 317th Regiment was the first to disembark at 1400, followed by the 318th Regiment at 2000 and transported in sections for a short motor march of approximately twenty-three miles into a tactical bivouac area in the vicinity of St. Germain-de-Varreville and Coigny, France on 6 August 1944.

Throughout the night, the Division continued to arrive. At 0100, the Divisional Artillery disembarked and moved to a bivouac area in the vicinity of Saint-Jores, at which place the Division's Forward Command Post was opened. The Divisional Artillery was followed by the 319th Infantry, which also had bivouacked in the vicinity, the 780th Ordinance Company, the 80th Cavalry Reconnaissance Troop which had assembled at St. Germain-de-Lanier, and the 305th Combat Engineer Battalion, which also had assembled in the vicinity of Saint-Jores.

The following day 6 August, the 305th Medical Battalion, Special Troops, and the Quartermaster Company, along with the 702nd Tank Battalion, which had been attached to the 80th Infantry Division, disembarked and moved to Fretout. Immediately upon entering the bivouac areas, the men were busied with general shakedowns, cleaning and adjusting equipment, and zealously preparing themselves for that which was shortly to come. But at the same time, the men contributed to the general improvement of the tactical bivouac areas.

While the 80th Infantry Division had been staging in France, the rapidity and strength of the breakthrough at Avranches by the Third Army's newly assigned VIII Corps and the success of the attack on the Brittany Peninsula had temporarily thrown the Germans on this front, into utter confusion. The enemy at this time had committed approximately forty-five divisions on the Normandy front and had managed to build up a mobile reserve of five Panzer divisions. This reserve, together with remnants of the units swept aside at Avranches, as soon as they could muster enough strength, counterattacked to cut the U.S. Third Army's rather weak supply line in the vicinity of Avranches and separate a potent portion of the Third Army from the remainder of the Allied Forces. To meet this great threat, the 80th Infantry Division received its first combat orders.

Robert T. Murrell
Company M 318th Infantry Regiment

Having had prior Military Service with the 325th Observation Corps of the old Army Air Corps and having served out my time, or so I thought, I was called back to duty on 21 July 1942, only a few short days after re-activation of the 80th Infantry Division at Camp Forrest, TN.

After being on assignment from the 80th Division as an instructor to the 2nd Ranger Battalion, I was returned to the 80th just before the Ranger Battalion went overseas. While in the states and being part of the Tennessee maneuvers, and Camp Laguna, CA where we trained in the Mojave Desert, then moving to Fort Dix, New Jersey, where we began to hone our skills we had been taught, and awaiting word to board the Queen Mary. And then, on to ETO.

Boarding the Queen Mary, on 28 June 1944, I remember the voyage across the Atlantic Ocean. I had been made Sergeant of the Guard and given an armband that had MP in great big letters and a big white button, which also had MP on it to wear on my jacket. I had the run of the entire ship. While others had a given time to eat, I was able to go into what was known as the Galley anytime and have a bite to eat or a cup of coffee. I was able to go anywhere on the ship including the bridge and the engine room, which I remember the engines to be really huge and throbbing with power to propel us across the ocean in a short time. While making my rounds across the fantail, I would delay long enough to see the wake in an "S" form as the Queen Mary would make a change of course every five to seven minutes. The reason was that a U-Boat could not lay a course on her fast enough to fire a torpedo and hit her. It was on the third or fourth day a drill had been scheduled for the crews of the Anti-Aircraft Guns to fire at drones being pulled by aircraft. But not knowing that a drill had been scheduled, I was really afraid we were being attacked, but after a while I determined it was a drill, after seeing planes pulling targets behind them. This was for the Gunners to test their skills.

Upon reaching Scotland, we boarded trains for a long train ride to the Manchester, England area, known as Tatton Park. The balance of the troops went to surrounding areas. Here, we were to hone our skills in weaponry and map reading. Daylight was very long, not becoming dark until close to midnight. In our idle time we would make rings from the silver Fluorine, about the size of a silver dollar. We would pound on the edge until it would flare out and then punch a hole in the center so we could wear it. I lost mine in France.

In crossing the English Channel and nearing the coast of France, we saw sunken ships and aerial balloons with cables attached to them to prevent any strafing or sea craft being able to get close to the landing site, which was Utah Beach. When it was our turn to be unloaded from the ship we were on, the LSI (Landing Ship Infantry) came in on an angle and punched a hole in the side of the boat. I remember the Captain giving the person operating the LSI hell, as he would be delayed due to the repair at the shipyard. It was like yesterday that I remember going over the side of the ship and down a rope ladder into the LSI, the short ride to shore and the ramp roping, the troops running down the ramp into the shallow water, and up to the top of our landing area, to be loaded on trucks. I saw my first large German gun emplacement on the hill alongside of where we landed, pointed out to sea. It had been bombed out. We were loaded on trucks and rode all day and when it was dark, we were then unloaded in a field. I recall hearing my first artillery firing, but was too inexperienced to know that it was our artillery. It wasn't long before I could tell the difference of outgoing, as opposed to incoming artillery.

Our route of march took us through St. Lo in a mop-up of the town and it was here I remember a sniper shooting at us from a church steeple as we came down a hill into the town. I also saw my first aerial dogfight between a German and an American plane as we drove down the hill, toward the town. Memory doesn't serve me as to which of the pilots had to parachute out after he was shot down, but I believe it to be the German. Traveling on trucks as we rode along, we saw hundreds of destroyed and burning vehicles from both sides, as well as bloated bodies of humans and animal carcasses littering the route to Saint-Hilaire, a distance of 75 miles. Resting overnight, we again boarded trucks the next morning, and driving to the vicinity of Vaiges, a distance of 62 miles, again, camping overnight, and an additional 6 miles the next morning to the vicinity of Charmes. We continued on trucks going through several villages, being fired on by snipers, finding mines, and blown roadways. We were warned about picking up any equipment, as it could be bobby-trapped. We continued on through St. Suzanne, and Sillé-Le-Guillaume, which was being defended by the 9th German Panzer Division. We encountered several roadblocks while receiving artillery and small arms fire. The rolling hills and thickly wooded area was a good area for the enemy to hold us back, but they did not have enough troops in the area to contain us. It was here we suffered several casualties, including one man being killed by sniper fire, several being wounded by mines, and one officer being wounded by a booby trap. Everywhere we moved, buildings had been totally destroyed by either bombs or shells, or pock-marked by perhaps .50 Caliber ammunition.

A large buildup of enemy troops southwest of Falaise with the mission to cut the supply lines of the U.S. Third Army, was to lead to the battle known as the Argentan-Falaise Gap. This was to be our first major battle, fighting through hedgerows one after the other. These hedgerows were five or six feet high and were made up of earth, rocks, and either trees or bushes, and sometime both, with openings, to go from one to the other. (One can compare these hedgerows to a farmers field he had put wire around, but instead of wire, earth and rocks, etc. were used.) An American soldier could be on one side of the hedgerow without knowing a German was just on the other side. It was difficult fighting in these hedgerows, fighting from one to the other, taking each one as we came to it, an advance of a few hundred yards, if that much. A tank going over a hedgerow would have its belly facing in an upward position and the Germans would fire an 88 into the bottom of the tank and destroy it. (At this point or there about, some tanks were fitted with plow heads to rip out these walls of earth so they could go through and not over them.) The capture of Argentan would complete the Argentan-Falaise Gap. The 318th Infantry Regiment in fighting through these hedgerows was assigned the objective of seizing Argentan. Setting up my section of machine guns of "M" 318th in what I thought at the time was a good place, on an embankment (lacking war experience) overlooking a roadway running from our right to left and running down in a curve into some woods, also overlooking a wheat field or some sort of grain field. Barbed wire entanglements were in front and also alongside us on the right. An enemy tank came up this road firing its machine guns at us as it approached. A Sgt. from one of my machine gun squads had the old Springfield rifle with a grenade attachment and he immediately put a grenade on the rifle and fired at the tank, with the projectile luckily going into the open hatch. Bye, bye tank crew. Shortly after this happened an artillery shell came in on us killing three of my men, including an officer, and wounding several others. Myself, I had my pistol belt ripped off by either rifle fire or machine gun fire I know not which, and a bullet going through my helmet neither of which touched me. As I tried to move under, and clipping the barbed wire with my wire clippers, several machine gun rounds hit the wire I was cutting; again I was unscathed. My first sight of war was a man's leg with the boot, having blown into the air, when he had stepped on a Schu mine, (a small round type mine designed to kill or maim anyone stepping on it) and returning to the ground with the heavy booted leg making a plop like sound. This is what I found war to be, my first reality of war and what it is all about. It didn't take long for me to become battle-hardened when I saw a dead German soldier, laying in a barnyard and a pig eating on him, causing me to laugh at his fate.

To our front was a wooded area, and the grain field between our positions and the woods. When we eventually fought our way into the woods, we found a curtain of greens (tree branches which were hung on wire stretched from tree to tree) hiding all movement from our eyes. Later in the battle and after we had advanced through this wall of trees, we found we didn't have good positions as the enemy could see every move we made. Our casualties were heavy.

The 317th Infantry Regiment came to our aid and after three days of heavy fighting, we were into Argentan, meeting up with the Canadian Army. The battle, which started with an enemy machine gun burst, became a baptism of fire for the regiment and the division, which, at last, had come to grips with a determined enemy. From the Morning reports of Company M 318th Infantry Regiment, this battle lasted from 19 August to 21 August 1944.

On 22 August 1944 in the vicinity of Pilou, France a member of my machine gun section, told me he had enough of this war and he was going to surrender. I did my best to talk him out of surrendering. However, he had his mind made up and got up and started walking down a slope to our left front with his hands over his head and the last I saw of him he disappeared into a wooded area. In 1983 on a visit back to the battlefield, I saw his name on the Missing in Action Wall, at the American Military Cemetery at Hamm, Luxembourg.

On 26 August 1944 we were loaded onto trucks for a 250-mile ride to the vicinity of La Riviére, France. The last major city we passed was Orleans, France and the next day we were again loaded onto trucks and traveled about 330 miles to Jalons, France. Again boarding trucks we were transported an additional 45 miles, de-trucking in the vicinity of Les Grandes Logas, France on 30 August 1944 where we engaged the enemy. As a Section Sgt. of machine guns, I would place my section of guns to give overhead fire for the advancing infantry. Many times I watched as the Rifle Company we were supporting would be firing from the hip in waves. One wave of men moving forward and then dropping to the ground and the second group would then do the same. My machine gunners would watch this and when they got close to our fire we would cease-fire. This was done by watching our tracers and where they were hitting.

The 3rd Battalion 318th Infantry continued in several minor battles. It was while we were engaged with the enemy at Belleville, France on 10 September 1944 that Tom Klee, my best friend and buddy, was hit in the head. Just a day or two before his being hit, he made a statement; he was tired of digging in. This night he laid alongside of me on top of the ground, and the Germans threw a counterattack at us. It was a bitter counterattack and in the dark, it was difficult to see the enemy approaching. It was in this counterattack that Tom was hit. It is my firm belief, that had he dug in as I had, while he may not have gone the balance of the war as I did, he may have lived to see another battle. After the counterattack was defeated, we made a stretcher of saplings and raincoats, and we carried Tom to the First Aid station where he died of his wounds a few days later. (A year or so after the war was over, Tom's father found my address in Tom's belongings and called me and ask me if I would come to the service of Tom's return and burial in the USA. Really not wanting to go, but yet feeling I must, I went. On my arrival in the town in Ohio where Tom was to be buried, Tom's dad ask me to come to his home. Taking me by the arm and seating me on a sofa, and him sitting down on the floor in front of me, his eyes making contact with mine, then ask; tell me how my son died. Another bomb had been dropped. Do I tell the truth? Do I make him a hero, which he was, as he had received a Silver Star? I sat for a while without answering. An inner voice, telling me don't tell the truth. As I sat and looked into that man's eyes, seeing that he was waiting for me to tell him what he wanted to know, I lied and spoke of how Tom fought hard in that counterattack. He was hit in the first volley of the attack. To this day, both Joe and Tom bear on my mind. I just cannot shake them.)

Shortly after crossing the Moselle River at Dieulouard and fighting our way through Loisy and Atton, the 3rd Battalion of the 318th Infantry Regiment had captured Mousson Hill and the enemy launched two unsuccessful counterattacks in a determined effort to drive the 3rd Battalion off the hill. This hill was a lookout point that made it possible to see for many miles around.

On the 15th of September, an enemy counterattack succeeded in cutting through the tenuously stretched supply line reaching from the bridgehead area to Mousson Hill and the Battalion. The enemy, as well as the adjacent terrain, retook Atton 1½ miles south of Mousson Hill. The 3rd Battalion and two platoons of AT Company and Company "M" with its machine guns and 81 mm mortars and TD units (minus Headquarters) were cut off from the bridgehead area. The battalion had run low on ammo and batteries for the radios along with medical supplies. Calls came for volunteers for a patrol to try to work their way through enemy lines for supplies; I volunteered to lead the patrol. Memory doesn't serve me as to who the others were on the patrol, but we worked our way through the enemy lines and received the supplies we were to take back. Medical supplies, mail, ammo and batteries. We had done well so far on our return to our positions, and was halfway through an orchard near the top of the hill, when the enemy spotted and fired at us knocking a box of rations off the shoulder of one of the men on the patrol, only for him to say "Damn, I'm hungry and no GD German is going to keep me from eating." He picked up the box, putting it back on his shoulder, and saying let's go men and we did, reaching our lines safely. (It was this action of my leading this patrol through enemy lines and return without losing a man or the supplies we were carrying on our backs and shoulders that I was awarded the Silver Star.) While we were on this patrol, L-4 Artillery Observation planes had dropped supplies in our area. After being surrounded for a few days, Company B 319th Infantry fought its way through to us, thus breaking the German circle of troops. It was while we were on this hill that Brig. General Searby, Commander of the Artillery, was KIA from a machine gun burst during a counterattack.

After being relieved by the 319th Infantry Regiment, we moved along with engagements in Millery where we fought the enemy from 22 September to 24 September 1944, when we moved to Bratte, France. It was here while assigning positions for my guns and as I walked a path on the edge of the woods where I had just placed my guns, I saw an ammo truck blown up on the road below me. Hearing voices I turned to where they were coming from and saw two Germans coming down the path toward me. Calling "Halt" and pointing my rifle at them, both raised their hands over their heads and surrendered. Removing their weapons and marching them back to where my first gun had been placed, I turned them over to be taken to the rear. It was then I discovered, I had the failed to throw my safety off on my rifle, I just about crapped. This action brought me the Bronze Star.

Sometime in September my section of machine guns was assigned to "I" Company, 318th Infantry with the objective being to capture the high ground (Hill 351) west of Morey, France. After the capture of Hill 351, we were told to stay there for the night. The enemy, which had vacated the hill, had dug foxholes on the hill, so we didn't have to dig our own, but rather use the ones they had dug. I had been assigned two new men that evening and I assigned one of them to a squad and the other I told to stay with me and occupy my foxhole. That night, the enemy not knowing we had taken their former positions and was using the foxholes they had dug on the hilltop, came back to use their old foxholes. I had told the new man he was to take the first watch and I would take the second and etc. It was while he was on watch the enemy came back. One of the Germans whose hole we were in, jumped into what I believe was his hole, his heel striking my thumb, and me saying damn, the new man said shh, (it was quite dark) and the German was bayoneted by the new man and taking the German's rifle, shot his buddy on the edge of the hole. Mind you, this man had no battle experience, but yet, he performed like a veteran.

We had captured a few of the enemy, and they were being guarded in slit trenches. When daylight came I surmise our artillery had not been made aware of our being on the hilltop, began laying an artillery barrage in on our positions. We quickly used the flares of the day to signal we were on the hilltop, however, the artillery either didn't see them or hadn't been given the code of the day, continued to fire on us, making it necessary for us to vacate the hill. While doing so, one of the enemy prisoners started to laugh, only for one of the rifleman of Company "I" to take a grenade from his bandoleer, pulling the pin as he did so and dropped the grenade into the slit trench with the statement, enjoy your last laugh. One less enemy.

It was rain and more rain that fell sometime in October, causing the rivers to flood. The ground became so muddy the troops could not move and the division went into defensive positions in the vicinity NE of Lixieres, France. We were there until 8 November 1944 when we moved to and engaged the enemy in Clemery, France. While here, I received a three-day pass to Paris. To me it was awe inspiring to see this city. The Eiffel Tower, Notre Dame Cathedral and the many other sights too numerous to mention, and be out of the battle zone. So that the MPs would know us as front line troops, we wore a green felt tab on our shoulder loop. Actually it made me feel good to see so many men wearing this felt, and know as I did, what war is all about and more or less rubbing it in on the rear line troops. If it was a case of trouble, you had a buddy on both sides of you.

Continuing to fight our way across France on 26 November 1944, and in the general direction of St. Avold, France, we came upon pillboxes at Fort Bambiderstroff, France. Fort Bambiderstroff sat down in a valley with a road coming down into the valley into the face of the Fort. The ground in front of it was completely bare of any vegetation with barbed wire entanglements. (On my return in 1983 the Fort, though it had been blown up with dynamite, the outline of the Fort and the bare ground was still there.) I remember this Fort as I entered it and found it had five floors below ground and tunnels to connect to other pillboxes. I led several GIs down the steps to the lower levels capturing several German soldiers as we descended its depths. I was awarded the Bronze Star the second time for this action.

We moved from there into St. Avold and Longville and several towns and villages and were in Bettwiller, France, being readied to cross over into Germany, when we received word to pack up and be ready to move out on an hour's notice.

19 December 1944, we received word to board our vehicles and move to Fischbach, Luxembourg a distance of approximately 150 miles, and to travel without delay. Word had reached General Patton of the German breakthrough in the north, and we were to help stop the German counterattack, in what we now know as the Battle of the Bulge. This trip was made in open vehicles, in weather which was at the freeze mark, and was in itself a battle to keep warm. Men huddled in their blankets and anything else they could find to help keep warm. Patton had given the order to drive full speed ahead and not to use the "Cat Lights" (the head light had a covering over it that when driving at night the lights pointed down at the immediate road in front of the vehicles so that they could not be seen from above and not at any great distance in front and they also resembled a cat's eye). Had there been any German planes in the air that night they would have had a field day with the column of troops on the move.

Arriving in Fischbach, Luxembourg at 1500 on 20 December 1944, and moving by foot to Colmar, Luxembourg on 22 December at 0600 and cutting across the fields we attacked Ettelbruck, Luxembourg. We went through a field west and south of Ettelbruck with the artillery firing white phosphate shells and their bursting a few yards ahead of us. Snow here was the worst they had, in many years. It was difficult to walk in it as it was close to a foot or more deep. After a very hard battle in taking the city of Ettelbruck, the 1st and 2nd Battalions were withdrawn from the 318th position in Ettelbruck to be attached to the 4th Armored Division to relieve the 101st Airborne Troops that were surrounded, in Bastogne, leaving the 3rd Battalion to cover the entire area, of Ettelbruck.

On 23 December 1944, just as I was approaching the two guns I had set in a draw facing NE, a direct hit was made on one of the guns; all the Crewmembers were killed. We continued to hold the town until 2 January 1945 when we went into Corps Reserve.

As I said before the snow was knee deep and the weather was the coldest it had been for years. If a man were to be wounded, he must keep moving or freeze to death. Water in the canteens froze. Snow was eaten instead of water. Company M 318 lost 1 Officer, 6 Enlisted Man, Killed in Action

7 Lightly Wounded in Action, 3 Seriously Wounded in Action, 4 Lightly Injured in Action and five Non Battle casualties, in the capture of Ettelbruck.

Leaving Ettelbruck, Luxembourg we traveled to Wiltz, Luxembourg on 23 January 1945, in Regimental Reserve and received hot food and a USO Show, leaving for Beaufort, Luxembourg on 27 January 1945.

While in defensive positions and engaging the enemy in Beaufort, Luxembourg from 27 January 1945 until 15 February 1945 when we moved to 1 Mile SE of Biesdorf. It was while we were in Beaufort, my good friend and buddy Bill Ewing was given a furlough to the States for 90 days. Captain Kessler, our Company Commander told me, to have Bill come to the CP, but I was not to tell him he was going home. When I got to where Bill was quartered, I said, "Bill, what the hell have you done, the Captain wants to see you right now, on the double." Going in and giving a very smart salute, and saying Staff Sgt. William E. Ewing reporting as ordered, and Captain Kessler telling him of his going home, without further ado, he turned and said to me I would knock you on your ass if you weren't such a good buddy, and then grabbed me and hugged me with both of us crying our eyes out. The war was over before he was able to get back to our company. After the war we visited back and forth with the other until his death.

Crossing into Biesdorf, Germany from Beaufort on 16 February 1945 into defensive positions we received replacements and engaged the enemy in the vicinity of Cruchten, Germany. Fighting our way south where we went through several towns and villages until we reached Serf, Germany and crossed the Rhine in an LCI into Weiskirchen, Germany. From here we begin to move very fast, Oberkirchen, Kaiserslautern, Waldfischbach, continuing on until we reached Kassel, Germany 3 April 1945. From Kassel to Siebleben, Apfelstadt, Gotha, Eggsätt, Erfurt, Jena, and nearing Chemnitz when we were halted, being told the Russians were going to take that town, but before we were told, Company M 318th, was given an assignment to reconnoiter positions on the far outskirts of Chemnitz. Pulling up to an Antitank Gun, we asked where the roadblock was and their pointing ahead of them, we moved out in our jeep only to see we had over run our own roadblock and was facing the German roadblock. The driver of our jeep, whose name escapes my mind, when seeing the German roadblock tried to make a 180 only for the jeep to be hit broadside. Jumping out on both sides we hit the ditch, looking from the ditch down over to the group of buildings, I saw several Germans gathered at a building down over the hill, and I put my rifle to my shoulder and fired a shot at them. To this day, I don't know if I hit one of them or not. All I know is we worked our way back to a group of buildings we had just passed, and where by chance we found four bicycles and pedaled our way back to our lines. I often wonder what the crew of that Anti-tank crew thought as we rode by them on bikes. This day, I shall remember all the days of my life, as this day was my third wedding anniversary (16 April, 1945).

The 80th Division was stopped before going into Chemnitz, due to a decision to let the Russians have that area. We then reversed our direction, west back to Gera and headed south by truck to Nurnberg, where the 3rd Infantry Division had just taken the town and we came in to mop up and patrol the town until 27 April 1945. It was while here I got to see the very large stadium where Hitler held all his rallies.

Again boarding trucks we moved to Holdorf, Germany 4 May 1945 and then to cross into Braunau, Austria on the framework of the blown bridge and where we were billeted and patrolled the town.

We boarded trains to Attnang, Austria on 7 May 1945. It was on this train ride that we had purchased tomatoes and onions along with bread and we had sandwiches made from the tomato and onion. We also had been able to lay our hands on several bottles of wine and we made merry. On 8 May 1945, War was declared to be over and the Company celebrated until we had to move out on patrol of the Mondsee Mountains, where we found a pocket of the enemy that did not know the war was over and had a short fire fight with them, finally convincing them the war was over they surrendered.

The German 6th Army surrendered to the 80th Division after General McBride had told the Commanding General of the German Army that all of his soldiers who were on the American side of the Inn River would become American prisoners while those who didn't get across by midnight would have to be taken by the Russians. The 318th Regiment helped to control the many prisoners of the 6th German Army who had surrendered to the 80th Division. After a few days of patrolling the town in keeping Law and Order, we were sent to Sonnhofen, Germany, a place where the German youth was trained.

While here the top three grades of Non Com's were given a building to use as a Clubhouse and I was made an officer of the club, and given the job of Liquor Control Officer. (Each of the top three grades of NCOs were to receive a bottle of whiskey once a month. This bottle could not be given to them and had to be rationed to them, so the club was formed where they received a card with 23 numbers around the edge, when they received their drink a number was punched and when the card was used out they were cut off.) I remember one trip I made with a German (his name was Bill) we had hired as a bartender who knew of a Potato Schnapps still, and told of our being able to buy the schnapps, but it was in the French area. He and I along with a jeep driver went into the French occupied area and received permission to purchase the schnapps, purchased fifteen gallon of pure uncut schnapps and brought it back to the club and cut it three times with water and served it over the bar. This club was the former chow hall for the youth movement.

It was from here that I received word I had enough points to be discharged. The first wave of what was known as the high point men had left and I was in the second group to leave. I was sent to Camp Lucky Strike to be processed to go home. I was asked if I wanted to change my patch to that of the 6th Armored Division as that was the group I was to come home with, I declined their patch and came home with my 80th Patch still intact. Boarding the Rock Hill Victory ship at Marseilles, France, making our way through the Mediterranean Sea, past the Rock of Gibraltar and for the 23 days it took to make the trip home over very rough seas, and to describe more fully, it would be like a match stick in a tub of water you were stirring up with your hand. Landing at Newport News, Virginia, I was sent to Camp Attebury, IN, where I was discharged on 26 October 1945.

Lt. Charles Coward
Company I, 318th Infantry Regiment
The Diary Written While in the Hospital

Leaving New York and the United States on 26 July 1944 on the SS Argentina in a convoy, arriving 7 August in Gurek Scotland, boarding a train to Hunition, England arriving approximately 9 August 1944, where we were classified and earmarked per our specialties of training. Our "special" groups were moved out promptly and along with hundreds of other infantrymen sent to Southampton where we were "sorted" out once again.

We were issued weapons and equipment and placed aboard a relatively small ship for the crossing of the English Channel to the shores of France! The crossing was uneventful except for our patrolling aircraft above and fast, British, torpedo boats weaving about: The threat of U Boats was still present. The chatter among us on board was more like "What the Hell, what's the difference where we are going... we know what we are going to do. And we're 'in for the duration'". Because we were a mixture of men not from any single, identifiable group, but from all backgrounds, rank and training... we naturally wondered WHERE we might wind up? Certainly, the 80th Inf. Div. was nowhere in mind!

The landing nets were put over side, LCIs pulled in below and over the railings and down to the wallowing boats. We quickly moved to the beach and disembarked, we had arrived on Omaha Beach 14 August. Task forces rounded up into "special" groups and we were ordered up and over the sand bluffs. Much wreckage and devastation was everywhere, burned out vehicles of all descriptions, abandoned equipment of all types and coiled up wire/steel buttresses shunt aside to make way for landing craft. The half-sunken ships forming a barrier immediately offshore sat stark and unrealistic against the horizon toward England. We were immediately transported to a Repel Depot. Passing through towns such as St. Lo, (obliterated by our B-17s), Lemans, Fontainebleau, and up to the vicinity of the Moselle River. Patton's 3rd Army had broken out at St. Lo, following the destruction of most of the German 4th Army at the Falaise Gap. I soon became aware that I was destined to be made part of this Third Army, but still did not know which specific outfit? I vividly recall the "glow" at night from the east... and the faint rumble in the far distance where heavy fighting had to be. The eastern horizon would flicker and the earth shook. A seasoned GI told us that the shells bursts, lights, and rumble were commonly referred to as "Corps Serenade," a term originating in the North Africa desert warfare.

I finally joined the 80th Infantry Division on 10 September 1944 near the town of Marbach, France where the Division was for all intents... resting... in a bivouac "resting" in an area three to five miles west of Dieulouard, France on the Moselle River, following heavy fighting at the Falaise Gap and racing across the miles in pursuit of the remnants of the German 4th Army, I soon learned that the enemy had taken up well dug-in positions along the Moselle River and we could expect the worst/best they could throw at us. Upon arrival I was assigned as Platoon leader of Company I 318th Infantry (3rd Battalion) and immediately went to each man to inform him who I was and what I was there for. I was amazed to discover that they had not had a platoon leader since leaving the US! A non-commissioned officer, S/Sgt. Dooley, had been their leader and he was glad to see me on the scene. I couldn't say at this point, that I was in any way glad/pleased with the assignment, because much had to be experienced and discovered; particularly with the 155 Long Toms emplaced a few hundred yards from our position, firing across the Moselle River. You may well imagine how I felt... "new guy on the block"... "how will he do in combat"... "will he lead us"... "take care of us"... "will we take care of him?"... a million unanswered questions.

It's impossible to reassure anyone about anything unless one had "been there" with first-hand experience: especially a 25 year old 1st Louie fresh from stateside and not a regular with the Blue Ridge Mountains Boys! I was, at least 98.6 and in excellent physical shape... well-versed in all infantry weapons and accustomed to taking orders as an enlisted man... and if necessary, "give orders" for the good of the mission and/or the GIs themselves.

I am not certain where I made the decision to ALWAYS "eat with the platoon!"... There were times when I was sanctioned in some ways for not eating with the CO and other officers who had occasionally requested I have food with them. They soon discovered that I would not... and I suppose someone entered a negative remark in my 201 file somewhere? Here, in the hospital, I feel the same... I wouldn't change a thing! I shall not expound on this point any further... just to say was/is my part of MY Leadership credo.

I had no sooner arrived as Weapons Platoon Leader of I Company... 3rd Battalion, 318th Infantry dug-in just outside of Marbach on 10 September 1944, until orders came down and I was informed we would be jumping off to cross the Moselle River on 11 September 1944. (They didn't waste any time for my "test" or to get my feet wet!). On the morning of 11 September we proceeded to a position, via Dieulouard on the banks of the river. The 305th Combat Engineers with the 317th Infantry Regiment had earlier forced a crossing head. Our own 318th Infantry came under artillery fire in attempts to assist the 317th consolidate their bridgehead crossing. Reports filtered down that the 317th had taken the hamlet of Bezaumont on high ground just to the east of the Moselle.

They also had driven southeast beyond Bezaumont, while elements of the 318th (Co. L) had crossed the river, northward, to the town of Loisy.

It was a bright day, although the entire Moselle River was at flood stage!... upon arrival to the river's edge we were confronted by a narrow canal with what appeared to be a dam beyond... leading across the river-proper. Our outfit forded the canal in water up to our armpits and once we made it to the dam we climbed up and shuffled across... single file with shells exploding in the river nearby. The top of the dam had wide, wooden planks placed on top thus making it easier for us to navigate with all of our equipment. The light machine guns were "broken" into smaller parts. As were the 60 mm mortars to make it easier to carry. The larger problem was having each GI carry as much ammo/mortar rounds as he could... plus his own rifle, belt, and bulky jacket... you name it! I at once learned that the most important piece of equipment was the "primus stove"... the question was always asked "Who's got the stove?" I don't know if all of the other platoons had "a stove"... but we DID and it was always #1 on our checklist. A bit later I also learned that the next in line of importance was the shelter-half... that small piece of OD canvas that "did it ALL"... particularly in the flooded rainy Moselle Valley. We wrapped ourselves in it, cover our holes and trenches with it, bound our wet feet with it... everything but make a tent out of it.

10

Our own Artillery supported us in the crossing very effectively... laying shells along the east bank not 200 yards to our front. The shelling lifted... almost magically as we neared the east shore. I had learned much from the Forward Artillery Observers and their invaluable contribution and bravery during a battle... they were always with us and in many instance in front of us... calling in targets under the most difficult situations. At times when they, themselves, were about to be overrun they would call their very locations to be shelled!

After crossing the river, we moved to positions approximately 1/4 mile east of the river, just below Bezaumont, reportedly held by the 317th Infantry. We dug in to secure positions against a counterattack. Soon after our arrival the Germans commenced shelling of the bridgehead area with fairly "good accuracy." The 305th Combat Engineers were erecting a pontoon bridge across the Moselle River, all the while being shelled.

We saw the first elements of the Field Artillery moving into positions to our right rear and also being greeted to the enemy shellfire. We watched the P-47s strafe what seemed to be just east of the 317th Infantry that held Bezaumont. We were to make contact with the 317th Infantry but as yet we had not, just reports that Captain Fountain (Company I Commander) had orders to leave our positions and pull back to positions just 500 yards south of the pontoon bridge and set up a road block on the road that run parallel to the river. Once again, we dug in near the river's edge. (Time 1800 dusk) A heavy counterattack was expected sometime that night or early the next morning and it was anticipated that they would zero-in on our dug-in positions. It worked exactly as planned! Captain Fountain, our CO, moved I Company back to the east bank where we once again dug-in to wait the expected counterattack. The pontoon bridge was extremely active with vehicles/supplies immediately to our left... no lights whatsoever... just the eerie sound of engines, tracks and muffled voices. Portions of our battalion established a roadblock on the roadway that ran parallel to the river (Time 1800-2000 hr. and dark). While in this position, we also watched the Ack-Ack (633rd AAA AW Battalion) move in and set up. We are under 88 fire that was inaccurate, and this made us dig a little deeper like mad men.

Most of the night was uneventful except for shelling; however about 0400 the next morning all hell broke loose in an area seemingly 2 miles north and northeast. (We could hear our armor crossing the river that night.)

Tracers were lighting the skies as the 20 mm arched overhead. Also we heard heavy shelling from tanks and their direct fire. We saw TDs pulling back but heard later that the Regimental Executive Officer Colonel Golden stopped them, how I don't know but they turned around. Our tanks "sailed" in and cleared the Jerries, with 50 Caliber ammo. Soon we had 20-mm rounds flying over our heads, along with artillery firing point blank into enemy armor that had penetrated to within 300 yards of the pontoon bridge. (Visibility fair.) This counterattack was beaten off. Around 0530 or 0600 spasmodic firing from German machine guns was coming from a distance, also our own .50 Caliber. We also learned that Company L 317th Regiment was nearly wiped out in the vicinity of Loisy and the 318th Regimental Headquarters was "chewed up" with the Regimental CO and Regimental Chaplain being captured... only to escape and return to our lines.

The next day 12 September 1944 under clear skies, we observed P-47 Thunderbolts on the scene dropping 500 lb bombs and strafing the area beyond Bezaumont and the areas northeast of our bridgehead. They were spectacular! We watched anxiously as one of the P-47s returned over our lines with smoke coming from his cowing... at about 500-800 feet!.. Once he cleared the river line a lone figure tumbled from the cockpit and opened his chute. He landed in a tree and his plane exploded when it struck the ground nearby... black, oily smoke hung in the still air.

That same day we were ordered to leave our positions on the river edge and our objective was... attack Loisy... a quick follow up to keep the Jerries off-balance. I believe the entire 3rd Battalion was involved with this one, along with the 4th Armored tanks. It was our first view of the carnage of the early morning Jerry attacks. A number of Sherman tanks were disabled and unmanned, but a larger number of Panthers... some still smoldering... was scattered across the landscape. Our line of attack was distributed among the Shermans as we approached Loisy... crouching low as the cracks of small arms fire came down on us. I do not recall any casualties in our sector.

I remember Loisy too well... .that was a town Company I reoccupied, following the beginning of our 3rd Battalion's attack toward Mousson Hill. As we came closer to Loisy, two Shermans preceded our company. They fired their 50s & 30s into the first buildings. No response. The Shermans cautiously advanced in single file, some 25 yards apart. Squads of infantry went ahead of the tanks, entering some buildings and skipping others. There were no reports of any anti-tank weapons so far? Approximately 30 structures made up the town of Loisy, one main street and two feeders, or side streets that were all messed up with rubble/debris. We understood Company L had been overrun during the early morning counterattack by the Germans.

As our company approached Loisy, the Shermans began spewing lead into the first nearby buildings. One platoon rode the tanks while the balance was on foot. Setting up our light machine guns in advantageous positions, one to fire down the street and the other through a hole in a large wall to cover the rear of the houses. We grenaded the area to explode any booby traps/mines which might be planted. We proceeded to go through the hole single file with all our equipment. (Approximately 30 buildings made up the town, one main street and two feeder—which were messy. Tanks were blowing everything to hell; several GIs were hit by the first burst of Jerry automatic fire! The Tanks when they heard the burst of the Jerry burp guns fired 75 mm rounds into the suspected enemy positions and were silenced with their 75s. An "S" mine was set off close by, by a GI which didn't explode but hit the man in the thigh, causing him to howl like hell, but, was more scared than anything else, all he had was a badly bruised thigh.

We cleared the town in approximately three-quarters of an hour, and took about 20 prisoners. Several German bodies were lying alongside the street and an abandoned automatic weapon rested nearby. A couple of German Medics were also taken. Several of the buildings were set on fire, and confusion was all over the town. We established a roadblock on the northeast corner of the town with bazookas and one 57-mm gun that had been brought up. The balance of us pulled back into the town and ordered to form a perimeter of defense on the northern edge of town. It started to rain and get cold as we sent out patrols of 6 men to see what was to the front of us, (approximately 400 yards) the patrols started out at dusk and got one hundred yards from the wood line (they were being covered by machine guns from our position) when they heard "Kamerad" and a shot, with everyone hitting the dirt, we knew it was an M-1 and again we heard "Kamerad" and then a white flag appeared. Seven prisoners were taken young kids and scared as hell. I relate to this incident, here, because of another "surrender experience" we had, weeks later, just outside of the town of Morey: That one was tragic! Incidentally, most of the prisoners seemed to be very young; however, the older non-coms sprinkled among them were arrogant hardened troopers. I recall one company grade officer being taken, and he was in "full-dress" uniform when he surrendered, also blond, arrogant and non-cooperative, even with his hands behind his head/neck!

13 September and it is raining hard all day, and it is cold and after securing the town we set up outposts of the town. Shelling still fell on us but was not accurate, just bothersome. We were briefed on an attack we were to make the next day. 14 September being a fair, clear day we started out on our mission of attacking and holding the town of Atton and proceed up the steep incline of Mousson Hill (High as Hell), take the top and fortified hill. Scouting reports revealed that little resistance, if any could be expected in ATTON, which we must do to start up the hill. It had to be assumed the Jerries were well dug-in, in fortified positions and ready to defend their ground at all costs. The top of Mousson Hill presented a clear view and domination of much of Alsace and on a fairly clear day one could see Metz to the north! Pont a Mousson is a city on the Moselle, just to the west of the mount itself. We heard later that the 317th Regiment had made a crossing to Pont a Mousson via assault boats, with heavy casualties.

Attacking at 0800 on the morning of the 14th heading for Atton. We had plenty of armor with us, 5 light tanks, and 15 Shermans. Mousson Hill was approximately 2 miles north of Atton and at the bottom toward Loisy (1-1/2 miles). From a distance we caught a glimpse of Mousson Hill. Our artillery had smoked the top of Mousson Hill to conceal our positions and we ran into heavy shellfire as we neared Atton. We sailed through Atton and concentrated on the open slopes leading up to the top of what our GIs nicknamed "Castle Dome". Rumor had it that a medieval castle was located on the very top, it doesn't take long for GI jargon to set in! It was rough climbing with all our gear, mortar tubes, base plates, protect the aiming devices, tripods, barrels, ammo boxes, rifles and bazookas, and the stove with shelter halves! The tanks were blowing everything to hell with their 75s and MGs.

The Infantry was spread out and Atton was taken easily. We then proceeded up Mousson Hill with 5 light tanks machine gunning every bush in, in their sights, we spit lead with our own rifles, etc. It was rough climbing and as we climbed we encountered three Krauts who wanted to give up, and so they did! When we got to the top we found Jerry dugouts unoccupied, did they ever look so queer, they had been what it looked like chiseled out of the rubble/rock and had been occupied for long periods. The smell was overwhelming and we could not re-occupy them. We found ourselves once again under cold, rain clouds and the Jerries had us pinned down in our positions. After our taking of the hill, the Germans threw a counter attack and during the attack on "Castle Dome", our 80th Division Artillery Commander, General Searby was killed. While we the infantry did not know him personally, it must have been a crushing blow to all those artillery who knew that if Castle Dome were to be taken General Searby would have seen every target to be fired on in, in Alsace-Lorraine. Those are the fortunes of war.

Soon after the 3rd Battalion made it to the near top of Castle Dome the Germans once again counterattacked and completely encircled the Mount. We were not aware as to the extent of the encirclement; however, we assumed that Atton had been retaken and perhaps the area about Loisy, if not Loisy itself? We were surrounded for four days, and the weather was bad, we could not expect P-47s to help us now. I believe that shells of every description fell on our position, including a large caliber shell from a distant railway gun? The rounds sounded like a freight train coming in, if the shell cleared the top of the Mount, then it roared over our foxhole positions to explode 200-300 yards down the slope, this side of Pont a Mousson. Each blast was ear splitting and we had no place to hide. We know the Jerries occupied dug-in, rubble like positions not 100 yards from us, on slightly higher ground.

We had several fire-fights/skirmishers with them from time to time. Too detailed to relate, here, but there were a few "heroics" performed and never officially recorded. On the fourth and final day of our being surrounded the dawn cleared and we could hear the thunder coming from the west: we watched as P-47s strafing and dropping 500 pound bombs, at tree top levels. From our location we were, at times, looking down on top of their wings.

There must have been 10-15 aircraft. We knew that the fighter-bombers were preparing the areas for a ground assault, hopefully to relieve us? It did not take long. A thin line of vehicles appeared beyond Loisy and the figures became larger as they drew closer. They are OURS, tanks and infantry, seeing the tanks with the 319th Infantry, in their counterattack to relieve us... finally arriving a la John Wayne! Wow! All who participated in, the battles for Mousson Hill. Castle Dome known for the severe number of casualties incurred. I vividly recall leaving my foxhole to report to the Company I CP, along the way, perhaps fifty yards or so, I came upon a scene where GIs were covered with shelter halves in the pouring rain and they were arranged in rows upon the ground. All KIAs. Reflections from the soaked canvas caught my eye, and I felt very sick. I had no idea where the wounded had been treated, or even their locations, there was simply, "no place to hide nor be safe."

Back to reality. The day we were relieved by the recuse column, we trudged off Castle Dome hoping beyond hope that perhaps we might get a little rest, lick our wounds and maybe a change of socks? Not to be. We forced marched to another damn hill directly below Mt. St. Jean some 5-10 miles distant. We found ourselves treading on the same ground we had covered days before. Of course there was much grumbling and moral was low, but those are the fortunes! I suppose the hill we occupied has a number, but we never knew those details at platoon levels. We found the hill was under continuous mortar fire for 24 hours!!! We took a night patrol out after being told by the CO, "Nobody is in there." Really? Well, we took several casualties from burp guns and mortars. And got the hell out of there. We called our CO, Captain Fountain, and told him to get his ...... over here and find out if anybody is there! We were blunt!

Stretch Miller
Company L, 318 Infantry Regiment and
Charles "Bud" Coward
Company I, 318th Infantry Regiment
Recalling Mousson Hill

Coward, who was an officer in Company I, and Miller, an enlisted man from Company L, collaborate on the battle of Mousson Hill. What Miller of L Company 318th Infantry and everything I remembered about I Company 318th Infantry of the crossing of the Moselle River is borne out except for the "pontoon bridge." Stretch Miller recalls crossing a pontoon bridge via Dieulouard to the eastern shore, and I recall a narrow walkway on top of a dam across the river. I Company used the path across the dam. Miller's description of "setting up and digging in" on the eastern shore near "some crossroads" sounds proper and his mention of another company also digging in nearby is familiar; that was us, Co. I. He clearly describes the German counterattack at 4:00 a.m. Co. I had vacated their dug-in positions earlier, and pulled back to the river's edge, realizing that the Germans would counterattack the position. Incidentally, Company I's original, dug-in position (mentioned above) was immediately below Bezaumont where the enemy had everything, including us, under surveillance: We came under spasmodic artillery fire while we were digging in. Coward states, during all of this, I had no clue where L Company, or any other unit, was located at the time!

Well, the counterattack was "right on schedule" and Company I was dug-in and "huddled," so to speak, in its withdrawn position: I would judge our position to be approximately 100-200 yds. to the west toward the Moselle River. Ordinance of all descriptions came over and into our positions and we could clearly hear the clanking of tank treads, not knowing whether enemy or our Sherman? Our orders were to remain dug in and to defend the "bridgehead" should the German's break through. I would estimate the firefight, at its height, lasted at least an hour, tapering off to spasmodic burp gun chatter and several large artillery rounds, from which side who, knows? News trickled down in the early morning hours how a high-ranking officer (Lt. Col.), brandishing a 45 automatic, literally forced several, fleeing Sherman tanks around to "force" them to confront the attacking Panthers. Again, we, in Company I, had no idea where L Company was during all of this. The bazooka man of L Company describes his action with a few others during all of this and a bit later that "a platoon" had been overrun by the enemy, the Chaplain captured, but who later escaped.

The dawn came with clear skies and P-47 support! They dropped 500 pounders and strafed for at least an hour on the positions just east of our dug-in location. We witnessed a P-47 limping back over our lines with black smoke streaming from its cowling, at low altitude. A figure tumbling from the aircraft and quickly a white chute. The pilot had to have landed within our bridgehead area and rescued. We will never know? The doomed P-47, itself, struck the ground near the river and exploded in a plume of black, oily smoke that lingered for hours in the calm air.

Finally, during the morning hours we formed up and were ordered to attack northeast, along the flat, open farmland to occupy Loisy, where rumor had it that Co. L 317th Regiment, had been "wiped out" during the German counterattack in the early morning hours. The flat farmland was littered with burned out and burning Panther tanks, plus a few Sherman among them. The distance from our departure line to Loisy was rather short perhaps half a mile, if that much? One would have to search the map for accuracy. We scattered ourselves among several Sherman tanks and advanced: Small arms fire crackled overhead, but Company I encountered little resistance and we saw no one!

As Loisy drew into sight we stood clear of the roadway leading directly into the town, and were confronted with a rather high masonry wall with a hole, large enough for one to pass through had been blown or removed in some way, at its base. We were at once alert to the danger that there must be a booby trap in the vicinity, so we "thoroughly" grenaded the hole area to set off any charges. We filed through the hole one-by-one (my weapon's platoon) until it came my turn. I had no sooner gone through the aperture when a sharp "POP" and a "Zinging" whistled next to me. I had no idea what had happened? It was a castrator "grenade" (a booby trap) that had not gone off, a miss-fire!

Meanwhile, we had set up our 30-cal. light machine guns trained down the single Loisy Street. Still no resistance? Other Company I platoon had entered Loisy at different locations and were making their way toward "the last building on the block." A Sherman tank positioned itself directly at the last building and a squad from our platoon approached nearby. Two Germans exited the doorway with their hands behind their heads, one of our GIs took them away and we proceeded to grenade the interior of the building including the basement areas. The structure was empty. Several more enemy surrendered (white flag routine) from the nearby wooded areas.

Now, this "last building," on the edge of Loisy, is the last man-made object between Loisy and the next "hamlet," Atton, located on what I judge to be on the SW slope leading to "Castle Dome" (Mousson Hill). It was through Atton, from Loisy, that we launched our attack on Castle Dome. We never paused for a split second in Atton. We had several Shermans with us and we used "marching fire" all the way up! We hip-fired our M1s and BARs at EVERYTHING all the way! Can't count the number of cattle watering stations we took out? Our objective was to take Castle Dome in order to allow us to view/control much of Alsace-Lorraine from such an advantageous location. Our comrade of L Company seems to allude to "structures" or "houses" of some kind, he also makes mention of Atton and I believe that is where he vividly describes the shelling and other action. Miller also notes that he learned that Company I, (Coward's company) had suffered severe casualties near the top of Castle Dome. He is so right! To clarify: The name "Castle Dome," I believe, found its origin in either our company, or at least in our platoon, they simply could not bring themselves to pronounce "Mousson Hill" every time they alluded to the stinking mess!

S/Sgt. Albert D. Dian
Cannon Company, 318th Infantry Regiment

The time was December 24, 1944. The Battle of the Bulge was very much in doubt. We were located in Luxembourg north of the capital. About the 14th or 15th of December, we were poised near Saarebourg in France for a big push by Patton's Third Army to pierce the West Wall, the 80th infantry Division moved at night, in a convoy, to help stem the tide of the Wehrmacht offensive. As we moved northward, the temperature kept dropping, and we experienced the first snow of winter. Arriving in Luxembourg City about dusk, lo and behold, the streetcars were running and no blackout was in effect. What a strange scenario! Artillery and machine gun fire was audible in the distance.

Proceeding to an area near Mersch, Luxembourg, we halted for a few days. The ground was almost too frozen to dig in but the snow was deep enough for insulation at night, enabling us to get a warm night's sleep.

Somewhere about the 20th, we moved northeast toward Diekirch and Ettelbruck. On our way, we encountered our first Nebelwerfers — the "screaming meemies" — multiple rockets fired at us with an eerie sound that was terrifying. At the same time, the walking wounded of the 28th Infantry Division was moving to the rear while we were advancing to take the positions they had held.

We passed by a typical guardhouse, the same type you see in old movies with guards in their comic opera uniforms. As we approached the guardhouse, the Nebelwerfers came raining down and the sentinels disappeared: "tout de suite" in the direction of the castle of the Grand Duchess in Colmar-Berg.

Proceeding to our designated area, we dug in our guns. Although an infantry company, the Cannon Company had six 105-millimeter howitzers designed to give the infantrymen ahead of us close support.

We set up our command post in an abandoned farmhouse and started to run our telephone lines to gun platoons. The weather for days had been miserable—poor visibility for our air force. This was probably the greatest advantage the Wehrmacht had, since they moved so rapidly on terrain they knew so well. Somehow (maybe a break in the clouds) our position was revealed to the German forward observer and we started to get hostile fire on our headquarters. Glass and mortar through the window made it expedient for us to retire to the potato cellar below the house.

Lo and behold, as we peered into the darkness, a mother, father, and a tiny baby were huddled there, terrified. We could only communicate with sign language. Their native language was a patois of French and German hard to understand. We shared cold rations with them for several days until our kitchen truck could move up to a safe area and provide us with hot chow.

Mail finally caught up to us and I had a package from one of my sisters in Cleveland, OH. She had read about how the little children in war-torn France, Holland and Belgium would not have gifts of any kind for Christmas. She didn't even know that I was in Luxembourg at the time.

Christmas Eve came. It was cold, no stars, and cloudy weather. Despite legends to the contrary, guns were still audible, both sides. I finally opened the package and it was an assortment of small, cheap trinkets. I believe my sister hoped I would distribute them to some orphanage.

By candlelight, I started to give the little boy "Edie," the name I best remember. At each gift, the mother and father would cry and thank me with gestures. Was this reenactment of the "Holy Night" in Bethlehem many years ago?

I know now how the Wise Men of old must have felt, since this tiny babe also lay in a bed of hay, smiling. Perhaps the Angels were smiling from oh high. I like to think so.

Before falling asleep, we said our silent prayer, "Peace on Earth, Goodwill toward Men."

Bob Duoos
80th Recon, 80th Infantry Division

Just after the war in the ETO ended, we were in Austria and I think the village was on a lake called After (?) Sea. Anyway, there was a large dormitory style building filled with pregnant German young girls—This place was where "ideal models" of young German men were sent for what would have been our equivalence to a three-day pass. And of course they were paired up with these girls. The babies were given to the State for upbringing and I believe were called "Hitler Youth." When a mother gave her third child to the State for upbringing, she would be awarded a medal. My spelling will be off but it was called a Deutschen Mutter medal. It noted the number of children and the date of the award. I found one of those medals and upon returning home, gave it to my nephew as a war souvenir. How I wish, I hadn't. I asked him a year or so ago if he remembered getting the medal and did he still have it and his response was "if you gave it to me, I still have it." I'm going to ask him again and hope he can produce it for me. He can keep it but I want him to know its value. No doubt, there are those who would deny such a thing ever took place. By the way, I remember the girls in the After Sea dorm was hanging out the windows waving at us and no doubt were lonely.

Robert B. Conner
Company G, 318th Infantry Regiment

I am not exactly sure why I am writing this. There are many possible reasons. One, I need something to do with my time. Two might be to create a segment of my "life story": that I intend to produce someday and which I hope to incorporate into a more compressive family history for my heirs. Or three, to document my military experience that seems appropriate now that we are celebrating the fifty-seventh anniversary of the "Battle of the Bulge" and the "Siege of Bastogne." The 16th of December 1945 is the day the German Army choose to launch its offensive in the Ardennes forest that became known as "The Battle of the Bulge." Maybe in some way, this will explain and answer the question that some of my kin might ask some day, "What did you do in the war?" (Editor Note: It is the Third Reason we pick up on.)

My military career and destiny really started when I was enrolled at West Virginia University in the fall of 1939. This was before our country entered the big war. Since WVU was a land grant institution, it was required to offer ROTC (Reserve Officers Training Corp.) and all undergraduates were to take two years of basic military on campus as regular classes. We just had two choices of a branch of service—infantry or engineers. Since the engineers' option was for engineering students, most of us ended up in the infantry. At the end of the sophomore year you could apply for the advanced program and after summer camp, following your junior year, you would receive a commission as a reserve 2nd Lieutenant when you graduated.

During my junior year of advanced military, war had been declared and the demand for young officers picked up considerably. The War Department changed the rules and mandated that all officer candidates would attend the Army Officers Candidate School of their branch before getting their commission. In addition, those who could arrange it were expected to speed up their graduation by attending summer school. I finished in three and one half years in February 1943 and went straight to Fort Benning, GA, to be among the first ROTC candidates to start the program. We were mixed with combat experienced veterans as we started our ninety-day program. We had not been sworn in the Army and had not been issued uniforms and I drilled in a black pin-striped suit with a white shirt and tie for three weeks before they figured out how to process us. OCS was not too difficult for us. We had excellent basic training at WVU and we were in top shape physically. We did get one advantage. Col. Orton who had been in charge of ROTC at WVU was transferred to Benning to be in charge of all training, including OCS. When our "tack" officers learned this, they were afraid we would be spying for Orton and treated us like special people.

I completed the training and was commissioned a second lieutenant in the infantry on my 21st birthday, June 5th. Several members of my class were assigned as company officers for the basic training companies at Benning. Just by chance the guys from WVU who had stayed there until June were assigned to the company I was with and we kept them and processed them until they could be scheduled for OCS. Here I was an officer and they were enlisted men. It was funny. They had heard so many stories about the Infantry School that they were scared to death and were afraid to even be friendly.

20

I became very close friends with three other lieutenants who had graduated with me and as luck would have it we were transferred together on several subsequent assignments. I have kept in touch with two of them for the last fifty years. One was killed in action. William Arden was from a delta town near Vicksburg, MS and Charlie Corwin was from Fargo ND. David Dowell was a football star and president of his class at Ole Miss Univ. He was the only one married and the only one to give up his life.

We shipped out of Fort Benning in the spring of 1944 as replacement officers for divisions that was preparing to ship overseas for combat. We stayed just a short while at Little Rock, AR, and then moved into Camp McCoy, WI.

We then left that Division and were sent home for a short leave before going overseas as infantry replacement officers. The invasion of Normandy started while we were on our way to England. While I was visiting home, Dad insisted I take a camera with me. I didn't own one so Dad suggested that I take Frank's camera, one of my brothers, who was serving in South America. I hesitated but Dad insisted. I found out it was a quite expensive camera when I ask at the port of embarkation if it was possible to take one. The officer I asked said it was O.K. and remarked what a good camera it was. I tried to find something to ship it home in but we were to ship out before I got it mailed. When I bought some film in England, the shopkeeper again told me it was an expensive model. I decided then that I should keep it with me at all times to avoid it be lost or stolen. I kept it in the right front pocket of my field jacket.

I was still with my friends and we were stationed at an old British Army barracks called Tidworth near the town of Salisbury. Here we had the job of basic training to regular army personnel who were being retrained to be infantry replacement soldiers. They weren't very happy about it and were not the easiest troops to work with. By the time we finished the training cycle, it was late August and the war had moved out of Normandy and Patton was moving fast beyond Paris. It must have been late September or early October that the four of us were sent to join different units on the mainland. As we were loading onto a little Dutch ship to cross the channel, we noticed that it was unloading large boxes that we finally figured out to be caskets. I said to one of our group that we would likely come back that way. Dowell disagreed, saying he was coming back in one piece very much alive. But he was the one who didn't make it.

In the middle of the channel, one of the soldiers aboard recognized the number on an U.S. Navy Destroyer and said his brother was on that ship. Word got to the two captains somehow and both ships stopped, put down little dories and the brothers had a reunion with a bottle of wine, with men from both ships cheering.

We landed on the invasion beaches and I remember trudging up a hill to an assembly area overlooking the channel, we boarded a train of boxcars and proceeded to Etemps a town on the outskirts of Paris where we were housed as replacements. We were assigned to Divisions and shipped out by trucks. I joined the 80th Division as platoon leader of the 1st Platoon, 2nd Battalion, "G" Company, 318th Regiment. The outfit had just made a major river crossing and suffered heavy causalities and was now in the rear of the front line getting resupplied with both men and equipment. The 80th is a reserve division known as the "Blue Ridge" Division and in peacetime is headquartered in the Appalachian region but by now it is almost completely replacement from everywhere. It was also one of the Divisions of General Patton's Third Army. When I caught up with them in early November, they were fighting in the Saar Valley, moving toward the Rhine.

My first combat was a small encounter. My platoon was to advance and capture a small town being held by the Germans. As we charged down on the village with our rifles blazing away, suddenly German soldiers started coming out with their hands above their heads, surrendering. This caught me by surprise and I had not been told what to do with prisoners. I must have shown my frustration, for the enemy seemed to think that I was going to mow them down. I finally got my wits about me and had a detail take their weapons and take them to the rear somewhere. We took the town without any losses and I had been baptized in combat.

After a few more days of fighting, we were pulled out of the line for rest and resupply. We were still in artillery range but our battalion commander insisted on formations and close order drill. This was a little coal-mining town in the Alsace Loraine area by the name of Freyming. I remember the tipple was brick and the shower and change room were white tiles. We had our Thanksgiving in this town and we had hot turkey with all the trimmings. After living on cold "C" rations, this was great.

We went on the offensive the first part of December. We took a small village, moved through it and dug in on the forward slope of the hill beyond. From the hill we could see where a German column had been strafed down in the valley. I had the men dig foxholes to settle in for the night. I walked across the front of my platoon chatting with the men until I got to the last hole. The Germans must have been tracking me for an antitank shell burst right near me and the foxhole. The soldier in the hole got a bad shoulder wound and I got a small piece of shrapnel in my neck. A medic gave me a Band-Aid and I thought nothing more of it, but I guess he reported it for I got my first Purple Heart for being wounded in action. I had decided to spend the night on top of the hill behind my men but the foxhole I started filled with water so I propped myself against a tree for the night a few yards away. When I got up and started back to the company command post, I passed the foxhole and beside it was a large artillery shell that had not exploded. Had I used that hole and that round had not been a dud, it would have been all over.

Things were fairly quiet for a couple of days but one night the captain called a staff meeting and said orders had come down that each unit must have a recreation officer and he jokingly appointed one of the other lieutenants as company recreation officer. Again, jokingly I protested that I wasn't considered so he announced that I would be the company mess officer. We laughed, knowing we had a good mess sergeant and he didn't get to do much since we had to exist on field "C" rations and there was little cooking done. Things were fairly static but just as we were about to move to another sector, the mess sergeant fixed a hot breakfast. He set it up quickly in a courtyard and the men formed a chow line. I happened to look up and noticed that Phillips, the mail corporal from the rear train, was first in line so I yelled with my new authority "Phillips, get the hell out of there and get back to the end of the line and when all the fighting men have eaten, you can eat." He did as he was told and other than my mail being slow, I didn't think much about the incident until months later in Halloran General Hospital in New York I spotted a soldier with an 80th patch and I ask him what outfit he was from. He replied 1st platoon, G Company of the

318th. I didn't recognize him so I ask him when he joined and he said in January. I countered that I left in December so we wouldn't know each other. He replied "Oh I know about you. You're the lieutenant that chewed the mail corporal in the chow line." I guess that meant more to the men than anything else I did while I was with the outfit.

It was now the middle of December and we were being trucked north toward Luxembourg because the Germans had broken through some of our replacement divisions and had started their last offensive, the drive to the sea. Some of the Germans were reported to be wearing American uniforms and carrying M-1 rifles to infiltrate our lines. When we started on foot again, I noticed several dead Germans in our uniforms. My rifle wasn't too clean so I traded mine with one from the dead frozen German had with him. It had turned cold and started snowing. I found a foxhole full of straw so I pulled my raincoat over my head and had a cozy night. When I awoke, my canteen was frozen solid and my rifle was frozen to the ground. We moved out of there through some open fields with some mortar falling around us, to reach some higher ground.

It must have been 23 December because the skies had cleared and the air force was out for the first time in days. While we waiting further orders, an exciting air battle developed overhead. A couple of US P-51 fighters had engaged a couple of German Messerschmidts. We saw one pilot get hit and bail out and all at once one of the German planes was flying directly at us just a few feet off the ground. I could have hit him with a rock. I guess he was out of ammo or gas and was hedgehopping to his base. It was back like in the movies. After the air show was over, we advanced over the top of the hill expecting all hell to hit us but nothing happened. We were now in the southern shoulder of the defense and I believe we were near Ettelbruck.

We did not know it but the 28th Infantry Division was stuck in Bastogne and General Bradley had ordered the 101st Airborne who were resting in Paris to move into Bastogne to help the 28th Division. Rather than pull back like I think they should have, they held their ground and got themselves surrounded and the siege of Bastogne began and General McAuliffe gave his famous "Nuts" reply when the German sought his surrender. Bradley ordered the 4th Armored Division to drive to the south into Bastogne to relieve the units inside the city. When efforts bogged down, General Patton pulled our 2nd Battalion over and attached them to the 4th Armored for a major effort on Christmas day. We were loaded into trucks and moved in the dark to a little village just south of Bastogne. We spent Christmas Eve in a barn out of the weather. Our Captain passed out battle maps of the area (first time I was given one) and proceeded to explain the battle plan for the next day. Somehow, we hoped that the war might end or at least an armistice declared for Christmas but it wasn't to be. We were to work with the tanks of the 4th Armored Division. They had been shot up pretty badly and were down in numbers just like we were. We had worked only with a tank battalion in our own division and they were more trouble than good since they always followed the infantry rather than lead it. We never got any support from them. But this outfit was supposed to be different. We were to stay under cover until the battalion of light tanks attacked the edge of the first woods, then we would go into the woods and clear it of any Germans until we got to the next open field. The first phase went great. We took a few prisoners and got through the wooded area without much trouble. When we got to the top of the hill, a battalion of medium tanks were supposed to do the same things the light tankers had done, move out, attack the edge of the

23

next woods and we would follow and go through the woods. When all of our men were in place I told the Captain that I would go over and tell the commander of the tanks so he could move out across the open snow-covered field and we would follow. The young lieutenant in charge refused to move. He said that his outfit had been shot up and he wasn't giving the command to move forward until we had crossed the field and cleared the next woods. We needed to neutralize the edge of the woods before jumping off so I asked if he had a forward field artillery observer who could call in some fire from the rear. I also asked him if he would fire some rounds at the woods before we took off and this fell on deaf ears. I reported this to my captain and we decided that the only support fire we might get was from our own little 60mm mortars. So we set them up and started lobbing shells at the next wood line. We had several hundred yards of snow-covered field with a few barbed wire fences to traverse so I told the captain that we should move out while the mortars were firing overhead. He was in very bad shape mentally and he refused to move out until mortars went out of action. This nullified the neutralizing effect and allowed the Germans on the edge of the woods to emerge out of their holes and pick us off like ducks in a shooting gallery. In order to get the men moving it was up to me to lead. So I stepped out as the point and the company followed in skirmish line firing their M-1 rifles wildly.

The men followed blindly and boldly. We advanced about a half way through the woods and the German small arms fire started getting more accurate. I had just passed a slight dip in the ground when suddenly I felt something tear through my left side. It didn't knock me down but I knew I was through. So I turned around to see if I might see that little dip and maybe get some cover there. While I was half turned, another shot got me. This one went through my neck and I felt like I had been hit with a baseball bat. It knocked me down and I couldn't move. I was scared to death. I was paralyzed from the neck wound. I later learned the German bullet entered the right side of my neck and hit the sixth cervical vertebra breaking off a piece of the "spicas process." This is a portion of bone that protrudes from the main body of the vertebrae. The impact jarred the spine and caused a misalignment or pinch enough to cause temporary loss of feeling and movement. I never lost consciousness. One of my men came upon me very shortly and looked down on me in dismay as though nothing like this was supposed to happen. He consoled me and assured me the aid men would be by shortly and pick me up. He then stuck my rifle into the ground and put my helmet on it to signify my location. Soon another soldier suggested he move the rifle to make it a little more visible. He did and moved on and in a few minutes the rifle fell over. I no longer had a marker and I was sure the medics would not find me. They did however, and loaded me onto a stretcher jeep and drove back to the aid station. I was checked over there and transferred by ambulance to the 39th Forward Evacuation Hospital. When the ward attendant came and started to cut off my clothes to expose the wounds, I told him I had a camera in the field jacket pocket and I didn't want it to disappear while I was in the operating room. He pulled it out of the pocket and some pieces of metal fell out with it. I then assumed that the bullet that went through my side had gone through the camera first. I later looked at the camera and there was a bullet still lodged in it. I had taken a third hit and didn't know it. Had that one gone on through the camera, it would have penetrated in the area of the heart. Frank's camera had saved my life. Due to a mix up of having two "Conners" waiting for attention, another soldier went before me into the operating room. I was listed as critical and supposed to have been first. While everyone else was eating turkey and full Christmas dinner I had to wait until they checked the extent of my wounds. They already closed the operating room when they realized they had overlooked me but opened back up in the basement room and the whole setup was much like the TV show "Mash." By the time I got through, the turkey was all gone and they only had some cold spaghetti. What a Christmas! One bullet through my side, one clipping my spine and the third stopped by a camera, really nice Christmas presents.

From the Evacuation Hospital I was flown to the 120th Station Hospital in England to recuperate. On the 14th of February I was shipped out to the 10th Replacement Depot in Paris, enroute to my old outfit. I noticed when I bent forward I would get electrical shock effect down my extremities. I knew something was wrong and I shouldn't go back to full duty until I had it checked out. After X-rays and etc., they thought I had a broken neck, after spinal taps, hitting me with a hammer to try to find where the tingles were coming from. One doctor wanted to operate and remove the piece of bone, but that was not to be. After a fashion, I was told I would have to live with it but over a period of time it would get better. I was also told had the bullet entered one quarter of an inch more, it would have severed the spinal column leaving me a quadriplegic if I survived. They decide I was not fit for combat or full duty and they would be sending me back to the states, and on 11 May 1945 I was released from that hospital and put on a Hospital Ship to come home. While on the high seas, VE day was declared. Upon docking in New York, I was sent to Holloran General Hospital for distribution. It was here I met the soldier from the 80th Division who knew of the chow line incident. I was sent home to the nearest General Hospital of my home so that meant Ashford General hospital at White Sulphur Springs, West Virginia.

I ask and received to be on the staff of the ROTC and I became an assistant professor of training to enlisted men in the Army's Special Training Program. On 6 June 1946 I married Anna Bowling. We now live on Preston Road in Morgantown.

Richard Radock
Company C, 319th Infantry Regiment, Medic Battalion
Relief of the Besieged U.S. Troops in Bastogne

Many of the veterans of the Bulge are writing about their units' participation in the relief of the 101st Airborne and other troops trapped in the Bastogne perimeter, even though we had 600,000 troops fighting in the Bulge and every unit and soldier contributed in some manner in the relief of these troops, even though it may have been indirect. These enemy troops had about nine divisions and assorted small units surrounded Bastogne and it took six infantry divisions, two airborne, three armored division, 1 CCB-10th Armored to destroy the Germans and push him back to the starting of their counterattack.

This story is about my division's (80th Infantry Division) role in the early shift of the 3rd Army troops from the Saar Valley and travel 150 miles from St. Avold, Bitche and Rohrbach which we were in this area for rest, refitting and maintenance of our vehicles, tanks, guns and equipment in preparation to assault the West Wall. General Patton ordered us to move north as fast as we could, the 4th Armored to Longway, the 80th Infantry to Luxembourg City and the 26th Infantry Division toward Liefrange 14 hours later, this was on 19 December 1944.

We were to set up a defense to stop the German 7th Army from penetrating southward and we were to attack the southern German flank quickly. The only divisions located here were part of the 28th Infantry Division and the 4th Infantry Division. Also, Patton sent up the 10th Armored Division to Bastogne to help.

We were assigned to General Milliken's III Corps. We were to pull out of the 3rd Army front line, load up all infantry troops, extra gasoline, ammo, rations, medical supplies and get ready to travel 150 miles at a great speed as fast as conditions warranted and set up a defensive perimeter around Luxembourg City and dig in about ten miles north of the city as the Germans wanted to seize this communications center. Leaving at 0530, we drove in a blizzard, the roads were icy and covered with snow, it was so dark we took a chance and drove with bright headlights that we may drive faster. It was Tuesday, 19 December 1944, and with a long drive with the entire division. We moved in a very long convoy. Our 305th Engineers went first to check the roads, and bridges for mines. Our division MPs were road guides and kept the convoy close so none of us would get lost. Then came the trucks with our 3 Infantry Regiments (317, 318, and 319 followed by the 702d Tank Battalion, 633d AAA AW Battalion, our Artillery Battalions (313, 314, 315 and the 905), then the service companies, headquarters units, then the Division Headquarters. All tired vehicles had chains on all wheels.

The trip was long and tedious, stops and go movement. And thirty-three hours of driving, and we had to get out many times to stretch, relieve drivers and eat cold K rations—there was no hot food or even coffee.

We arrived in Luxembourg City and found a lot of rear echelon troops of the 28th infantry Division, mostly clerks, mess workers, cooks and headquarters troops. They were glad to see us.

26

We placed guards at strategic cross roads, billets and command posts and medical facilities.

Our infantry took positions north of the city to defend and protect it from the Germans, as they were ready to launch an attack on the city. One of our infantry regiments loaded up in trucks, moved north of the city, registered their guns and fired on the enemy on 22 December 1944. The rest of the division set up a defense north of the city and were ordered to attack at 0600 hours on the same day.

We attacked and advanced 14 miles in 48 hours in deep snow and caught the enemy by surprise and slaughtered about two-thirds of a Grenadier Division of the Wehrmacht 7th Army.

The 80th Infantry Division would move toward Ettelbruck, the 26th Division toward Wiltz and the 4th Armored toward Bastogne. The 80th Blue Ridger destroyed an enemy artillery battalion in Ettelbruck and we stopped the German drive on Luxembourg City. We also seized a 4-mile stretch of the German main supply road from Trier to Bastogne.

Two battalions of our 318th Infantry Regiment were ordered by General Patton to provide infantry support to the 4th Armored Division. They loaded on trucks and motored 22 miles toward Bastogne. The Germans kept up pressure on the Bastogne perimeter. The 101st Airborne Division and other troops were surrounded. The 80th Division fought with tenacity and advanced 5 miles to clear Merzig of enemy troops. On 23 December 1944, clouds lifted and our XIX TAC had a field day bombing and strafing the enemy. My Company C, 305th Medical Battalion Collecting Station was located in Ettelbruck so I had set up an ambulance shuttle post in Heiderscheid to cut down travel time for my ambulances which were assigned to the three infantry battalion aid stations of the 329th Infantry Regiment. My job was to evacuate the wounded soldiers immediately including the enemy and civilians, with great speed so the wounded would not go into shock or hypothermia. Other ambulances would transfer the wounded and drive them to our Company C Collection Station located in Ettelbruck. Since the 80th Division was ordered to move to Ettelbruck and join the XII Corps, the 35th Infantry Division took our positions.

On Christmas Day 1944, we slugged it out with the enemy for three days but we held our ground. We captured many enemy soldiers and pounded them with a thousand rounds of artillery and mortar shells. Good news this day as the 4th Armored, 37th Tank Battalion, led by Lt. Col. Abrams, rolled into Bastogne through a narrow corridor. The besieged troops were glad to see them. Lt. Walter Carr of 2nd Battalion, Company E 318th Infantry Regiment with a four-man patrol, slipped through the enemy lines and made contact with an engineer outpost on the outskirts of the Bastogne perimeter. He then was escorted to the 101st Airborne Headquarters and was given an overlay of the defensive positions, conditions of the wounded and supplies needed and ammo.

The major crisis ended at Bastogne but many tough battles were to be fought as the Germans had about nine divisions and small units surrounding the perimeter around Bastogne. The next few days, the corridor to the city was widened and ambulances and supply trucks moved into Bastogne. All of the wounded and civilians were evacuated. Many fresh troops relieved the paratroopers and other besieged troops.

The trucks hauled ammo, blankets, rations, guns and medical supplies into Bastogne. There was much bloody fighting yet, as the Germans had the tenacity and made counterattacks even though they were not productive in capturing territory.

After a couple of weeks Hitler ordered his troops to retreat east to the Fatherland to defend the West Wall. The Germans abandoned their panzers, heavy guns, and trucks and retreated on foot to Germany as they had no gasoline, ammo, rations or medical supplies. They even left their wounded.

The siege of Bastogne was over and can be attributed to the 600,000 US troops who fought a gallant battle. Our cost was about 81,000 casualties, 47,139 WIA, 8,600 KIA and 21,144 MIA. The Germans suffered much worse in casualties and thousands were taken prisoners.

Each soldier who participated in this campaign in the Ardennes deserves much credit for a job well done, no matter what his job entailed.

Lynn Bryan
Company F, 317th Infantry Regiment

I was in the 2nd battalion; I joined my company (F) on 1 January and did so in a rather abrupt mode. I took my basic training at Fort Bragg, N.C. in the Field Artillery. Upon completion of my basic, September 1943, my MOS was Prime Mover Truck Driver. I arrived in Scotland in January 1944. Apparently there were too many truck drivers in the UK so I was sent to school to become a company clerk. I shipped to France in September of 1944. After three months as a clerk typist I was relocated to Compiegne for two weeks of infantry training. At the end of my training, December 30, I was a passenger on a six-by that, we were told, was taking us to the "front." We stayed in a hunting lodge somewhere in the Ardennes overnight. At the time I was 19 years old and wondered if I would ever make it to 20 in the coming New Year. The next day we were again loaded on the trucks and after a 12-hour ride and going through a burning village along the way we unloaded and formed into separate small groups, according to which platoon and squad we had been assigned to. It was very cold and there was about two feet of snow on the ground. I was ordered to join a group of five other guys. A Sgt. told us that we were assigned to Company F, of the Second Battalion, 3rd Platoon, 3rd Squad. We took off through the thick snow laden woods and after about two long hours arrived at the company headquarters. After a brief stop we were then sent to our assigned foxholes. I found out that we were on a front line defense position and warned not to show any light whatsoever. The Sgt. told us that there were Germans only about 300 yards directly in front us. He then proceeded to hand me a BAR and told me that I was now the BAR man for the squad. So, that is how I spent January 1, 1945, I experienced three months of heavy combat before I was 20 years old on April 2, 1945.

Crossing the Our River

It was about 2000, dark, with a cold brisk wind driving the rain into our faces. It was about the fourth week in January 1945. We were in the Ardennes Mountains of Luxembourg. We had been bivouacked for the last week in a forest and had moved out early in the day. We were only told that we were moving to a new location. We had been walking for over eight hours with ten-minute rest stops every hour. We had only our three-day supply of cold, dry "K" rations to eat. We were getting rather tired to say the least. As dusk settled in, we found ourselves on a small one-lane dirt road. We were at the top of a hill overlooking a small valley through which a river ran. This road led down to a group of four buildings, which was approximately a half-mile away. We were cold, tired and the cold rain was running off my helmet and down my back, soaking through my wool shirt.

When we were about half way down the hill we heard a squeaking sound behind us, and someone shouted to get off the road, we were in two files, one on each side of the road when a flatbed truck brakes squeaking with protrusions hanging over the sides drove down between the two files of men nearly hitting some men, the load was one I had never seen before. Two more trucks loaded the same way, also came through the files of men with similar loads and turned into a farm. We were puzzled as to what the trucks was carrying. We soon found out what the loads of equipment were when that night a very bright light lit the skies. Looking at the light we found that was the load on the trucks. Searchlight to light the sky. It was like a moonlit night.

It continued to rain very hard and the cold rain was now about one half snow. As we got closer to the farm buildings we saw they consisted of a small farmhouse, a large barn, and three other buildings made of thick stone. The walls were approximately one foot thick. We continued to walk toward the barn. The closer we got the bigger it looked and I thought I heard running water. As I looked out in the darkness, I decided that it was the river we saw at the top of the hill. The road we were on continued on to a stone bridge that was a pile of rubble, it had probably been destroyed by artillery fire. The head of the column headed into the barn, I was about the third from last to go into the barn. The floor was about eighteen inches below the road. Stepping down we found the floor was an earthen floor. There were no cattle in the barn. It was now about 2200 hours and as soon as I got into the barn, I flopped down for sleep, bone weary. We had marched about fifteen miles with full combat packs, with rifle and ammo. It was now pitch black and guys were lighting their lighters to see. The noncoms and the Lt. had flashlights to give a bit more of light.

The Sgt. woke us up a little after dawn. We ate our cold rations and were allowed to heat water in our canteen cups for hot powdered coffee. It was approximately 0700 or 0800 hours when the Lt. entered the barn and told us to gather around him, he had something to tell us. In a subdued voice we were told we were going to cross the river in a pontoon boat and assault the Germans on the other side. I had never assaulted across a river before under enemy fire. I did not know what to expect.

On the opposite side of the barn where we entered was a set of steps leading out toward the river. After the Lt. went out the door, we were told to do the same thing. We were about to cross the river. The bank was covered with thick bushes and led down to the river and looked to be about five feet high and ran alongside of the barn. A path leading alongside of the river looked to be a cattle path to the river. I also saw a barbed wire fence. An orchard was to my left, looking a little further I saw a two-foot stone fence at the far edge of the orchard. We were told we would have to climb across the barbed wire fence and gather on the other side of the stone wall and wait for him to join us, and we would be doing that in the next few minutes. He said we would make a run for it one man at a time and he would be the last one to get there. He explained to us, we would probably run into heavy sniper and mortar fire as we crossed the river from the heavily wooded hills. We heard a couple of mortars land in the orchard area as we ate our rations. I had a strong phobia of drowning, as I don't swim.

I could taste the acid coming up in my throat. A rush of adrenaline made my heart beat like I was running a 440 dash back in high school. A hot wave of panic went from my head to my toes, making my skin tingle. My throat was getting drier by the minute. For a fleeting moment I wondered, to myself, what would happen if I refused to go? Fortunately for me, my Basic Military Training and discipline pounded into me and held sway. I figured copping out was not a choice for me. I did not wish to be labeled a coward by my buddies. I would not be able to take that shame. I had to do my share.

It must be remembered it was very cold, the temperature being below freezing that night, and cold freezing rain was falling. Later I found it was six below zero that night. Our main concern was to try to keep warm and stay alive, and all the weight of our equipment was another hindrance in the crossing. If I were to fall or be dumped into the river, I would surely drown. In the meantime with all this on my mind the Lt. was giving us instructions as to what we were to do when we reached the other side. When the word was given to go, I found all that equipment; I heard bullets zinging all around me. It took all the willpower I had to make it to that fence. Besides, I had to vault over the barbed wire before getting to the fence. After vaulting the wire, I ran for the fence and waited for the other men to join me. After reaching the river, I saw what looked like it may be a boat. It was made of rubber, and was like an elliptical sausage. It was about twelve feet long, about three feet high and had six handles along the top, apparently to carry it with.

After about ten minutes the Lt. joined us and told us to listen up. On his order we would jump up, run for the boat and grab a handle on each side and carry the boat to the water. The Lt. laid there for about two minutes to catch his breath and shouting "let's go" and jumped up and headed for the boat. We jumped up and ran for the boat grabbing a handle on the side closest to me, and the other grabbing a handle, we started to move the boat toward the river, it was a very heavy boat. All the while, bullets were hitting all around us. By the time we got about half way across, the river current being about ten to fifteen miles per hour, we started being carried downstream and we started to paddle like mad. Everyone was paddling at his own cadence and the current was moving us swiftly downstream, I looked at the rubble of the old stone bridge and I started to get worried, there may be a possibility that we could end up in the bridge rubble and capsize. Without thinking, I called out to paddle in cadence and yelled, "hut, two three, four." In just a few seconds we began to paddle in cadence and started to move toward the far bank.

The riverbank where we were about to land appeared to be quite flat and sandy. There was an open field directing behind it that was about 200 yards wide. It was covered with grass and sloped up to a small dirt road that ran alongside the base of the wooded area. Across where we were about to land I saw a pillbox of medium size. It was built off the road into the steep hillside just behind it. No one had bothered to mention the bunker let alone telling us if it were occupied or not. I was puzzled we were not getting fire from it.

We did not see any signs telling us of a minefield, but we worried just the same of perhaps stepping on one. As we hit the shore line with the enemy bullets hitting all around us, they had been shooting at us all the time we were paddling across, but the sound of the paddles was such we didn't hear them. As we landed Sgt. yelled to pull the boat onto dry land.

I had no idea where to go the Sgt. was close by and was yelling to spread out and keep moving. By this time the mortars had stopped, as the angle was such they couldn't get to us because of the slope of the hill. Getting up and running as fast as I could with my BAR, I headed for the pillbox in front of me. I fully expected machine gun fire from it, but upon reaching it I found it to be empty. The door was open, so I ran into it and flopped down, on the concrete floor, panting like a dog. Looking around we found water about two inches deep and water seeping in the backside from the hill. I did not care; it was a sweet home for a few minutes. On the front side of the bunker was a very wide slit, about twenty feet long and looking down at the river where we had just landed. Had the bunker been occupied, we would have been mowed down like grass. Another lucky day.

Being nineteen years old, I did not understand very much about the war. I did not get wounded, when a lot of my buddies either was wounded or killed. I just could not understand why I wasn't hit as they were.

It was cold and damp in the bunker and it was getting dark and I began to shiver as I watched the snow falling around me. We had no contact with any of the officers or Non Coms since we left the boat. We waited approximately two hours in the bunker and suddenly we heard footsteps coming toward the bunker, we all were on the alert immediately as we didn't know if it was friend or foe. We had been given the sign and counter sign; this is a code used to know if it was a friend or foe. We heard someone call out "MASHIE", the song for the day, we quickly returned the countersign "NIBLICK" and we were all very happy to hear the countersign. A GI with a flashlight came in the doorway, and told us we were to follow him. The rest of the squad and the Lt. were in a barn down the road. It was pitch black and a cold sleet was falling. I could hear the river to my right as we went to the barn. We all realized we were in enemy lines and the river was between us and safety. Following the messenger through the door of the barn, I noticed it was built like the one across the river, only half as big. There were no lights in the barn as we stumbled over the doorsill. We were told to call out our names as we came through the door into the barn and find a place to sit down.

The Sgt. and the Lt. started talking in a low voices at the other end of the barn after about a half hour after we had dozed off, speaking in a subdued voice, just loud enough to be heard, he told us that the pontoon boat had to be taken back across the river so that the rest of the platoon could come across and join us. No one wanted to volunteer to do the taking of the boat across the river. The Lt's job wasn't an easy one and not as he would have liked it to be at this time. He would have to make a decision as to who would take the boat back. I was startled out of my daydream when I heard my name called to take the boat across. Take three men, and you are in command. Take the boat back under fire and in a swift current was not my way of being in command. I called out the name of the three men who had been in the Pillbox with me and headed out the door with them, hoping we could find our way back to where the boat would be.

We found the road we had come from the boat, we were opposite the old pill box we had been in, we followed down the slope after walking through what we thought may be a mine field and found the boat.

Looking across the river, we were about twenty yards below where we floated the boat into the river. Dragging the boat up river so that the current would carry us to the place we wanted to land the boat. After twenty or thirty minutes of dragging the boat we launched it and started for the far shore. I figured if we paddled hard enough we could make it OK. The river was flowing to our left so I knew we had to try to keep heading as far to our right as we could to counter the current. Sitting on the edges of the boat I told the men not to paddle until we were far enough the enemy couldn't hear our paddles hitting the water. As we approached the middle of the river we began to pick up speed very rapidly more than I would have liked for us to do. Paddling like hell and with all the strength we had in our arms after some frantic paddling I could make out the outline of the shore. We were approaching very fast and I could see we were going to miss the landing spot, where we could beach the boat. We then hit the steep bank with bushes along the bank, I reached over as much as I could to try to grab a limb or something. Not being able to do so, and seeing a possibility of going into the rubble of the bridge and hoping the water wasn't too deep as I can't swim. Making sure I had a hand on the rope at the front of the boat when I jumped and I sank into water and mud knee deep. Four guys were sliding down the bank to give us a hand. One of the men grabbed my hand and helped me up the bank. One of the other men grabbed the rope and now it was their boat. Again, I felt lucky to be alive. I sat down and took off my overshoes, which were full of water and feeling I was back in the real world and waiting for someone to tell me what I was to do next. Our CO, a Captain saw me and realized I was the one who brought the boat back to them, I was to go back in the same boat and guide the men on how to get across and to rejoin my buddies on the other side. As soon as we got in the boat, the Captain took over and told everyone to paddle hard and in cadence. I guess he was watching how we crossed and followed suit. As soon as we landed, I was told to take the men to the barn where the rest of the squad was quartered.

It must have been a little after midnight and I was totally exhausted. After reporting to the Lt. in the barn, I took the time to take off my overshoes, shoes and wet socks. Reaching under my shirt, and retrieving the warm and dry socks I had next to my body and put the wet socks back under my shirt next to my body to dry. Donning my dry socks, my boots and overshoes, I went to sleep.

The next morning, after a cold "K" ration for breakfast, the Lt. formed up our squad and told us we were going to move to the middle of the hill and dig in. It was below zero and the ice-cold rain we had to contend with was miserable. Our position was about one hundred yards above the barn we had left earlier and it overlooked the destroyed bridge about two hundred yards away. We maintained this position for four cold miserable days. We were told hot chow would be waiting for us down by the deserted pillbox and we were to go down one by one after dark. Hot chow was like heaven.

Digging our foxhole and having a good start, something happened down the road, and we were told that the Lt. had told the platoon Sgt. to take three men and search the gully between our positions and the mess tent down the road. Passing this gully on our first trip for hot chow we saw a sing on a post that read "ACHTUNG MINEN". As soon as the Sgt. saw the sign, he told the Lt. about it, but the Lt. in a very firm voice said that is an order, the Sgt. looked at him for approximately 30 to forty seconds, then turned and called three GIs to go with him. Taking off with the three men, they started up the gully each following with a good spacing between them. About half way up the gully, the Sgt. stepped on a mine. We heard the explosion. As the Sgt. tried to crawl out of the gully, his hand hit another mine and blew off arm and head. The man directly behind the Sgt. got hit by some of the shrapnel and the other two managed to get out unharmed. The blackened, headless, armless, torso of the Sgt. was left sitting upright in the middle of the gully. We had to look at this each time we went to chow, very sickening sight. After this happened we all hated the Lt's guts. Everybody just ignored him and stayed away from him as far as possible. He had lost all the respect we ever had for him.

During the first day in our foxhole, I saw something taking place down by the rubble of the bridge. Looking through my field glasses, I saw a group of engineers build a bridge across at that point. Using a mobile crane they were laying a pontoon bridge into place. This would mean tanks and more help would be coming over to help us. As I was watching, I saw a puff of black smoke in the midst of forty engineers working on the site. Those who had not been wounded or killed dropped what they were doing and took off for safety. When things quieted down they returned to their task of building the bridge, and caring for their wounded. In the four to six hours I watched this the shelling came approximately five or six times. My hat was off to this group of Combat Engineers, whom I always looked on as rear echelon troops, I sure changed my mind after this. When we received the order to move out, they were approximately seventy-five percent finished.

The best foxholes are the ones where you dig a shelf on one side and if it is for two men, then one for each man, and deep enough if it rains you won't have to sit in the water. We would try to keep them dry with a cover of either a raincoat or some other cover over the hole itself. You were always on the alert to any sound that seemed to be close to you, even if it were a buddy approaching, you made sure it wasn't the enemy. One day, a foxhole about twenty yards from our hole, we found a dead GI lying on the ground between us. How he got there was a mystery, a real puzzle to us. We were the only ones on the hill. Whenever you find a body like that, you are to mark it by either sticking his rifle with the bayonet on it into the ground and hang his helmet on the rifle so the people assigned to pick up the dead was able to spot it and tag it before loading it on a truck. I often wondered if all these men were found.

After the fifth day right after chow, we were told we were moving out and to assemble down on the road at 0900. It had started to snow through the night and the ground was completely covered. It was cold and we could see our breath like we were smoking. We formed two columns with the Platoon Sgt. and Lt. in front. This was the same Lt. we no longer trusted due to the mine disaster. I didn't realize how the others felt about him until we were given orders to "move out". He started up the road believing the rest of us were following him. Which normally we would have done without question. Not this time! The platoon Sgt. was about five paces behind the Lt. and as he glanced behind him he stopped dead in his tracks. Not a GI had moved. We just didn't trust him and we were too battle wise. By this time the Lt. stopped and saw we hadn't moved a step. In a very loud and angry voice, he hollered for us to get off our asses and get them in gear and move out. Not a man moved. As far as we were concerned he had lost command and we were not about to follow him. He turned to the Sgt. and said something, which we couldn't hear and the Sgt., looking at us, took a few paces toward us and with a stern face, gave us, the command to move out. We all hesitated for about ten seconds and then the guys in the front started to move out. The Lt. had a puzzled look on his face like he didn't know what the hell was going on. He disappeared about two days later. I guess, in the strictest sense, we had mutinied.

The narrow one lane dirt road led around the hill where we had dug in earlier. It looked like it headed up the hill into the heavy forest. The temperature had dropped and my hands and feet were very cold. I was happy to be moving as it helped to keep me warm. After marching for a few minutes, we passed a small opening set back from the road; I looked over and saw a German helmet on the top of a rifle stuck in the ground, by its bayonet. For the first time I felt a kinship for him. It was as miserable for him as it was for us. I felt sorry for him as he had as much choice as I did and had to be in this godforsaken place.

We continued up the road for about an hour, we were marching on a road that looked like an old logging road and also we were in a deep heavy snow-laden forest. Snow that was crunching under our boots. We soon came up on a very large concert bunker set back off the road and it had been pounded pretty badly. Thank goodness it had been abandoned. My first thought was, thank God it was not occupied. I looked over toward the front of the bunker and noticed something sticking out of the snow. I couldn't quite make out what it was. I didn't recognize it right away. As we got closer I was startled to see that it was a dead German's bare arm sticking up. I could just make out the outline of the snow covered it was attached to. I looked around and saw five other German bodies lying in the snow. The exposed skin on the arms and legs looked very pale, almost like alabaster, it was eerie. Nobody said a word as we walked by; each had his own thoughts.

After about four hours of marching we finally reached the other side of the forest looking out we could see a large open grassy area directly in front of us. It looked much like a grazing area for cattle. There was a small village about a mile away at the far end of the open area. We were told to dig in and set up a defense line. We were also told that we had to be combat alert, one guy in each foxhole, on guard, at all times. We were told that we could possibly expect an attack during the night. I did not realize at the time that I was looking down the little German village that was the town of Stockigt. I did not realize it at the time, but it would be the scene of some heavy fighting for us in the next few days.

Edgar E. Bredbenner, Jr.
Company B, 318th Infantry Regiment
We Never Got to England

This was a day I will never forget and it was probably the longest day of my life. The 80th Infantry Division had moved from central France to join the Third U.S. Corps along with the 26th Infantry Division and the 4th Armored Division to attack the southern shoulder portion of the Bulge area. It was a long, cold ride in open trucks with no blankets or overcoats and we spent almost two days without stopping. At the time we had about 15-16 men in our squads and we attacked Ettelbruck, Luxembourg, on 22 December 1944. We fought there for three days, losing many men, all officers and all our automatic weapons. This attack was called off because of the cost in men and on Christmas Eve we again loaded on open trucks to join with the 4th Armored on their attack on Bastogne, Belgium. This was another long cold night.

Early on Christmas morning we moved out and we were immediately fired on. A burst of a burp gun hit me in the neck and ear; I took off my helmet and shredded the towel around my neck. Medics patched me up and we continued through the thick woods deep on the right flank. Tanks were on the road on our left, but we could not hear them; the air was so heavy and the snow swirling about. We had sniper fire from the rear, right flank and from the front. Artillery fire and mortars shattered the trees about us, but we kept moving forward into the attack, losing many more men. About 1300 a tree burst hit me in the thigh and opened my leg up. A medic patched me up, gave me a sulfa powder and morphine and said to hike back to the aid station, which was five miles. No stretcher-bearers were getting through the waist deep snows and the enemy had closed in behind our lines. Three of us started back, but without our weapons. One man had his heel shot away and the other had been hit in the back and none of us were bleeding, it was so cold and in the deep snows. We found wounded men, trying to get to the aid station that had been shot and killed by snipers and their equipment gone. We had a few firefights, but when we returned fire the enemy melted away in the woods. The medics had no blankets for the wounded. We had no overcoats, Shoe Pacs or any of the needed camouflage clothing. If wounded you walked your way out, if you stayed you froze to death. No fires were allowed and we saw no buildings at any time. After a P-49 sprayed us, we reached the aid station about dark. We were checked out and placed in ambulances to travel to an Air-Evacuation Hospital, near the French-Belgium-Luxembourg borders. We were told we would be flown to England and probably to the USA. We all fell asleep in the warm ambulance and all of us had severe pain from frozen feet and legs, and did they ever sting. We were placed on stretchers and put aboard the plane after a change of bandages. About 500 feet up three German fighters fired a short burst and hit the plane. But, we were lucky. They evidently saw the landing strip lights and realized that this was a medical area and flew off. One engine was out, the plane was on fire, some of the men and nurses were wounded, or killed, and the co-pilot was out of commission. The pilot was wounded, but brought the plane around and we landed on the airstrip. We were back mobile again and helped to remove the dead and wounded. Ten minutes later the plane exploded. I was moved to an operating area and I sat in a chair while a doctor gave me seven shots of Novocain and opened up my thigh to the bone. I sat there and watched him. Today, I would probably pass out. After being operated on at the Air Evac Hospital

I was sent by ambulance to Commerce, France to the 50th General Hospital for 80 days and then sent right back into combat. (The ironic item is that I was told that probably after I arrived in England I would be sent back to the states???) They were short of Infantry for sure. I never got to England.

R. J. Trammel
Company D, 318th Infantry Regiment
Every Christmas Since... Extra Special

Edward Bredbenner hit most of the high notes of the action by the 1st Battalion of the 318th Infantry Regiment (Old Virginia Tires). He left out, we were pulled out of the line at Ettelbruck on the 24th and married-up with CCA, 4th Armored along the Arlon-Bastogne highway just south of Warnach where we opened up our sleeping (?) bags and laid them on top of the snow for a Christmas Eve nod or two—there was no way to dig a hole in that frozen ground. Our cooks somehow gave us pancakes for Christmas morning breakfast although the syrup froze soon as it hit the mess kits. We jumped off in the attack at daybreak (about 0800 DDST). Our Line of Departure was a fence line on the edge of a deep draw which was right under the Krauts' outpost line and they opened up on us before we cleared the LD. Our objective was now secondary to restoring some kind of cohesive attack to clear the road from Warnach to Tintange which wound through hilly terrain with a high granite wall on the north side and a relatively gradual slope on the south of the road. Unfortunately, it was thickly wooded serving as host to a tree farm.

Bredbenner's "B" Company had the right flank and truly took a beating from tree bursts by the Kraut assault guns and mortars firing from the high ground in the vicinity of our objective Tintange. Captain Sam McAllester in an effort to get his company out from under this terror got permission to deviate from the battalion's plan by going farther to his right with an envelopment, which succeeded in getting the scenery changed. With this aggressive action and help from an air strike on the objective by the XIXth TAC, the emergence from "The Valley of Death" was accomplished about 1530 hours. The battalion had lost its trusted veteran CO LTC Mike Tosi in a bloody Ettelbruck encounter during 22-23 December and had a new man at the helm on the 25th. We got even a newer guy on the 26th who turned out to be an outstanding combat leader for the remainder of the war, then Captain Charles Gakin.

I don't recall the reports of various companies' unit strength when the 1st Battalion was relieved by elements of the 35th Division on the 28th/29th, but heard consensus reports that the whole kit and caboodle was hauled out with 6 deuce and a half, so 20 men per company average including headquarters personnel sounded about right.

As I was being evacuated on a medic jeep about noon on the trail en route reliving the 80th's representatives in the "Relief of Bastogne," the 1st and 2nd Battalions of the 318th, and each received the Presidential Unit Citation for their efforts.

I was a Second Lieutenant assigned to "D" Company in early September and intermittent absences received my mail at "DOG" Company until July 1945.

Being there on 25 December 1944 has made every Christmas Day since... extra special... and painful when remembering those guys who didn't make it through that tree farm en route to Tintange.

Kenneth Roettger
Company E, 317th Infantry Regiment
Receives a Christmas Gift
The Day Santa Flew a P-47

A few hundred riflemen shivered and crouched in frozen foxholes waiting for death. For more than two days we neither had food nor sleep.

Starting about half strength, our battalion in two days had lost nearly half of the remainder and many weapons.

Foxholes were so far apart men had to shout to each other and this one thin line was the entire depth with no way to stop armor. Through the still winter air came the unmistakable sound of German tanks. It was but minutes until we were overwhelmed by hundreds of enemy. It was Christmas Day 1944.

It all began 10 days before, when Hitler launched the last great Nazi offensive, which developed into the Battle of the Bulge. At that time I was a rifleman.

Piled 25 to 30 men in open trucks, we skidded over icy and crowded roads for the entire day and night. Fog, dampness, and cold added to the misery.

Huddling together without food we didn't know or care that this would be called one of the most astounding moves of modern warfare. General Patton pulled three divisions from one attack, moved them 150 miles over poor roads under terrible weather conditions, and attacked in a new direction in less than two days.

During the night, fog and enemy air attacks caused the trucks to become lost but by morning all had reached the battle area. Debarking without sleep, we dug in, in front of the towers of powerful Radio Luxembourg. With the German army shunted, the regiment turned to the offensive.

This began a three-day period of probing by both sides in the midst of the Ardennes Forest. Every day seemed the same: miles of marching, intense cold, swirling fog, mysterious woods, and general confusion.

The Ardennes landscape under overcast skies resembled the dark abode of evil spirits from tales of the Black Forest. Every rock became a menacing danger in the misty shroud. The forest was so thick that an entire army could hide among the firs. The unreality was heightened by the utter silence as the fir needle floor and banks of fog muffled sounds. Adding to the difficulties were the many steep hills and narrow streams that rushed between them.

Marching was especially hard because of the weight we carried about 30 pounds of combat equipment including our rifle, grenades and ammunition.

But the worst were the clothes. I wore (starting from the skin out) shorts, two sets of long underwear, two pair woolen pants, two wool shirts, a sweater, field jacket, scarf, and overcoat. On my feet were two pairs of socks, combat boots, and overshoes, while on my head was a cap, towel as a scarf, helmet liner, and helmet. Two pairs of gloves completed the outfit. We kept these clothes on 24 hours a day for weeks, for even with all this we were constantly cold.

But the Army decided men could carry more. Because the Germans were infiltrating dressed in American uniforms, everyone was issued the one item of equipment the Germans didn't have— gas masks. Later passing through a field, we could see each man hit the ground when a German machine gun opened up. Almost as though it was planned, each soldier shed his gas mask right there and that was the end of that plan.

Despite the weight, we stumbled 10 to 15 miles each day with temperatures dropping to 20 below zero. The water froze in our canteens but on the night of December 21 snow fell and we ate that to slake our thirst. Most of us drank from an open rushing creek until we discovered bodies in the water upstream. Food was mostly "K" rations. Fires were forbidden since they would draw enemy shells, so everything was eaten cold.

At night it was necessary to dig a hole to stay alive. Foxhole digging in the frozen dirt was a tiring, discouraging project. The ordinary folding shovel we carried soon broke in the hard crust, but soldiers the world over are natural scroungers. Within a few days nearly every squad had a full size shovel or pick taken from an overturned truck, or a burned out tank, a deserted barn, or a captured enemy position. Even so, it took over and hour for two men to chop out a shallow hole.

At night, if possible, blankets were brought up to our holes but frequently this could not be done and two men just huddled together in one hole. It might seem hard to sleep sitting up fully dressed in a frozen hole each night, after the day's trials it was almost impossible to stay awake. Yet our lives depended on one man staying awake. All had heard of men found dead in the morning with German bayonets in their chests. So one man would sleep for an hour while his buddy watched and then they would exchange throughout the long night. It was a wonderful feeling to be alive when dawn came, but then, with the realization of what the day would bring, one questioned the very value of life.

As I climbed stiff and frozen from the hole to march on aching feet, I wondered if hell wouldn't be welcome as a chance to get warm again.

After three days we were completely exhausted. Except for a few minor brushes and occasional shelling no real battle had been fought but casualties mounted. Each army felt for the other in the fog-shrouded fields and forests of the Ardennes. Were not our minds numbed, it would have been eerie, as if two giant ghosts played hide and seek in the swirling gray mists.

The fourth morning we knew things would happen. Orders had been received for the regiment to attack the ridges south of Welscheid, Luxembourg, which were occupied by strong German forces.

Throughout the gloomy days, as we moved forward, we saw more and more signs. Smoldering buildings, abandoned meals in emplacements, and tracks in the snow all indicated the nearness of the enemy. The final proof came late in the day when five tanks joined us as the entire battalion crossed an open field. The tanks looked so strong that we felt naked in comparison. They seemed to be protective big brothers.

Suddenly spears of flame seemed to shoot out from three of the tanks. A moment later came the boom of the hidden 88s. The men in the tanks never had a chance; they were cremated instantly. The fires were so intense riflemen nearby were badly burned. The two surviving tanks were ordered to leave as we continued.

Now we entered the wildest terrain for which the Ardennes is known. Rugged, almost vertical hills covered with fir forests became darker like a scene from a horror movie. It was the start of one of the most terrifying nights I have known.

As the official army history of the battle reports: "Sometime after midnight the forward battalion started into the assault over a series of rough slopes where man was outlined by the bright moonlight reflecting from the glazed field of snow. The enemy, waiting with machine guns on the reverse slopes, had all the best of it."

As one of the lead companies in the action I will never forget how as the battalion crossed a small field between hills, machine gun fire tore into our ranks. From then on we kept to the woods and hills as sporadic firing from both sides and flanking probes continue. The night in the forest became so dark that our widespread formations became a single line with each man trying to keep his hand on the man in front of him. Up a steep ravine the line clawed until fiery tracers caused an angled decent. We started back up another incline and then shells began to fall over the entire area. Each explosion gave a bright light that blinded us for minutes. The routine became climb, duck, climb, and duck. Hitting the ground while climbing a steep hill consisted of just holding on to a tree or brush since we were already against the ground.

Another firefight caused us to go down again. Here it was so steep we couldn't walk but slid down the icy slope, hugging trees and crushing through brush. At the bottom our battalion was a confused mass of men. Some weapons and ammunition were lost and a few men became separated and hurt. As the confused group started up still in another direction, I found myself near the end of the column. Everyone was so exhausted from the all-day and night maneuver that we had to stop the climb every few minutes to rest.

At one rest stop, a man fell asleep and didn't warn the end of the column when the unit moved on. As a result a dozen were left behind, lost in the middle of enemy action with no idea of which way to go and able to see only a few feet. Shells continued to fall and rifle fire was heard from what seemed like all directions.

Waiting several hours until dawn, we climbed straight up through the forest. The sound of digging came from the top but it was impossible to tell if it was our outfit or Germans digging in. As we crept closer, a string of GI curses was a most welcome sound. It was our men and we were saved.

Saved, that is, until full daylight revealed our positions. During the night movements we had deeply penetrated the enemy lines and now sat on top of the ridge, completely surrounded. We had not eaten since noon of the preceding day, and now we knew we would get no food until we worked our way out of the trap.

All that day we prepared our defensive positions, waiting for the enemy to attack. We could hear their horses and wagons as they brought up ammunition and weapons. Except for artillery and a few patrols they left us alone.

During the day the weather improved as the clouds began to break. Possibly the Germans wanted to wait for it to clear up before hitting us. Above the clouds came a noise of aerial combat and then the sounds of a plane diving under full power. The ground seemed to shake when it hit at least a mile away.

That night it was decided that we could get out of our trap the same way we got into it. For hours we crawled down through the woods from that ridge. Every time a flare went off or a shell exploded we froze, but this time darkness and the rough country were our allies.

Almost like a miracle we made it to a field where foxholes were completed shortly before dawn on Christmas morning. As the sun came up, we were overjoyed to see it and a perfectly clear day. Our joy was short lived, as the position became obvious. We stretched across the middle of a wide-open field at the foot of German held hills. Any artillery observers on those hills could look right into our holes. Quickly orders were given to move back.

But it was too late and the withdrawal became a rout, as the entire field seemed to explode. Mortar and artillery fire fell everywhere. The frozen ground splattered the shells so almost all the metal fragments flew around instead of digging large holes. I felt a blow on my foot but kept running. When the survivors reached the edge of the field we hid behind trees and in ditches until the firing ceased.

Then we dug holes and formed a thin defensive line waiting for the attack we knew was coming. No one was thinking Merry Christmas—but then our presents arrived.

A low roar grew to thunderous proportions as a squadron of American fighters circled over at a low altitude. Then, sweeping single file so low over our holes that we felt their prop wash, they fired rockets into the German area. More came with the bombs and finally they strafed with their guns.

The smoke from the hills told the story. The German attack forces had been smashed. While the Battle of the Bulge meant many more weeks of brutal fighting under impossible conditions, this was the turning point of the battle for our outfit.

I've never seen any artist portray Santa Clause flying a P-47 but he must have been at the controls on that Christmas morning, for he brought us the greatest gift possible—our lives.

Joseph Drasler
Company L, 317th Infantry Regiment
War, The Greatest Curse of Mankind

It never stopped raining, day or night, during the time we bivouacked on Omaha Beach. Every time we took a gander out of our tent door rain was splattering on the sea of mud that surrounded us. It was early November 1944. Out of sheer necessity we sloshed through boot top gumbo for chow.

On a dismal cold morning we were surprised to see a convoy of Army trucks, known as the "Red Ball Express" arrive in camp. We climbed aboard still loaded down with fully stuffed barracks bags, gas masks and rifles.

Squeezed into the canvas-covered vehicles, we looked like the proverbial "sardines in a can" as we began the bizarre journey that would finally end in Nancy, France.

The convoy moved by dark of night only, over rough improvised roads, temporarily repaired bridges, around deep potholes and flooded areas, with the leading vehicle employing nothing but its "cat eyes" lights, to avoid detection by enemy aircraft. When the last truck of weary new recruits unloaded. It was not so much the end of a night Marist ride as it was the beginning of the darkest days of my entire life.

We were now in Gen. Patton's Third Army, 317th Inf. 3rd Bn. L Co., under command of Lt. Miles W. Smith, or "Smitty" as we got to know him, under the most difficult of battlefield conditions. Quicker than one could say "Holy Cow!" the grim reality of war, in all its frightful aspects, hit home like a bolt out of the blue, when the order was given to "Put on extra clothes", stuff knapsacks with extra socks, shirt, and underwear, and drop barracks bag at a barn hastily converted into a collection center, as we marched past. This was it—the brutal reality of war.

No more sleeping indoors sheltered from the frigid weather. No more hot meals or a place to shave and wash up.

From now on it would be life in the open, sleeping in foxholes, occasionally in an abandoned barn or building that offered shelter from the bitter cold. It was initiation into life in the cold and rain, surviving on K rations and a canteen of water.

L Company immediately moved into a thick pine forest to protect a flank of the city against enemy counter-attacks. Constant guarding against infiltrating enemy troops and maintaining surveillance day and night left precious little time for sleep or letters home.

Addendum to the Published Story of My Participation
In The Battle of the Bulge
From The Book "Veterans of the Battle of the Bulge" (1991)

As an infantry rifleman in General Patton's Third Army during a period of six months, I was in combat at Metz, St. Avold, St. Vith, Farbersviller (where half of my unit, Company L was lost), Wiltz and defended the area around Neiderfeulen and Ettelbruck, in Luxembourg, where again Company L was wiped out almost to a man.

I fought in the Battle of the Bulge from Dec. 23. 1944 to Jan. 27, 1945. And in the Battle of the Rohr from March 31 to April 15, 1945. Fought in three campaigns, Ardennes, Rhineland and Central Europe across France, Germany and Austria. Directed fire against enemy personnel and light vehicles. Went on combat and reconnaissance patrols to locate enemy gun positions and to learn the strength and disposition of enemy troops. Did outpost guard duty in the front line to prevent a surprise attack by the enemy. Served overseas for 18 months.

During combat I underwent numerous strafing from enemy planes and attacks by German 88s. I remember the awful sound of burp guns and screaming meemies. Saw the utter destruction, death, devastation, human agony and sorrow of the war. My basic training was at Camp Fannin, Texas, where I qualified as expert rifleman. Earned the Combat Infantry Badge and served as rifleman and first scout on the front line with the 317 Inf. Regt. 80th Div.

After wading ashore from LST's at Omaha Beach I lived in foxholes much of the time while battling through the heavily forested country. Learned to subsist on K, C, and D rations, and very little rest or sleep. Later, when the enemy was on the run and we were dashing across Germany. I rode on tanks, jeeps, armored cars or any other mobile vehicle, in pursuit of the enemy. After the war I was part of a Special Task Force stationed in Pusan, Czechoslovakia.

My most memorable moment, profoundly felt and everlastingly remembered, occurred on Christmas Eve, 1944, following an all-day battle, men of the 317th Infantry, 80th Div. engaged in an attack to secure a hill in the vicinity of Neiderfeulen, Luxembourg, that would forever after be remembered as "Bloody Knob".

The 305th Med. Bn. Field Hospital hallway and waiting room was jammed with wounded GIs, seated on chairs and laying on the floor, anywhere room could be found for another litter case. Hours later, after receiving treatment for my frozen toes, I was assigned a cot in the corner of a room facing a little cheerfully decorated Christmas tree that captivated my emotions completely. One look at that little tree so symbolic of the season triggered such a flood of tears and emotions I could do nothing but let them flow. The thought of loved ones back home, recollections of dead and wounded, assisting two of my closest stateside buddies (Sylvester Perciabosco from Omaha, Neb. and Dick Thorne from Elizabeth N.J., both badly wounded), off the Hill through all that, I remained rational and in control, but the sight of that twinkling little Christmas tree.... it was incredible.

In retrospect, the resistance we encountered at Wiltz and Farbersviller proved to be only a prelude to what was to occur at Bastogne. On the afternoon of 19 December 1944 we boarded trucks and moved 150 miles north to Gonderange, Luxembourg, where in the next three days swift preparations were made for carrying out 317's role in the Battle of the Bulge.

With little food or water remaining after maneuvering over the frozen, inhospitable countryside, we encountered enemy resistance in the vicinity of Neiderfuelen on Christmas Day— a day I will never forget. It turned into one of the bloodiest battle's L Company and its supporting companies would fight during the entire war. In frigid weather, over frozen snow-covered ground, the attack began up an open hillside that stretched for miles to its top. A hill that would be remembered forever by 317th dough's as the "Bloody Knob." Withering artillery, mortar, machine gun and rifle fire greeted us from all direction.

We forged ahead through murderous opposition, driving the enemy from one position after another. It was pure hell, fought in the worse weather conditions ever experienced in those parts. Casualties like wildfire, overwhelming our medics and leaving wounded men to depend on battlefield buddies to get them back to a road, where they could be picked up and rushed to the hospital. On two occasions I helped wounded men off the hill. Buddies who were so disabled they were helpless against enemy counterattacks. Their letters I received after the war expressed eternal gratitude.

When darkness descended on that sad day, confusion was so widespread no one could locate their CPs. It took days before we were able to regroup. In one fierce day of battle, I and about a dozen survivors of L Company became the "old timers" of the outfit. And at the end of that day of infamy, I also ended up in the 305th Medical Battalion hospital in Neiderfuelen, with frozen feet.

Relief of Bastonge was completed. The German hopes for a major break-through had collapsed. German troops soon lost faith in the ultimate victory and enemy resistance disintegrated into isolated points of resistance.

How true the words, "Soldiers are citizens of death's gray land." The most experienced soldier finds it difficult to recreate a true picture of the horrors of war. And even the electronic media with all of its technical know-how, produces mostly phony scenarios. In 1945 I was in a Division Parade where General Patton reviewed the troops. At the time the 80th Div. was being redeployed to the States, our Regt. was attached to the Quartermaster Depot in Munich, Germany.

I have pleasant remembrances of a 10-day visit to the French Riviera, a visit to Hitler's "Eagle's Nest" at Berchtesgaden, two trips to Paris and a few shorter Army passes. Reflecting on the vicious combat in the Battle of the Bulge and at Farbersviller, it is gratifying to recall incidents in which I was able to assist some of my buddies who were badly wounded, under conditions of warfare when there were no medics to help them. One of them was Silvester Perciabosco, from Omaha, Neb. who came over with me from Camp Shanks. He was shot through the arm. Another was Frank Amego, a Porta Rican who was shot through the ball of his foot. I helped both of them off a hill above Neiderfeulen in Luxembourg to a safe area where they could be picked up by jeep and taken to a hospital. The hospital was at Hollenberry where I also ended up with frostbite and trench foot. I also helped my wounded buddy Walt Hevess (New York), in the battle of Farbersviller, moving him back to safety where he could be evacuated.

Sgt. Day G. Turner
Company B, 319th Infantry Regiment
Medal of Honor

Sgt. Turner was one of the four men of the 80th to receive the Congressional Medal of Honor posthumously, and is the only one of the three still buried in Europe. He died on 8 February 1945 and is buried in the American Military Cemetery, Hamm, Luxembourg. He also was awarded the Purple Heart with two Oak Leaf Clusters. His citation follows:

"Rank and organization: Sergeant, Company B, 319th Infantry, 80th Infantry Division. Place and date: At Dahl, Luxembourg, 8 January 1945. Entered service at: Nescopeck, PA Birth: Berwick, PA. G.O. No. 49, 28 June 1945.

"Citation: He commanded a nine-man squad with the mission of holding a critical flank position. When overwhelming numbers of enemy attacked under cover of withering artillery, mortar, and rocket fire, he withdrew his squad into a nearby house, determined to defend it to the last man. The enemy attacked again and again and was repulsed with heavy losses. Supported by direct tank fire, they finally gained entrance, but the intrepid sergeant refused to surrender although five of his men were wounded and one was killed. He boldly flung a can of flaming oil at the first wave of attackers, dispersing them, and fought doggedly from room to room, closing with the enemy in fierce hand-to-hand encounters. He hurled hand grenade for hand grenade, bayoneted two fanatical Germans who rushed a doorway he was defending and fought on with the enemy's weapons when his own ammunition was expended. The savage fight raged for four hours, and finally, when only three men of the defending squad were left unwounded, the enemy surrendered. Twenty-five prisoners were taken eleven enemy dead and a great number of wounded were counted. Sergeant Turner's valiant stand will live on as a constant inspiration to his comrades. His heroic, inspiring leadership, his determination and courageous devotion to duty exemplify the highest tradition of the military service."

1st Lt. Edgar H. Lloyd
Company E, 319 Infantry Regiment
Medal of Honor

1st Lt. Edgar H. Lloyd was one of the four men of the 80th Infantry Division awarded the Congressional Medal of Honor during World War II. He is one of the three men who are deceased and who were awarded the Medal posthumously. His date of death and place of burial are not yet known to the 80th, but he is not listed among those still buried in Europe. His citation follows:

"Rank and Organization: 1st Lieutenant, Company E, 319th Infantry 80th Infantry Division. Place and date: Near Pompey, France, 14 September 1944. Entered service at: Blytheville, AR. G.O. No. 25, 7 April 1946.

Citation: "For conspicuous gallantry and intrepidity at the risk of his life above and beyond the call of duty. On 14 September 1944, Company E 319 Infantry, with Lieutenant Lloyd was serving as a rifle platoon leader, was assigned the mission of expelling an estimated enemy force of 200 men from a heavily fortified position near Pompey, France. As the attack progressed, Lieutenant Lloyd's platoon advanced to within 50 yards of the enemy position where they were caught in a withering machine-gun and rifle fire crossfire which inflicted heavy casualties and momentarily disorganized the platoon. With complete disregard for his own safety, Lieutenant Lloyd leaped to his feet and led his men on a run into raking fire, shouting encouragement to them. He jumped into the first enemy machine-gun position, knocked out the gunner with his fist, dropped a grenade, and jumped out before it exploded. Still shouting encouragement he went from one machine-gun nest to another, pinning the enemy down with his sub-machine-gun fire until he was within throwing distance, and the destroyed them with hand grenades. He personally destroyed five machine-guns and many of the enemy, and by his daring leadership and conspicuous bravery inspired his men to overrun the enemy positions and accomplish the objective in the fact of seemingly insurmountable odds. His audacious determination and courageous devotion to duty exemplify the highest traditions of the military forces of the United States."

2nd Lt. Harry J. Michael
Company L, 318th Infantry Regiment
Medal of Honor

2nd Lt. Harry J. Michael was one of the four men of the 80th Infantry Division awarded the Congressional Medal of Honor during World War II. He was one of the three men who are deceased and awarded the Medal posthumously. He died 14 March 1945. His place of burial is not known to the 80th, but he is not listed among those still buried in Europe. His citation follows:

"Rank and organization: Second Lieutenant, Company L, 318th Infantry, 80th Infantry Division. Place and date: Near Neiderzerf, Germany, 14 March 1945. Entered service at Milford, IN. Birth: Milford, IN. G.O. No. 18, 13 February 1946.

"Citation: He was serving as a rifle platoon leader when his company began an assault on a wooded ridge northeast of the village of Neiderzerf, Germany, early on 13 March 1945. A short distance up the side of the hill, Lieutenant Michael, at the head of his platoon, heard the click of an enemy machine-gun bolt. Quietly halting the company, he silently moved off into the woods and discovered two enemy machine guns and crews. Executing a sudden charge, he completely surprised the enemy and captured the guns and crews. At daybreak, enemy voices were heard in the thick woods ahead. Leading his platoon in a flanking movement, they charged the enemy with hand grenades and, after a bitter fight, captured 25 members of an SS Mountain Division, three artillery pieces, and twenty horses. While his company was establishing its position, Lieutenant Michael made two personal reconnaissance missions of the wood on his left flank. On his first mission he killed two, wounded four, and captured six enemy soldiers single-handedly. On the second mission he captured seven prisoners. During the afternoon he led his platoon on a frontal assault of a line of enemy pillboxes, successfully capturing the objective, killing ten and capturing thirty prisoners. The following morning the company was subjected to sniper fire and Lieutenant Michael, in an attempt to find the hidden sniper, was shot and killed. The inspiring leadership and heroic aggressiveness displayed by the Lieutenant upheld the highest traditions of the military service."

Abe Lashin
Company K, 319th Infantry Regiment
A New Replacement

Some sugar. I got the glad eye from the baker's daughter, and I thought,
"What a hero I could be...
with a little sugar I could have my first love affair right here in France. Hubba-hubba..."

For the next few days, I started to collect little packs of sugar and even liberated a larger box of the sweet stuff. As luck would have it, I got one more pass into Marseille, and made my way to the "boulangerie" and deposited my "loot". Unfortunately, there could be no overnighter, so all I got was profuse thanks, and a shy kiss from mademoiselle and that was the end of my love "affair...." and it was back to the pick-up point and "home". About a week later we got copies of the Stars and Stripes, a GI newspaper. The headlines screamed that the Germans had broken through our lines up in Belgium and Luxembourg. Lots of American losses. The weather had been bad; snow, freezing cold and fog. Under this cover the Germans had moved three Armies and surprised our troops, overrunning them and supposedly heading for Antwerp to cut off our supply port and supply lines. This created a bulge in our lines and the battle to flatten out this bulge by troops for the next month was to become known as The Battle of the Bulge.

Our location was a hundred miles south of this onslaught, but everybody seemed to be getting a little edgy. Sometimes we heard distant thunder of artillery. Or was it thunder....

One night as we lay sleeping, there was a distant drone of an airplane. The GI on guard duty must have panicked and thought he heard an armada of bombers and called out. "Air raid... air raid everybody up... air raid" Well. You can imagine what happened next. Everyone safely asleep in their fart sacks dreaming peacefully, when awakened by this yelling. Not realizing that we were sleeping in pup tents that you can only sit up in, not stand up in, most everybody jumped up from their sleeping position, and I mean UP, so that their head hit the canvas ridge of the tent and pulled the tent, pegs and all out of the ground, and stumbled around and into each other, falling down, getting up clumsily, trying to shake off the canvas tent from around their bodies.... Hilarious, to say the least. Finally, someone, on the loudspeaker, calmed us down. The camp was a mess, but it didn't matter. We got orders to move out later that day; so we just snoozed into the dawn's early light as best we could, and began folding our tents later in the morning. These late night flights later became known as "piss call Pete," or "Bed check Charlie". They were usually observation non-combatant planes either theirs or ours.

After a hot breakfast, we collected our gear, including folded tents, and marched off to the trucks waiting for us. Each platoon climbed on board their truck, and it was off to the railroad depot. There, waiting for us, were these old rickety-freight cars, a long line of them. They were called "40 and 8's". The reference here was that each freight car could hold 40 personnel or 8 cattle or horses... I believe that these cars were used during the First World War and since.

Anyhow, it was our luck that the car my platoon was assigned to previously had 40 cattle, and we spent half the day cleaning out the floorboards and washing them down. We were going to be" housed" in these cars for the next couple of days, or so we were told. With lurches and alternating jerky stops and go we were way north, bouncing along the tracks, trying to be as comfortable as possible. We made food stops and pit stops as we rode. Some guys could not contain their bodily functions between pit stops and had to protrude that part of their body to accomplish this "evacuation"... I do believe that I handled this last sentence with a great deal of tact... but this is war. As we rode we were able to view the French countryside, and there before our eyes we could see the spoils of war. The results of artillery shelling was very evident; demolished buildings, destroyed motorized vehicles, large and small, people scrounging around the rubble for who knows what, fields pock-marked from the results of shelling, or maybe they were abandoned foxholes.

Late in the evening of the fourth day, the train came to shuddering stuttering stop. The night air was crisp and cold, and we were darn glad to get off and stretch our legs. Our bodies, and whatever else we could stretch. At the train station, we read the city sign, Brumath, a small town in the Alsace-Lorraine part of France. Our barracks or duffel bags were placed on trucks waiting for us... only our bags, not us. We were going to hike in this moonlit midnight madness, with overcoats, field packs, rifles, web belts still no ammunition), and helmets for about 10-12 miles to the town of Bischwiller.

Commands were given in hushed tones, and the companies moved out, route march. There was very little conversation, if any at all, as we marched along the street curbs, our boots making a clatter on the pavement in the stillness of the moonlit night. We marched for 50 minutes, then took a 10-minute break. More often as not, as we marched past a residence you could notice a window curtain part while the resident peeked through to see what that "racket" was.

Finally, after a few hours, we arrived at Bischwiller, dog-tired and pleading for rest and sleep. The platoons and companies peeled off into various type buildings. Company F was given accommodations in an old factory with most of the machinery gone so that we could spread out and be comfortable. There were long officer meetings with information feeding down through the Non-Coms, and finally to us about our situation, where we were, what Army we were attached to, how to behave if we go into town, no fraternization, and keep your lips sealed.

Christmas was upon us, and we were going to get turkey with all the trimmings... oh, happy day. The day after Xmas there was some rumbling, some rumors were in the works about people moving out. What company, or platoon, or who...???

The word got out, "Everybody fall out in the yard.. Important announcement." Capt. Davenport, our CO, read a General Order... "The following men called will be pulled from the ranks, and sent to another outfit as reinforcements. You men will pack your gear, take your bags and fall out after breakfast tomorrow morning for motorized transfer..."

Wouldn't you know it? Lashins' name was called out loud and clear. Finally got my transfer. Since we were a full strength infantry company, reinforcements were needed. Probably up north where the fighting was getting fairly hot, and those line company's rosters were being decimated.

Geez... another truck ride, and we were going further north with the weather getting colder and colder... And these two and a half-ton trucks were open and we were freezing. We "reinforcements" huddled as close together as possible to keep warm. As we got closer we could hear artillery, see dismantled tanks and vehicles, and lifeless bodies still in the fields or next to the vehicles. The smell of war has arrived, here it is... You are now combat operational... Whatever that could mean.

There were signs on the roadsides that indicated we were "Entering Luxembourg through the courtesy of the 80th Blue Ridge Division"...

The laden trucks drove into the grounds of a large multi-storied mansion or more likely a... medieval castle... There were armed troops milling about, hustling and bustling around other trucks, jeeps, armored personnel carriers, ambulances.. Snow everywhere, fires being stoked in 50-gallon steel cans to keep the milling GIs warm, if they were standing still. The sun was shining brightly, but there was a nip in the air. Getting hungry, I opened up a "D" ration bar, and started eating from it. Little did I know that each half inch by half inch section of this bar of chocolate was only to be eaten at intervals, not a few chunks at a time. It was very concentrated. I was to be greeted later in the evening with a case of the GIs... what a way to "go"... You learn as you go along.

Well, the trip from Alsace was over, and we were now part of the 80th Division. This Castle was the regimental HQ, and we learned that this magnificent edifice belonged to the Duchess of Luxembourg. She was in safe hands living in London waiting out the war, and HQ was temporarily leasing the premises. The reinforcements dropped out of the trucks, half frozen stiff from the ride. I swear that I could not feel my legs below the knees. Everybody was jumping up down and getting the circulation going, trying to listen to the orders being given.

Groups of names were called and a HQ Non-Com took us into the building and led us to a large room where we would bed down for the rest of the day and night, and be ready to move out in the morning after breakfast to our respective units. The Non-Com led a bunch of us to the door of some room and called out a few names. Lashin was one of them. He opened the door for us to enter. Wow, this was the biggest bathroom I have ever seen in my life. The floor was intricately designed mosaic tile, the walls were a soft hue with graffiti, in the artistic sense, of playful figures, maybe cherubim, or angels, or something. The ceiling level was quite high with more decorative light fixtures. The cabinets were ornately fabricated with thick marble counter tops. The basins and bathtub were a light marble with the accessories (hot and cold-water taps and spigots) probably gold—I can't believe that I still can recall all this.

There was a concealed niche in this grand room where a water closet was located. Alongside it was what looked like another water closet. The lot of us being naive had never seen a "bidet" before. One curious guy got real close to the bidet, and started fooling with the attachments. As he bent over, he hit the "right" one and got a squirt of toilet water right in his kisser... Laugh, we thought we'd croak... As if this wasn't enough, with daylight still permeating the room, we went over to the windows and saw that this castle was on the edge of a plateau with a valley below studded with snow-covered trees and paths. What a breathtaking beautiful sight to behold... We rested until dinner, and I couldn't wait to get back to our room where the after effects of that chocolate bar took hold. I slept fitfully that night, considering a tile floor not very accommodating.

51

I slept with my clothes on, wrapped in my blankets, with my pack as my pillow I don't think the Auto Club would give this evenings accommodations a triple A rating. Location and ambiance, yes, but not the bed. The next day dawned cold and brisk, and after a nice hot breakfast we fell out in the courtyard of the castle. Names were being called for "distribution" to the various companies of the 319th Infantry Regiment. After a while my name was called along with an ole Alfred buddy, Ed Lester. We picked up our gear and headed for some trucks that were warming their engines. We hoisted ourselves in and we were on our way driving through the beautiful snow covered countryside.

The sun started to break through and I could tell that we were traveling north. We passed some villages that looked like they bore the brunt of some devastation. If some buildings, farmhouses for the most part, weren't completely demolished you could sure see the shrapnel and bullet holes in the stucco'd exterior walls. In the snow-covered fields one could also see where mortar or cannon shells exploded searing and discoloring the pristine white snow... In the distance the thunder of exploding shells could be heard. Yes, we were nearing where the action was and is....

As we rode, we snuggled real close to keep warm in these open trucks. We arrived at one little village where a few names were called out and a few GIs dismounted with their gear and joined some company. A couple more stops and my name was called along with Eddie's and a guy named Sandsmark from Long Beach, CA. He was also from the 274th and as young as Eddie and I... more battle babies for the grind ahead. We were directed into a farmhouse set back from the icy road where the truck stopped, and were met by some Sergeant. He took our barracks bags and ushered us into another room occupied by the 1st Platoon, 3rd Squad, S/Sgt. Joe Buncic, "presiding," Sgt. Glen Mitchell, Asst. Squad leader.

Welcome to Company K, 319th Infantry Regiment, 80th Blue Ridge Infantry Division, Maj. Gen. "Horrible Horace" McBride commanding, 3rd Army, General George S. Patton, commanding. Platoon Sgt. was George Sifkin. And our Platoon Leader was Lt. Howard Rosenbloom. We learned that the Company was in a holding position taking up "residence" in this village of Heiderscheid. The 80th, we learned arrived at Utah Beach sometime in August and went right into combat across France with the 3rd Army and saw quite a bit of action ending up somewhere near Alsace Lorraine. When the Battle of the Bulge started in mid-December, Patton had them trucked up north to start to pinch the bulge from the south, giving a damn good account of themselves. They were now in a rest or holding position.

Somehow, I felt good about being with a combat-experienced outfit rather than being with the 274th of the 70th Division who were brand new and green troops facing a rough enemy. I later found out that the 70th in their first baptism of fire rose to the occasion facing SS troops at the Rhine and did themselves proud earning unit citations in combat. A few GIs from my old platoon in Co. F, 274th paid the ultimate price. But, that's the way things go, I guess.

So here we are getting introduced to the members of my new squad and platoon. I remember names like Sgt. Ott, Jim Trailer, Torn Peria, Pop Morgan who I swear looked like he was somebody s grandfather, Kraft, Harry, Griffith, and Sandsmark and Lester. I learned later that the 4th Armored Division was the 3rd Army's wedge with the 80th Division in the middle and the 5th and 26th Yankee Divisions flanking us. My dear ole Uncle Joshua Stern was an infantryman doughboy in WW I with the 26th.

Sgt. Buncic made an attempt at introducing us three teenage "combatants," Sandsmark, Lester and myself. The guys looked like a weary bunch trying to get some rest. So their acknowledgments of these new recruits was downplayed a bit. We were hardly settled in when some GI, apparently from another outfit, came storming into our room calling out, "Any youse guys seen a P-38 in this room when you occupied it....?" There was some disinterest and mumbling about from the half asleep resting troops, but it was a frustrating few seconds or a minute or so before I decided that I would offer and answer for this antsy GI looking for his P-38. I thought that would ingratiate myself with a little humor, so I responded, "Didn't see no P-38, but I saw a B-17 go through that rear door." First there were some snickers. Then the irate GI made some expletive comment that made me cower and wish that I was in the deepest foxhole in Europe.

Sgt. Buncic took the ball from there, and made some comment about my humor and not lasting too long. He further stated that he would call me "Charlie" didn't want to know my name... and he call Eddie, "Johnny". Boy, what he must have thought about these fresh unshaven alleged infantrymen joining these battle-tested GIs.

Bit of explanation is required here about the P38 incident... A P38 is a .38 caliber German Luger pistol. That poor guy who was looking for that pistol probably liberated it from some Kraut officer and wanted to hold onto it as a souvenir of war. He was dead serious about his loss and here I was, this raw replacement mouthing off trying to be funny. It is true that throughout my life I have always tried to find some humor somewhere, anywhere, anyplace, anytime... As a matter of fact where many GIs carried bibles in their breast field jacket pocket, probably on the left side, I carried a soft covered book, called "A Thesaurus of humor", and published by the Infantry Journal. There were over 350 pages of jokes of about a hundred categories... Pick a category and I can look up a joke for you.

Well, that P38 incident was soon forgotten, and I tried to get into the loop of battlefield friendships. I can recall that maybe two of my comrades in arms made conversation with me. There was a fellow named Kraft who suggested that I stick close to him and do what he does during any fighting. Seemed to be a nice guy... Came from Iowa, I think. Another fellow, Sgt. Glen Mitchell was a Texas walking preacher in peacetime. He found out that I was Jewish, and he would corner me in conversation about what I knew of Judaism, our rites, our holidays, our ways of living... etc. He was a very interesting character.

Sgt. Buncic, out of Pittsburgh, was a no-nonsense type of guy. He was a good leader and you had to toe the line with him or he'd let you know about it. A case in point happened one night when Eddie and I had to pull guard duty in a perimeter defense around this village while in the holding position. It was shortly after we joined up with the 1st Platoon. After leaving the 274th, and riding north in the open trucks for two long cold days and nights we were pretty tired added to the first days with our new outfit. Nevertheless we had to pull a duty time frame between 2200 and 0200.

The earlier guards returned from their duty and awakened Eddie and me. Sgt. Buncic took us to our post and gave us the password and response. If I remember correctly it was "Mae West" and the response was "Life Jacket". He left us there and said that we would be relieved at 0200 for the next shift. Man alive, but it was getting cold that night. The snow that was in the foxhole had melted from the body heat of the guys before us and it was somewhat muddy at the floor of the hole. We shoveled some of the mud out and put some more pine needles and branches on the floor and settled in for the four-hour shift.

Our wool knit caps were on our heads and ears under our helmets and we wore our overcoats over our field jackets. Our leather palmed gloves kept our hands reasonably warm. Our M-1 rifles were loaded, round in the chamber and the safety lock on. And we waited and listened and listened... One way that I used in "combating" time was to count which also helps in staying awake. So, I started counting. I didn't have a watch so there was no way that I could tell the time. We would have to rely on the Corporal of the Guard to come by now and then and check on our positions and ask for the time.

Were you ever told by your doctor to count sheep to help you GO to sleep? And here I am counting numbers to stay AWAKE. Every now and then I felt myself dozing. Eddie was next to me, but I don't know "where he was". You can't do too much talking in the foxhole, especially at night, because sound carries very far in a still cold atmosphere. So there wasn't much conversation between us.

In any event, time was passing and I think we were in a never land of half dozing and half trying to stay awake. What was happening about this time our Sgt. Buncic was making the rounds and checking the posts. Apparently, he approached our post quietly. And whispered out the password, "Mae West" and there was no response so, another "Mae West", and nothing. He crept up closer behind us and noticed our inert bodies and helmeted heads bobbing and weaving a bit, signifying a sleepy head or two. Then came another louder password which shook us up a bit and as we were groping for the "Life Jacket" response. Buncic hit our helmeted heads together.

There was a lesson to be learned here. You do not cover your ears with a cap and you move around your hole looking in different directions, back-to-back with your foxhole buddy. It was fortunate indeed that we were in rear position, because I don't know how close we came to a court martial, and shot at dawn.

Well, the dawn came and we were still alive, later that day we got dressed. Picked up some K-rations and we were going to march to a neighboring village of TADLER which we out posted for the next couple of days. It was only a few miles away but my feet were starting to "bark". My boots were small, my feet were growing and I requested that my Squad Leader get me a larger pair of boots. My combat boots were new issue, and these GIs never saw them before. They still had GI shoes with legging laced up I couldn't use 2 pair of socks in my boots, so I had to do with one dry pair till they came through with a larger pair of shoes.

New Year's Eve was spent quietly in Tadler, including the next day, the first day in January, 1945 and just about the rest of the week. We hung around the area, cleaned equipment, marveled at the beauty of the snow covered trees and winterized vistas of the Ardennes forest and quaint villages The local inhabitants seemed to go about their business as usual, as did we, maybe a patrol or two, having hot meals since the kitchen came up to us and took residence nearby.

At the end of the week we packed up our gear and one very early morning we marched back to Heiderscheid. Later that day we were briefed about our next combat mission. I went to sleep with my own private nightmare... Will this be it for me....??? What will it be like..??? Will I perform properly....??? Just when I thought I was getting back to sleep we were awakened about 0230. Had a hot breakfast. My last meal...??? And we jumped off at 0345. I read the Company morning report for January 6th, that's why I know it was 0345, 'cause I didn't have a watch.

We formed up after breakfast and marched out of the village with our boots crunching on the snow and ice-covered roads. Before we took off, K rations, ammo bandoleers, and grenades were handed out. It wasn't a half hour later, or so, when we heard "outgoing mail". Our supporting artillery were making their presence felt by giving the village of DAHL, our objective that day, a good pasting.

As we crunched along the road, single file on each side, enemy artillery got word of our presence and they started hitting on us. By now daylight was upon us and our dark jackets and/or overcoats made us stand out like sore thumbs. We dove for the ditches lining each side of the road and tried to burrow ourselves down to China. Nobody near me got hit, but after a few minutes I heard a yell from out in the snow covered field to my left, "Hey, you guys, is there any room in that ditch you're in....??? He called out his name and it was one of the guys in our platoon. The guy next to me called out that there was and told him to haul ass over here in between explosions.

The next thing I saw was this big guy running through the snow drifts in the field, hopped over, or most probably crashed through the wooden fence, and landed in a heap on top of me. Did that ever knock the wind out of me? I could hardly get the words out of my mouth to get off me and give me some space when he pulled out a GI hard pack of Lucky Strike (green) cigarettes and practically stuck one in my mouth saving, "Thanks buddy, I'm Boffman, got caught out in the field. Let me light you." Before I could say that I don't smoke, his Zippo lighter was lighting my cigarette, then lit his. If I wasn't lying down after that first deep drag, the dizziness that I felt would have keeled me over. That reflex action inadvertently filled my entire lung capacity with nicotine smoke. Wow! "Take small drags, buddy, you won't get so nutty, or else, don't inhale." he offered. Yeah, thanks a lot, impairing the morals of a minor I thought.

After a while the enemy barrage lessened and we got the word to get up double time and take up positions at the edge of town. This apparently was going to be house-to-house fighting. Kraft told me to stay close to him; that is if my aching feet would keep up with him.

We hit the edge of town, single file on each side of the street. I was on the left side of the street walking past some small houses the troops up ahead had cleared. All of a sudden we took "incoming mail". It was hitting the street up ahead of us about a few hundred yards. Almost immediately the guys ahead started dashing into the nearest building, cleared or not. I followed the guys in front of me and made my mad dash up a few steps of a front porch, crashed through the door which was slightly ajar, skidded on the hard tile front room or parlor, still unbalanced into the same tiled kitchen floor and through the rear door which was off its hinges, and landed in a heap on a snow bank in the rear yard just missing a cow dung heap by a few feet. Welcome to your "Baptism of Fire, soldier...."

It was all I could do to pick up my helmet and snow encrusted rifle and crash back into the house. My comrades-in-arms thought it was very funny. When I looked at them. They just shook their heads and turned away. It would that I was on my way to being the platoon comedian.

The enemy shelling was continuous, and amidst all that had happened in the last few minutes, it was aggravating my "plumbing system". I needed relief, and the toilet was NOT in the house. The outhouse, it was pointed out to me was in the rear yard beyond where I flopped down earlier. Oh brother!! I am not going out there again, especially, since my platoon buddies were telling me that soon after we kick the Krauts out of an area, they counter-attack. They usually have the area zeroed in and then they let us have it and sustain more of our casualties. That was why everyone was taking up a position window on both levels of the house, or at a door.

But, when you gotta go, you gotta go. I started looking around the kitchen area for someplace to relieve myself. The sink was too obvious and too exposed and the kitchen was occupied. There was a small door under the stairway. I opened it. It was the pantry, and the lady of the house had many jars of preserves of different fruit and vegetables stored on the shelves.

Well, what to do? I pried open a jar with a small amount of whatever was in there, and finally let loose my "torrent" in the privacy of my little pantry pee-house. I wasn't going to pass through the kitchen, open the door or window, and toss this jar in the yard, so I found the deepest darkest corner of the pantry and stashed it on the floor, covered it up with other pantry articles, and silently made my apologies to the family, but this was war and sometimes field expediency has to take over. I've had a guilty conscience about this for many a year, but I would hope that when the family returned to their home after liberation, that they would trash the larder and start fresh. I hoped and prayed for that.

Back to more serious things, I started to look around for a window or door or some opening to view any action coming up the street, but they were all occupied. So there I was in the middle of the front room trying to look over shoulders of the other GIs in my platoon.

Outside and further up the street one could hear shelling, machine gun fire, including small arms. I overheard that the 1st Battalion must be in one fierce firefight. And we were waiting for the fighting to come in our direction.

As time wore on, the noise of combat lessened. We learned that finally the enemy was contained and repulsed, and that the village of Dahl was considered liberated by mid-afternoon.

Later, it was learned that Sgt. Day Tuner, Co. B got the Congressional Medal of Honor in that fire fight earlier that day, albeit posthumously, but he took a lot of Krauts down.

Somehow, later that day, we moved to another building taking up defensive positions. Incidentally, in this little house were a few Kraut prisoners that we were supposed to keep an eye on until they could be sent to the rear, probably Battalion HQ? They were in this room and Sgt. Sifkin picked me to watch them. He told me, "keep 'em quiet, keep their hands in front of them, and don't get distracted. I'm calling HQ."

There was a chair opposite of the corner from these three Krauts. I stood next to it with one foot on the seat and my M-1 pointed directly at them. Needless to say. I was really scared. Here was the enemy captured. They might have killed some of our guys in the last action before they gave up. I wasn't alone in the room. A few other squad members were relaxing, making small talk, not paying any attention to the prisoners that was my responsibility.

Suddenly, I realized that the prisoners were starting to murmur among themselves pointing to a barrel in another corner of the room. I could see that it was filled to the rim almost with apples. One of the prisoners motioned to me and to the barrel. Saying, "Apfels, Essen apfels....???" They were supposed to be quiet, but I deduced that they were hungry and wanted to get a few apples. ...I should have told them to shut up and stay put or I'll put a round in your gut... However, being the decent good guy that I am, I motioned to one of them that it was OK and I pointed to the barrel with my M1. One of the Krauts started to get up and head for the barrel. This motion caught the eye of Sgt. Silkin, and he roared into the room, firing a burst into the ceiling with his carbine and kicked over the barrel of "apfels".

Oh, how the good lord saved me. Out spilled most of the apfels, including a few pistols, and a "burp" gun. I could have sworn that the next burst would have "done in" the Krauts in that room. Silkin was livid. If I wasn't so green and un-knowing, I bet he could have hung me by my thumbs. That was quite a lesson that I learned that day never again will I trust my enemy. I will shoot first, I hope, if I get the chance. Geez, this enemy were seasoned veterans.. You can't play with your emotions with them, and you never give them the benefit of the doubt. I think that I hyperventilated for a while, and went back into my little "pee house" in the pantry to "clean" myself.., a result of my being scared to death.

Everyone in that little house was on alert after that to-do. It wasn't but a few minutes later that we heard some noise coming below, probably the cellar. Everyone hushed up and we scrounged around the first floor boards looking for a trap door. After pushing aside a chair over an area rug, we saw the frame of the trap door. The Sgt. stomped on the door and yelled out something in German, like, "Kommen sie hier..." "eine minit..." "rouse...." Our rifles were at the ready, and some grenade were ready to be pulled as he opened the trap door.

The noise was clearer now. It was the stifled cries of some child, maybe more than one or two. As daylight flowed into the dark cellar, we could see a man with a couple of very young blonde haired little girls. Wow!, how close were we to fire into the cellar. The man was the owner of the house. His wife, we didn't know where she was. He opted to stay in the cellar, after he got some food from the pantry. He thanked us for liberating his home, no less his little village. He probably knew that there would be a counter-attack and he would be safe down there. We assured him that

57

the Germans would not be back. We were going to outpost the town, defend it, then move on to continue moving the enemy back till they are out of Luxembourg.

Some MPs came by and picked up the prisoners, and we settled down and took defensive positions in and around the house and the barn, some guys went into the barn. Some took positions in a couple of foxholes and the rest were at windows around the house.

Then it started. There was shelling and explosions at the other end of town. We would attempt to re-take the village. A little later orders came through to return to Heiderscheid, and another company will take over our position.

We packed up our gear, and started to make our way back. Just as we got to the crossroads, an 88 opened up followed by machine gun fire directed at the crossroads. No way could we continue. It was getting pretty late and cold. Our scouts pointed to our Platoon Leader, Lt. Rosenbloom, where the enemy fire was coming from. Instead going across an uncharted field, he told Sgt. Buncic to take his squad around the base of the rise where the fire was coming from, and see if the fire could be "neutralized." We only had about 7 or 8 men in our squad, but we took off, taking cover among the snow covered trees to a position we hoped would be the rear of the enemy's position with our scout leading the way.

This rise was a little more than a molehill. Fog was moving in which helped conceal us. It wasn't easy climbing up two or three steps and failing back one, slipping in the snow, trying to grab a tree sapling if we could to assist our climb. It was amazing that there was very little talk or bitching to alert the enemy up there at the top.

Anyway, we made it to the top, and spread out. We couldn't hear voices or see anything, except for the 88 firing, and a few seconds later heard a machine gun fire, all concentrated on that crossroads below. Finally, we were close enough to see the situation we couldn't believe our eyes. There was only one old German soldier loading from a stockpile of 88 shells, pull the lanyard, then trudge over to the machine gun that was fixed in place and fire off a bunch of short bursts, then trudge back to the 88 and repeat the process.

Sgt. Buncic checked our position and gave a silent signal to attack and take the Kraut prisoner. Go... Buncic fired a burst at the feet of the Kraut, and told him to get his hands up. With the Walkie-Talkie, we told the Lt. that we are in possession of the hill and guns. He could hardly believe what we told him, one old duffer holding up our company. His people made him stay behind; to continue what he was doing until he ran out of shells and ammo. He must have been about 60 years old, wearing a long overcoat with part of a white bed sheet draped over him.

We went down the hill with our prisoner who seemed to be glad the whole charade was over, and we marched back to Tadler. I had a chance to write some V-mail letters back home writing silly things, mainly because I was so exhilarated in being alive in my baptism of fire. The Lt. who censored our mail must have thought I was a little loony. My folks kept all those letters, and I have them in my possession today. I also noticed that I was shaving almost every day. I'm becoming a "man" out here.

Excerpt from the reminiscences of Edwin Tester, my ole foxhole buddy from Co. K 319th Inf., 80th ID... "We were moving out to attack the next town. We were dressed in a white cover over our uniforms so we would blend in with the snow. We were crossing an open field when all of a sudden you cried out, I lost my glasses in the snow, and I can't find them."

I stopped to help search for his glasses; we struggled in the snow looking for them. When we did find them, we looked up and everyone was gone, except for the two of us standing in this open field.

We got very nervous and started to run across the field toward the woods in hopes of catching up with our outfit. But, they were long gone and suddenly there was firing and several German troops were coming through the woods towards us. We started a firefight with them and I believe we killed the German officer leading them and the rest fled.

There was another incident I remember which was a funny one but did not involve you but rather myself and a group of German POWs. I will tell you that one next time we meet.

It is really strange that we both wound up in the same hospital at Bar-Le-Duc, though I think you were there before me and shipped out of that hospital before I got there I went back to the US on May 12, 1945 on a hospital ship and wound up in a hospital in North Carolina. I was suffering from frostbite, also, but I don't think as bad as yours and also from a bad case of pneumonia which almost killed me. We must have been in the same hospital and perhaps at the same time. I was discharged from the service in August 1945 and returned home to renew my college career. Though this time at Rensselaer Polytechnic Institute. What a life, what a world....

Isn't it strange that the above related incident is absent from my mind? However, there is a tiny recollection of my being part of a chase involving some fleeing enemy troops. But, I can't seem to connect the first temporary loss of my eyeglasses with this short combat event.

If I placed myself in the above-mentioned situation of 57 years ago. I could imagine the panic I must have felt in the midst of battle to have lost my sight... then regaining it. If I am not mistaken, I should have had a second pair of eyeglasses in my field jacket. Did I realize that at the time, put those on, and forget the lost ones? Who knows...?

Anyhow, what I will tell Eddie later when I see him, is that I had a soft covered book, entitled, "A Thesaurus of Humor," published by the Infantry Journal which I kept in my left breast pocket of my field jacket. On the blank inside cover of this pocket hook are the names of my fellow platoon members, the town names we recaptured from the enemy, the names of the hospitals where I was, and the hospital ships that carried me across the Channel and the Atlantic Ocean, and sketches of the "Meat Wagons" ambulances that bore me to the various hospitals. That's why this info helped me with my recall for my memoirs...

One day our squad was volunteered to do a patrol and contact elements of the 26th Yankee Division, my Uncle Joshua's WWI outfit, and coordinate some information or tactics, or whatever patrols are supposed to do. I asked the Sgt. again about my new boots, but nothing had arrived. My feet weren't making me very comfortable for walking; however, I didn't want to complain.

During breakfast, while eating, I tried to massage my feet, put on new socks that I had wrapped around my body to warm them, and into my old boots. It seemed to help a little bit.

It was just starting to get light as we moved out of town. We were routed through a neighboring snow covered wooded area. Then the trail started to rise and we were starting to climb through deep snow, trying to grab for footholds, cussing under our breath, and wishing we were back in a warm house resting.

All of a sudden we got a signal to stop and listen. We heard some rustling of tree branches up ahead and we dropped to the ground and undid the safety on our rifles, and waited. And there it came, through the wooded area, as smug as could be, a proud looking stag... just looked at us and kept walking down the hill, then started to run when he realized how close he came to being venison. I don't know why but our squad leader told us to fix bayonets, after another stag ran past us down the hill he probably felt that something spooked them up ahead.

This was beginning to spook the hell out of me now. What was up ahead? The two scouts pushed up ahead and we spread out behind them. This was to eliminate an ambush that could get us all done in, in one fast firefight. We moved along as silently as we could. Our breathing making curls of vapor in front of our faces, with my eyeglasses fogging up something fierce. In all the cold, I was sweating and my brow was giving off steam which was actually clouding my specs. I wish I were home... What am I doing here...? Well, what the heck are we ALL doing here, so I said to myself, "Shut up, dogface, and keep your ears open at least."

All of a sudden, up ahead, I thought I heard gunfire, because everybody hit the ground. I plopped down into a snow bank, face down, and when I looked up, I couldn't see anything. Snow and sweat took its toll and I really couldn't see I yelled out "I can't see, can't see...." Jim Trailer crawled over to me and asked, "Where are you hit....?" I responded, "I'm not hit, my glasses are dirty 'and fogged up". Where is everyone?" He answered, I think he said, oh, for Christ sakes, get up and follow me, clean your glasses." Fortunately, we made it through the woods in good order, and contacted a patrol of the 26th that took us to their HQ. Our Non-Coms went into a huddle with their counterparts and the rest of us settled down for lunch. I opened some C-ration tins, and concocted a sort of hash with some spam and a soup of some sort, and heated it in my cup, and ate it with some crackers or biscuits, followed by some coffee, and a piece of a chocolate bar. I was learning to mix and match my rations to make them more palatable; it was fun. We shot the breeze with the 26th GIs, talked about ourselves, about home, usual stuff....

Since contact was made and mission completed, we started on our way back to our base. We were lucky that the weather held up and was clear albeit cold. After that long hike, then rest, my feet were really starting to bark. Almost felt like my lower extremities would burst through the seams of my snow-covered boots. But I kept up with my buddies, and we came out of the woods and trudged into our platoon area. I happened to take my rifle off my shoulder, and l held it as though it was a cane; to assist me as I walked. Sgt. Buncic noticed this, and yelled at me, "get that rifle at shoulder arms.... "it's not a GD cane... Don't let me see you doing that again...." Oh, man he was right, of course. I inquired again. But no news of any new boots for me. Guess I'll have the Chaplain punch my TS card.... again.

It was about mid-January now and the Company marched to, I believe it was the village of Goesdorf, which we outposted with a Tank Destroyer Battalion on the edge of town. I pulled early morning guard duty. It was freezing cold, and it was snowing, too. The heat from my body penetrated through my heavy GI overcoat melting the snow on me and in the outposted foxhole. It was a muddy mess by dawn's early light.

The next day late afternoon, I pulled guard duty again with a guy from my platoon, name of Nelms, a regular red neck from Carolina. We were in a foxhole next to a big Sherman tank when all of a sudden a trio of planes, could have been fighter bombers from our 9th Air Force, flew over very close to us, climbed, turned around and made another run at us, and this time they dropped what probably was a 500-pounder about 100 yards from us covering us with the smell of cordite and dirt, snow and debris. What the hell... our own planes are attacking us what's going on... On another run they strafed two tanks and other vehicles near us, and we scrunched down deeper and deeper into our foxhole.

Somebody do something....!!! Sure enough, the firing stopped. The planes returned and waggled their wings at us and flew into the blue yonder. Just then, there was a mad scramble from the tank destroyer personnel to mount their vehicles and change the color panels. Those morons forgot to change their proper color panels for the next day on the night before, and our planes thought it was a Kraut trick.

Imagine how close the possibility of ending my combat days by friendly fire came that morning. Whew!! The next few hours Nelms and I made small talk, but one item of conversation I had with him still sticks out in my mind to this day. He started by saying, "You know, it's strange that we have a guy like Rosenboom, an infantry Lieutenant and leading our platoon. He's a Jew. I thought that all the Jews were in the Service Commands, typing or in supply behind the lines...."

If blood could reach a boiling point, it was nearing that point within me. Damn, I'm not a violent or an aggressive person. In my young age, I have never been faced with such bigotry and imbecilic racist views. After a moment or two and catching my breath, I tried to enlighten this moron that the military is made up of all American citizens from all walks of life facing a common vicious enemy. In fact, the guy sitting and sweating it out in this very foxhole with you, who may have died alongside you if the bomb had been dropped closer is also Jewish. But what's that got to do with the price of beans. - - - . What are you, besides not being Jewish?

There was no more conversation for the rest of our guard time in the foxhole. As a matter of fact, I wanted to speak to Sgt. Mitchell about this, but I let it go, hoping that we would not meet up again in the same hole.

Since we were in a holding position the last few days, we were waiting for other combat groups to straighten the front lines abreast of us. I believe that was the scuttlebutt, before we could move into a combat situation, and move forward through the Kraut's ranks. This gave me a lot of time to catch up on my letter writing, and re-read previously sent letters from home, my old school chums Bobby and Dave, and a couple of girlfriends who were corresponding with me.

So, during the next few days we marched between the towns of Tadler, Dahl and Heiderscheid. It was sunny, but brisk and cold. The towns were near each other, outposting them, doing some patrols. During one of those patrols we captured some prisoners. They were split up between the platoons to hold onto until they could be sent back to Battalion HQ. Two of those POWs were teenage kids, snotty nosed, grimy looking, skinny, clothes "three sizes" too big on them... is this part of the "master race"? They were entrusted to be our responsibility, our platoon, our squad, and MY responsibility. Again, I am watching prisoners. This time, I guess they thought that I could handle the situation, oh yeah....

Preparations were being made for an attack on a small town of Nocher. Our platoon was located in a two-story farmhouse at the edge of town. I was on the second floor. We had just finished eating what you might call "dinner" out of our rations, C or K, or some other letter of the alphabet, or 10-in-1 rations and were getting ready to bed down for the night.

One of the instructions that were given us about getting shelter in two-story buildings is to keep inadvertent movement down to a minimum, especially, as you passed a window or other wall opening. The enemy if they had any kind of surveillance of that building could pick out shadows, if at night, or any movement to indicate that the building was occupied. This could be followed by their shelling us with the bad news to follow.

Sure enough, some guys moved about between guard posting, or maybe, someone went downstairs to the outhouse. All of a sudden, our quietude was shattered by a series of bursts starting at the far end of the barnyard, and then one must have come through the window and exploded in the fireplace, loosening the floor joists and the stairway. Part of the second floor was on the first floor. I wound up on the floor below, unhurt, as were many others, by a miracle. There were other casualties, and while the medics were tending to them, I tried to find a place to lie down and relax, if that were possible. The Lt. radioed artillery, gave them our position and where the enemy shelling came from and told them to fire for effect.... We heard no more from them....

Just as I was dozing off, one of the guards coming off duty, trying to find a place to sit down, stepped on my feet.

I must have let out a blood-curdling yell, followed by a bunch of expletives. Sgt. Buncic heard me, and so did the Lt. They decided that I should join the wounded back to Battalion Aid where I could get some further attention.

Lt. Rosenbloom accompanied us, because apparently he had been hit in the face by flying shrapnel or fireplace concrete pieces. I finally got to see a medic at the Aid Station. He used a sharp knife or a scalpel, or something to pry my boots off my feet, and removed my socks. I can remember that my feet were icy white, with veins bulging. They even looked puffy-like. Anyhow, the medic told me to look away so as not to see what the heck he was going to do. Geez, what the heck was he going to do? While I was contemplating that, unbeknown to me, he was picking my toes with his scalpel to see if I had any feeling. I didn't feel a thing or a sting nor did I flinch.

There were other stories heard, here and there, about medical personnel using a cigarette lighter very close to the suspected frozen toes or feet to see if the GI had lost any feeling in those areas. I don't know which would have been worse just to prove severe frostbite.

"What's up, doc?" I asked. "What's going on?" The Lt. who was nearby came over, and asked the same question. The medic answered, he's got severe frostbite, bilateral. But, we can't evacuate him right now. We have no transportation. And besides, we were getting enemy fire on the road back to the field hospital I can warm his feet temporarily, and bandage the area that I cut.

"OK", said the Lt. "Do you have any extra shoes and dry socks for him after he thaws out? We need him back at platoon."

He scrounged around and came up with a dry pair of socks, and a pair of shoes that seemed to fit. Lt. Rosenbloom watched this, and then both eyebrows raised, and his voice screamed out, "Get those boots off this man. Those boots are German. I don't want him wearing enemy issue."

The medic answered, "Well, what we can do is rip up a GI towel, wrap his feet with it, tape it tight and we have a size 12 GI shoepac or galosh that will fit him temporality. Will that do?" So, what was what I was going to wear for now?

After a while, my feet did seem to feel better, so the Lt. and I left the Aid Station and trudged back to the platoon.

What a weird looking pair of feet I had. It was ridiculous, fighting a war like this. "What with the persistent pain, and wearing these ridiculous clodhoppers, how am I going to keep up," I asked myself again.

It looked like I was going to be stuck looking like this for a while. Lt. Rosenbloom had a sulfa bandage on his face. I assumed that evacuation would come after the next attack on Nocher.

They gave me the responsibility of watching the two teenage Krauts. At the same time I was given a new MOS, not a rifleman, but an assistant bazooka ammo carrier. A good sleep was precious that night, and I took advantage of it. The two kids just huddled in a corner shivering and crying. They were no threat to anyone. It was still very dark and cold outside when we were awakened. Someone said it was 0400, as the last guard watch came in. The kitchen had come up the day before and we had a hot breakfast. Hot oatmeal with armored cow (canned milk), dried eggs, toast, I think, hot coffee, sugar and "a/c" again. That really warmed our bellies. The mess GIs handed out more C and K ration packages for us, I guess, in case the attack took us past lunch... a walk in the sun, a day at the "office" ...hah....

Just when I thought my feet were coming around, they started to pain something fierce. I looked at them after breakfast. Both feet seemed warm, but the spots where the medic punctured my toes were getting discolored, and that was where the hurt was. The Lt. and Sgts. were not around. They were being briefed on the attack. What to do? I talked to my feet; I caressed them and told them to hang on just another day. Strange, the "barking" abated. I rewrapped my feet, put on the shoepacs just as the Lt. and Non-Coms re-entered, "Let's move out" was the word heard. Sgt. Buncic gave me two bandoleers of bazooka ammo, plus two bandoleers of 30-cal ammo for my M-1 rifle. My additional rations were in my backpack, including my mess gear and my entrenching tool hanging from the pack. I put on my web belt loaded with additional ammo, my bayonet, and first aid pack. Canteen newly filled with water; did I forget to mention the two grenades hanging from my pack straps in front of me?

"Don't forget to keep an eye on these two kids till we get into Nocher", Sgt. Buncic said. "Take a position at the rear of the squad next to the Bazooka man." As we left the farmhouse, we turned left straddling the road. Wow, was it cold on this bleak early morning. There was a heavy fog hanging out over the area. I could hardly see the lead man of our squad up ahead. We left the town proper and were out in open farm country what I could see of it.

There was distant shelling and once in a while we could hear "outgoing mail". Our boots and shoepacs made a crunching noise on the snow and ice of the road, until we came to a crossroads. We left the road and turned into an open field. The fog and mist was still very evident, and we had to rely on the guys in front of us for going in the right direction. There was no sign of this being a minefield. Whew! What a relief.

After trudging on for some time, I felt a slight breeze come up, just as the sky started to lighten up to greet the morning. The fog and mist were leaving us. Uh oh.... That wasn't good news. Here we were company strength, spread out, but wearing our dark olive drab overcoats or field jackets, silhouetted against the pristine white snow in this open field, a few hundred yards from a forested area where we could reach cover, if necessary.

My two prisoners were ahead of me. To lighten my load, I had given them my canvas bazooka ammunition carriers to carry. Just then there was shelling up ahead. The enemy had seen us and was dropping mortar fire on us. We were getting "incoming mail." We were urged to continue to the wooded area on the double. Shells were bursting around us. Oh, just great, the Krauts give us a creeping barrage forcing us toward them, and then they opened up on us with machine gun fire... There was some. Disorientation as we scooted forward Helter-Skelter. Oh damn! I lost track of my two young German prisoners. Back at the farmhouse, I learned their names, so I started to yell for them. "Woe bist du?" where are you? More yelling. Squad leaders urging us on, then as I thought I was entering the wooded area, I don't remember anything, until…

This part of my life is a deep shadow. Apparently, the Company made it through the woods, entered the town of Nocher, and wrestled it from the enemy without too much difficulty.

What occurred in the next few hours, up to maybe 24 or 36 hours, I have no recollection. What comes to mind very vividly is a medic walking me to my company area, where someone there located my platoon hangout. It was in a small house set back from the snow-covered road. The guys in my platoon were resting, some smoking, and some digging into a can of C's. One guy was reading a bible from which he looked up as I walked into the room. The Medic said, "I think he is one of yours name of Lashin." The bible reader, Sgt. Ott, looked up. "Lashin", he called out, "I had you listed missing in action. Another 12 hours and I would have had to send your mother an MIA telegram. Where have you been?"

More vague references to my where about, but the medic pointed out, "he was hit. See the ripped hole in his helmet, probably where a piece of shrapnel hit it, but did not penetrate all the way through the plastic liner and heavy woolen cap, but must have given him an awful headache and may have knocked him out for a while. He wasn't wearing gloves, and his hands seem to be frostbitten, and where did he get that get-up on his feet"? I was still wearing the wrapped towels and shoepacs. Those hours lying in the snow must have really done me in. Nobody in my squad could account for me or my where about. They were probably looking out for their own asses and I don't blame them.

The company combat medics usually sweep the field of battle afterward looking for wounded or KIAs. That was, I guess, how they picked me up when they saw that I was alive and breathing...., but lying in the snow....

Sgt. Ott reported to my squad leader that I was still alive but not very functional. He felt I should be evacuated. Sgt. Buncic told me to get something to eat and we'll call for a Jeep to take you to the Aid Station. I could have used some aspirins since my head was still aching a bit. I had to open my K ration box with my teeth. My fingers were of no immediate use. I guess I didn't want to bother anybody to feed me. One of the guys was having the shakes and he was being tended to, and what was left of my platoon was nursing their own post-battle trauma.

Somehow the whereabouts of my two teenage prisoners didn't come up, and there was no need of the bazooka ammo during the attack on Nocher. So I assume that they figured I left it out in the field, unless it was picked up by somebody else. Still the bottom line for me was . . . where were those kids? After a while I didn't care. My part of the war will be temporarily halted as the Jeep arrived and put me on board.

The Jeep stopped in front of the 2-story farmhouse, which was the Aid station. There were a couple of meat wagons (ambulances) warming up their engines. There were three GIs already on litters tiered in place inside one of the ambulances, and they were waiting for me.

Whatever I had with me, except my clothing. I gave up which was my dear rifle, web belt with attachments, air-conditioned helmet and liner, backpack, etc. My shoepacs were removed to let my feet breath. My lower extremities were really ugly and discolored. Was it becoming gangrenous? They dusted them with sulfa or penicillin and loosely covered them with gauze. Oh, did they hurt...? The medics lifted me up and locked me into a space inside and we took off. It was warm inside, and it felt good.

The ride was comfortable, albeit a bit bumpy, because of ruts in the road, or shell holes not filled in. We were on the road for about an hour or so when the driver and his shotgun let out a scream and the brakes were applied so hard that the ambulance spun out of control and slammed into the side of a building that was just a few feet off the road.

The result was that we patients got tossed about pretty good, and two of the wounded were hurt even further. The back doors were thrown open by the drivers and some other GIs to check on us after we stopped. We were hurting but nothing that needed immediate attention.

What had happened was that as they made a turn in the road into this town, they came face to face with a German Tiger tank with its 88 long snout—stopping inches away from the front windshield. On seeing this, they panicked and went into that spin out.

The only saving grace was that this tank was already neutralized. The Tank Destroyer outfit in this town had knocked it out earlier that day, we found out. And so was the ambulance. The accident left us without transportation. The TD GIs radioed for a replacement. Within an hour, after they fed us, we were on our again.

The drivers finally made their way to Bar-Le-Duc, France, where the Medical Corps had taken over an old asylum and turned it into a temporary station hospital. We thanked the drivers who apologized to us, but we shook it off, and wished them well. They had a hell of a job to do, also.

There was a bed already and waiting for me. First, I went into a treatment room where my clothing was removed and probably burned, because I had a feeling what my underwear looked like. There was local help that washed the grime of war from my delicate hairless body, gave me pajamas, and then the nurse re-dressed my wounds and Georges wheeled me back to my ward. Georges was a local denizen who worked as an orderly and helped the doctors and nurses. He was a long time employee of the asylum during peacetime, so he knew the place pretty well, and was quite attentive towards us GIs.

Georges and I spent some time together. I practiced my high school French on him and I helped him with his English. He was married and had a few young children, and oh how he blessed us, Les Americans, for coming here to free France from the unholy yoke of the German occupation.

Each day we received certain rations, like candy. Cigarettes, V-mail writing paper, maybe other sundry items. Since I didn't smoke, I gave George's all my cigarette rations and some of the candy and chewing gum. I'm sure some these items reached his little children and the others like the Lucky Strikes went to the Black Market to buy whatever necessary things his family needed. He was overly thankful to me for the few days that I was there. Before I left, he gave me a small French coin, a sou with a hole in the middle of it, 5 centimes, as a thank you or good luck charm. I thanked him, and to this day, 55 years later it has always had a place on my key ring.

On the day that I left, the Head of Medical Personnel at the hospital gave me my General Orders for a Purple Heart, which already had my name engraved on the backside of the medal and pinned it to my pillow. A proud moment.

According to the local edition of the Stars and Stripes, it seems as though our troops have broken the backs of the enemy and straightened out the "Bulge". It is now about January 26, 1945, and I was given orders to go to another Hospital in Thionville, France.

The treatment that I received at Bar-Le-Duc was exceptional. They cared for my feet every day. The nurses arranged my sheets and blanket at the foot of the bed so that my feet were exposed. They hurt so much to the touch that I couldn't keep them under the covers. I still couldn't walk, but I did pretty good maneuvering my rickety old WWI wheel chair.

Well, it was back in the old "meat wagon" again, and on to Thionville. It wasn't a long ride and we got there safe and sound.

The doctors there examined my feet again, and continued with the penicillin to keep the infection at bay.

They were still sensitive to touch so the nurses continued to "short sheet" my bed covers.

It was now about the beginning of February, and there was some latrine rumor that we would be leaving France. To where we did not know.

The news was optimistic in relation to our troops continually pushing and punishing the Krauts further into Germany. This could not occur without casualties on our side and I assume that they needed available beds close by for evacuation. Since many of us patients at Thionville and Bar-Le-Duc were out of danger and in a convalescent mode, we were ripe for transfer.

The word finally came through. It wasn't to be ZI (Zone of Interior), the good old USA, but Old Blighty, England. This time we were transported to the local train station at Thionville. and we left for the north coast through Paris.

This was a hospital train so we were arranged in tiers, about three high, something like the troop transport I came over on, except the bottom most berth was three feet above the train floor.

The berth they put me in was perfect for sightseeing. I could look out the window and see the countryside and in and out of the train station in Paris.

Finally towards late afternoon we arrived at Le Havre, France. Medical personnel came on board, helped us out of our berths and put us on stretchers and carried us out to the docks where we boarded the US Hospital Ship Jacob Huddleston.

It was a beautiful white transport, with painted Red Crosses, so clean with pretty nurses, and warm inviting beds. We ate well, listened to the news on the radio, and followed by music, Glenn Miller's AFN band. I slept well that night. Early the next morning we left Le Havre and crossed the English Channel. It was a little bumpy, but we made it to the English coast, where, I am not sure, probably Southampton.

Debarking was a long process, and since I was still not mobile, I was stretchered to a waiting ambulance with three other GIs.

Walking was not possible I just couldn't put any weight on my feet yet. I decided that I would ask for some physical therapy, because I could feel my ankles tightening up. The muscles at my ankles were regenerating very slowly, and if I made any attempt to walk, it was very awkward. I must have looked like a flat-footed duck with my butt sticking out and bent over.

It seems as though the severe frost bite on my feet had taken more of a toll than first contemplated by my doctors and myself I made up my mind that I would get these feet back in shape, the shape that they were in when I won medals in track, and was the second fastest man in my infantry training company. That's over 200 men......

Although I was transported within the confines of the ambulance, I was able to glimpse through the front windshield and back door window and see what I could see of the beautiful green English countryside with the rolling hills and lush colorful meadows with cows and sheep alternately lazily grazing thereon.

Finally, we arrived at a United States Army Hospital Plant 4150. The village nearby was called Cirencester. The wards were Quonset huts. There were about 10-15 bedridden wounded GIs from different outfits, couple of potbelly stoves down the middle of the room, the beds along each side of the room. At the front of this ward was treatment room and some offices, and a couple of sleeping rooms for on-call nurses and doctors. While not on call they had their own quarters elsewhere.

The grounds, what I could see of it beautiful... so green and lush with landscaping and trees. I wanted so bad to get out of bed and walk around this area. I really got started on exercising my lower extremities to try to strengthen them. It was starting to come around pretty good getting towards February 21 and, my 19th birthday.

That morning, after breakfast, I was able to put on slippers and my robe and hesitatingly strutted up and down the middle of the ward. I was so elated, that a surge of silliness came over me. I went to my bed and got hold of my pillow and punched in the ends, and set one punched in end on my head. Just before this I cut out a star from some see wrapping paper and pinned it to the front of my "Russian Cossacks hat". Then I ambled over to the pot-bellied stove and pulled out a red hot poker, and called out in a Russian accented flow of words and expletives... that I have just come from the Eastern Front and... where are those GD Krauts....??? I'll skewer them....

At this point, Lt. Lundgren, my doctor, and Lt. Naomi Somers, my nurse, came into the ward for morning rounds... How I escaped a Section 8, a trip to the funny farm... is something I never found out. Can you imagine what I looked like standing there in the middle of the room....??? Well, I can still picture it in my mind's eye.

Some of the patients thought I was a nut case. Maybe I was showing off too much in front of them, being able to get silly while they were nursing wounds. Well, at least I was doing something about "nursing" my wounds by exercising my feet, and getting out of bed. Some of the guys got a good laugh out of it, as did I.

It was a strong possibility that Lt. Somers spoke to the doctor and told him that it was my 19th birthday, and I was still wet behind the ears, and at least, happy that combat was a thing of the past for me. The prognosis was quite a few months of eliminating the gangrene which was responding very well to the medicine, and then rehab to walk properly before put on combat boots again.

A Louisiana boy, name of Kennedy shared my birthday, on the 21st, with me. Lt. Somers brought in a birthday cake for us, and shared all, including the nurses there were some other little gifts and one, I still have to this day was a toilet ditty bag with toilet articles. Those articles were all used up in time, but I still have the ditty bag which contains every letter I had written while in service, from Ft. McClellan, Ft. Wood, overseas with the 70th and 80th Divisions, the hospitals in France and England. My Mom and Dad and sisters had saved them all.

Getting back to my hospital life, I was now able in good weather, to go sit outside, and drink in the atmosphere. The hospital was located near a RAF airfield, and every once in a while we could see Spitfires or Hurricanes, come in to land. I was fascinated by it all. We didn't have to worry about enemy planes because it was now well into March and the Krauts were getting pinched darn good from East and West. Their air force was no force at all.

Believe it, or not, our English ward orderly, was named George, also, just like my Old French friend, George's, in Bar-Le-Duc. He was a right Charley, also, and we had a lot of fun with him around.

For whatever reason, I found out that I was being moved again. This time to USAHP #4145 near a village called Middlebrook Stoney, or maybe it was Bicester. Some of these names stick in my mind today, but this hospital was to be my last venue in England.

Before I left, within the last couple of weeks, I started to get a lot of back mail from the 70th and 80th Divisions, and believe it or not, some packages from my mom with her cookies and other goodies which were wrapped and re-wrapped a few times following the APO numbers across France and Luxembourg and England. What a Postal System....!!!

Toward the end of the first week of April, I was told to start packing whatever belongings l had, for I was going to be flown back to the good old USA. The discoloring on my feet was disappearing fast and I was able to get socks and shoes on now, while I continued to exercise my ankle joints.

It was April 10, 1945 that I left and driven to the north of Southampton, where I had arrived from France, a couple of months ago. I, along with a host of other GIs going home were milling about a large ship which was the TT (Troop Transport) George H. Barry... another George!!! This time the passengers were not all hospitalized personnel, but returning GIs for re-assignment, or Airmen with over 40 or so missions, and Red Cross personnel.

The ship hauled anchor early the next morning, and we set sail through the English Channel, saying goodbye to the war to France, Luxembourg, England, and times in between. We were not in convoy on this Merchant Marine ship. We sailed alone which was a little hairy, because the war was still going on, and there were German wolf packs, and submarines out there, in the Atlantic. However, we had US Navy personnel on board able to man the rear guns, depth charges, or whatever, for defensive purposes. The ship was fairly new and sailed at a pretty good pace and zigzagged every few minutes or so, so that the undersea enemy would find it hard to get a bead on us.

The first day at sea was uneventful, until we heard a "Now hear this.... this is the Captain speaking." We all stopped what we were doing and with baited breath we waited for the remainder of the announcement... "We just received news from Washington, D.C. that our President, Franklin Delano Roosevelt, died this morning at Warm Springs, Georgia." (There's another George....) It was April 12, 1945.

What a way to start on our way home. After the announcement, you could hear pin drop. There was almost total silence throughout the entire ship. After a while, what may have seemed like an eternity, there was some murmuring here and there. It was obvious that it was about the President's death, and what a shame; he led us through the depression and the war... which was practically over at least in Europe, anyway. And now, what was the vice-presidents name....??? Truman, Harry Truman? Can he follow through? What happens now with the war in the Pacific? The Germans are on the run, and how soon to victory. Can Truman lead us...??? All these subjects, I can recall, were on everyone's lips.

After a while shipboard life returned to normal. We were alone at sea. All we could see was our zigzagging wake in the ocean behind us. Accommodations and food were fair. Enlisted men were in one space, and officers and Red Cross personnel were in other spaces. During the day, on the loudspeaker, we had a sort of make-believe ballroom or music hall. The Merchant Marine personnel would play records, the music and songs and big band sounds of the day.

One day, another shift of record playing mariners took over, and the majority of music was country and western, what was known then as, Hillbilly music. After many hours of listening to this kind of music, day after day, and demands for more popular music, there was grumbling in the ranks. The gripe was that there should a better mix of music. Not one kind over another. The mix after some time was not acceptable to many people.

It reached a point that one day there was an insurgence, or shall I say a raid on the radio room where the records were being played. Needless to say there was some physical confrontation, some records were broken, nerves frayed, blankets, pillows thrown about, loud and boisterous language, etc...

One can guess the outcome. The authorities couldn't pinpoint the main culprits, so everybody suffered. The radio room was shut down, no music, and we were fortunate in that no one was put in the brig. After all, just about everybody on this troop transport were either wounded and recuperating combat veterans, airman with many combat missions, and we were all letting off a little steam.

So ended our second emotional upheaval and we all returned to regular shipboard the weather was kind to us. Being in the North Atlantic, it could get pretty rough if the weather turned against us. We were into our second week at sea and nobody seemed to know when we would see landfall. It shouldn't take this long to cross. When I left Boston harbor last December, it was only a ten or eleven day trip. I could tell that we were traveling west because the sun always set at the front of the ship, and rose behind the ship. What a mariner, I am.

It was noticed that food portions were getting smaller. Scuttlebutt had it that we were too long at sea and food was going fast. Too much zigzagging takes time away than just going straight. Some of the sailors were casting lines over the ship and catching fish. This effort became part of our daily menu. Boy, I tell you, days were getting longer and longer and we were all praying to see land. And soon.

Finally, on April 23, 1945, we sighted land, and guess where? Boston Harbor, right back where I started from with the 274th Regt. on the S.S. Mariposa. Excitement was rampant throughout the ship. Home at last, or at least, partially. Everybody was busy putting their gear and

70

possessions together, and making sense out of the directions we were getting on debarking. As we neared the pier where we would dock, the Boston fishing fleet met us and threw streams of water saluting us, tooting their horns with tug boats chiming in. What a spine tingling feeling we all got from this ovation... everybody on deck waving and yelling. As the ship docked, there was a band that struck up the "Stars and Stripes Forever", followed by other martial music, Red Cross coffee wagons, shore personnel waving and going about their work to receive us... Buses and ambulances ready to take us to the nearest military station.

Finally, there I was walking, a little limp maybe, down the gangplank, and like a few other GIs, as I reached terra firma, I knelt and kissed the ground, actually my palm was flat on the ground and I kissed the back of my hand. Think I'm crazy smooching the dirty turf of a waterfront pier... Telephones and a Western Union office were made available to us while we waited for orders to board our transportation. Since the family didn't have a phone that I knew of I went to the WU office, waited in line and sent a telegram that I was safe and home and will write soon. At the time I didn't know that I had a two-week furlough coming up before my new destination.

The family saved every bit of mail that I sent home while in the Army in the US and overseas while in combat and in the hospitals where I "lived". This day happened to be my sister Eileen's birthday, April 27th.

While at Standish, we were given physical examinations head to toe, appraising our injuries, aches and pains, etc., paid to date, including my combat infantry pay, overseas pay, and given more clothing, ODs and suntans. Then the best part, while they evaluated our situation, sent us all home with a 2-week furlough. Look out Brooklyn, here I come... My wallet was flushed. I picked up my barracks bag with all my "possessions" and my orders to report to Camp Bunter Convalescent Hospital, North Carolina, after the 2 weeks were up. I guess that I was lucky. Some guys were sent back to active duty, and some were discharged on the spot. They must have had the required points for discharge.

There was a system of points that the military conjured up to be used for discharging all GIs. So many points for length of service... so many points for overseas duty... so many points for days in actual combat and a star for each zone, so many points for any medals: Purple Heart, Bronze Star. Silver Star, etc. It was possible, in fact I am sure, that I didn't have enough points. My military service at this point was only about 13 months, including overseas service of only 5 months. My only decorations were the Purple Heart and Combat Infantry Badge. The Bronze Star was awarded me over 50 years later by the Dept. of the Army.

Perhaps I needed more attention at Bunter. My feet were still very sensitive to hot and cold and I couldn't stand for any length of time. The range of motion at my ankle joints were minimal, probably due to some muscle or tendon impairment. But I was doing exercises to retake the flexibility I needed to walk and run properly. For Pete's sake, I was only 19 years and 3 months old, I mean young. Sports was my "reason for being". It was important to me, besides, there was also my career... What career? I had no idea what I wanted to do. Well, I was young, plenty of time to figure this out. I, obviously, would be going back to school... got to pick a college, but what career subjects... all in time. Right now, we are saying goodbye to Standish and some of our buddies we spent time with on board the Barry and in the barracks, and off to New York City.

The train to New York was in Taunton, Mass (the same train that I took to sneak home Thanksgiving before I went overseas) I boarded the train, in uniform with the "fruit salad" at my left breast pocket, feeling very proud, and lugging my barracks bag. While on the train, my mind wandered to a few short months ago. I was a soldier, in combat. I saw and heard and felt the destruction, the ear shattering noises, the pain personally, and the discomfort, the uneasiness of who of my buddies may have been wounded or killed. How could I have been so lucky? Was I at the right place at the right time...? I know that I was because there were certain instance where that was so. I was shot at, bombed and strafed (albeit by our own Ninth AF mistakenly). Someone up there had to be looking out for me. Being a lowly Private, decisions were being made for me, go there, stay here.. Your turn is from 0200 to 0600, you're on patrol today, go with your squad go up to the 2nd floor, stay away from the windows, follow me, stay close, do what I do... fire into those trees, fix bayonets, we are going into that stand of trees. WOW! I think that I was beginning to sweat with all those mind boggling thoughts running through my head. What will it be like seeing the family again, my dear Mom and Dad, my sister's Yvette, Eileen and Rosalyn? Other members of my family and friends, my two closest friends, Dave and Bobby.

Well, before I knew it the few hour's train ride was over and the conductor was yelling Pennsylvania Station, next stop. I was in Shaky Lane now. Could I remember how to get home? Are the same trains running to Brooklyn, the Sea Beach Line, and the Culver? I checked with a Travelers Aid person and she told me, yes, and where to go. I guess GIs were well looked after. The war in Europe was just about over. It was only a matter of a few days to May 9th, and the nation would go crazy, forgetting for the moment there were GIs, Navy and Marines still fighting in the Pacific. An oxymoron, eh? The war is over, the war is still going on!!

The next step was to find a phone. I found out that the family had a phone installed and armed with that number, I called, and told them where I was and that I would be home within the hour. This was about late afternoon now.

The Sea Beach Line took me to the Flatbush Avenue transfer point where I took the "creepy" Culver to the Ditmas Avenue stop. Whee! I'm home. If I was nervous or excited, I don't think I felt it. I felt high. Those thoughts coming home on the train were still with me, but the reality was that I was HOME. A guilty conscience creeps into one's thought, how come I made it when so many didn't? Do I deserve it, should I have deserved to go on with my life?

The train doors opened, I stood up, lined up behind who also were getting off. I got it in my mind to stop "wandering" and shook myself back-to-reality. I proceeded along the long platform to the stairs leading to the street. As I approached the head of the stairs a familiar figure loomed in front of me. As he spied me, he called to me and my spine tingled. He rushed at me and gave me a big kiss and a bear hug that I will always remember.

There were some tears flowing, to be sure as we walked downstairs to Ditmas Avenue, then to East 2nd Street, #640 Apt 3C. My Dad and I walked in the apartment and there was my dear

Mom, tears of joy and more hugs and kisses. My sisters were still in school. Hugs and kisses to come later with them. Home at last, at least for the next couple of weeks of furlough.

The Army is not finished with me yet. The whole family was home for dinner for the first time in the last two years so. There was so much to talk about, so much to say. I must have gone and on about my military service and what I did overseas. Mainly, because the last time I saw the folks I sneaked in to Brooklyn for only a few hours before I went back to Standish (Boston) POE and shipped out on the Mariposa for Europe a couple days later.

The family had kept practically all my mail while in service and showed me the letters and postcards keeping them for posterity. This included all my V-mail while I was in combat and in the various hospitals in France and England. In some of those missives I couldn't believe that I had written such inane immature writings. My censors must have thought that I was a Section 8 case, but considering that I was only barely 19 years of age and still wet behind the ears, they let it go without much ado. As long as I didn't reveal any top secret information that the enemy might intercept if they captured our mailman... oh yeah...

A long night's sleep was the order of the day next and I surely slept in that night. My mom had gone through my barracks bag that I brought home with me and I'll bet she was up half the night doing my laundry and ironing my khaki suntans and hanging them up. My winter Class As were still the order of the day. My seedy dress jacket which was given to me in England before I left was a bit long in the sleeves and the pockets on one side were in disrepair, looking like it caught some shrapnel. It was all they had that fit me at the time. My mom darned it as best she could and ironed it so that looked fairly presentable. However, I think I only wore it once to take some pictures with the family. The rest of the time I wore my Army field jacket.

It was now the beginning of May, and there was a high fever pitch for the war in Europe to be over. Sure enough, the news on May 9, 1945 was that Germany surrendered unconditionally. And, I can tell you there were lots of people yelling and cheering and celebrating. But, there was some restraint, of course. The war in the Pacific was still a war. The Japanese were not giving up. Our boys, they are men by now, are still fighting getting hurt, dying while island hopping, getting closer and closer to the enemy's shore.

Well, that was thousands of miles away. For however short it was, my participation in the war was over, and I was home. The country was still on a wartime basis and many prayers were going out to the Pacific for our servicemen to stay safe and maybe the Army, Navy and Marines will concentrate their efforts in only one war zone and get over with soon so that we can see the end of all hostilities.

The two-week furlough was ending, and I was starting to pack gear, my belongings, since my next destination was Camp Bunter Convalescent Hospital, North Carolina for a physical checkup and a determination of military future. With my orders in hand, I made my way to Penn Station in Manhattan, as I had done a few times before, and boarded the train south to probably Charlotte or Durham. I don't know which city, but the army bus was there to pick me up and take me to Bunter.

Camp Bunter, I believe was a training facility for infantry or some other facet of military service. In one section of the two story wooden barracks was to be our home. The barracks were called "wards" since we were all hospitalized personnel who came here from other facilities for rehabilitation and convalescence. Rehab was right. My feet were still giving me trouble. I couldn't stand steadily for any length of time, my ankles ached which caused me to walk with a slight limp. I couldn't take hot bath or my feet would turn a pretty color of blues and purples, etc. I looked forward to doing anything that included sitting or lying down.

Within a few days of arriving at Bunter, and acclimating to the climate, which was getting warmer and warmer as we approached the months of June and July. My physical checkup was good from the ankles up. Everything checked out, but I needed some therapy for my feet. I did a lot of exercises to strengthen my feet, and still looked forward to sitting down. I was having nightmares about not being able to play ball like I wanted to... like beating out a bunt to first base for a hit, or going out for a pass, or running through the line for a big gain or a touchdown... Will my feet ever get better for me to continue in sports which I love so much?

Therapy continued, my skin around the ankles was scaling and peeling off, I was getting new skin, can you believe that... I was making friends in my ward, and we shared a lot of tall war stories. When I felt able and was given the OK... I got my first weekend pass to go into Henderson, the nearest town to Bunter. A fellow infantry man from the 90th Division, Frank Dixon, from Philly was my pass buddy. We left after dinner one Friday and kind of strolled through town, and found ourselves in a residential neighborhood. We were told that there was a church nearby that had set up cots in the basement for GIs who were on a pass and needed a bed for the night for free.

Anyhow we got a bit tired, so we picked out a lush green lawn in front of a large Victorian home and relaxed a bit before moving on. As we relaxed, a young child, about 9 or 10 and an older teenage girl came outside and introduced themselves.

Their first names escape me to this day, but their family name was Farrell. Frank was the outgoing guy and he introduced us. He referred to me as "Lash" ...because that was what the guys called me back at Bunter. Abraham or Abe maybe stuck in some people's throats, like..., oh, he must be Jewish... Not wanting any confrontations, I would be called "Lash", or "AL", my initials which was etched on everything I owned.

Well, the little tyke said, after introductions, I recall, "What kind of name is that"? I'll call you "Gremlin", probably because I kidded her and joked with her before introductions. I think that Frank had an eye on the teenager. He was a couple of years older than me and tuned into the opposite sex quicker than anyone I knew at the time.

At this time the parents came out of the house to see what was going on. After talking to the girls, the mother, with gracious southern hospitality, invited us into the house, fed us and wouldn't hear of our spending the night in the church basement. Her two sons were still in the military and she had their spare bedroom to offer us. We were "forced" to accept her generous offer. So Frank and the Gremlin slept peacefully, had a great breakfast, thanked them profusely, and went on our way.

Meanwhile, back at the ranch, life went on. Some of the guys were rehabilitating very well, and the powers that be were discharging them, not sending them back into service. That was good news for the rest of us, that is, the possibility of going home in the next few months, maybe.

Some occurrence, which seems a bit vague to me, but which is corroborated, in the text of a letter I sent from Bunter to home, is that my old foxhole buddy, Eddie Lester, caught up with me at Bunter, and what a reunion we had. We both had no idea where or what happened to us after Luxembourg. We filled each other in. Eddie told me he got pneumonia and frozen feet and was evacuated, and I told him my story. Son of a gun made PFC.

Back at Bunter, some good news reached us. The authorities decided that all mobile personnel would be going to school. Some of the barracks that weren't being used would be used as classrooms.

Since it was summer recess with July and August coming, there were teachers and professors from the local high schools and Duke University who will be on "campus" and give lectures and classes in a variety of subjects from Algebra, History, Physics to Zoology. What a list. It was mandatory to select a class and attend or it would be KP for the rest of your stay at Bunter.

I was looking at the list and I came up to Drafting, Architectural. A female teacher was giving this class from Duke and the classroom was next door to my ward. WOW! I always had a knack for drawing. I enjoyed it while in school creating certain artwork. There might be something to this drawing of plans for buildings, homes, factories offices, etc. I thought that there might be a building boom after the war. Why not get involved. Besides, the teacher and the location fits like a glove.

That was it. Later that day I signed up for the class and the next week I sat down at my first architectural drafting board, on a drafting stool that swiveled. There were pencils, triangles, scales, a T-square, of course, erasers. And I was ready. And, oh, the teacher. I was in love right away.

She presented the drafting course in such an interesting manner that I fell in love with architecture. What an amazing profession to be able to put down on tracing paper all sorts of lines, information and notes explaining the line work. All this with input from Mechanical, Civil, Electrical and Structural engineers, then making many sets of blueprints, giving them to various Contractors who bid on the work to be performed, then commence the actual construction and erection of a building of whatever occupancy.

I was so serious and attentive to my work that the teacher took notice of this. I was the first one in class and the last to leave. This I decided would be my profession, an Architect. Of course, the fact that she would critique my work standing very close to me so that her perfume overwhelmed me didn't exactly deter me from my decision.

Finally, one day, after five or six weeks in class, I got the notice to be ready for discharge on August 23, 1945. I was going home for good. The last advice from the teacher was that I had an aptitude for Architecture and to follow it up when I get back to civilian life, at 19 and a half years old. My whole life lay ahead of me. There was lots of merriment around camp. About a couple of weeks before I was to be discharged, our Air Corps dropped the first atom bombs on Hiroshima followed by Nagasaki. It was time for the enemy to surrender. What devastation? Surrender took on the USS Missouri early in September 1945. Peace at last.

One hairy incident took place just before we were discharged. Some southern GIs started playing their hillbilly songs (that was what they were called then... not country western) so loud that it was very disconcerting to the other guys who wanted quiet before leaving, and there started a real barracks fight. Beds were up rooted, mattresses were tossed down the stairs, footlockers opened and emptied records were broken or hidden. The MPs were called, but before they could see our devastation, most of it was tidied-up. If anybody in authority had seen this our discharge would have been to the stockade, and pay deducted for the damage.

August 23, 1945 came, and after breakfast we lined up for the last time of our military life and received our official Honorable Discharge papers, back pay and free passage home by train. We sewed a cloth replica of the beloved "Ruptured Duck" on our uniforms over the right breast pocket of our sun tans and our "fruit salad", medals to you, over left breast pocket, and away we went to make our way north again to Penn Station and home to Brooklyn and my future.

Lester J. Schlager
905th Field Artillery Battalion
Close Call

I was in the 905th Artillery Battalion, a T/Sgt. directing Artillery for the 2nd Battalion of the 319th Infantry. We were getting close to a town. The town was down in the valley. The field we were in was mud, we were sliding all around the place. The Germans started firing their 88s at us. Our Corp. Artillery started firing on top of us too. We were sliding in all directions. There were (4) houses in front and to the left of us. I headed for the 1st house. As I got to the door, one of the guys yelled, over here Sarge. I spun around and headed for the 2nd house. The Infantry guy behind me kept heading for the 1st house. When he opened the door, the house and him were blown to shreds.

I went to Milwaukee, WI to enlist in the Marines. I was sworn in with 28 other draftees. I called my wife to have her come and meet me. As I was leaving the room, I was called back, to take another test, which was color blindness test. The book was opened and I was asked what I saw, I said nothing, another page was turned, again I said nothing, then the man turned to the last page and when I said nothing again. I was told I was color blind and I was out of the Marines. I went to the Navy and was also told I was color blind, I then went to the Army and was accepted.

We went from Milwaukee to Fort Sheridan on a trolley car. The first night I was in the army the Sgt. told me I could go to the movies, but I must sign out with him. About three quarters way through the movie, I happen to think I hadn't signed out, so I made a mad dash in the pouring rain back to my barracks to sign out before I got into trouble. However, when I got there, I didn't know which barrack was mine, but found it after a fashion. Sneaking in, I hurriedly undressed, and in hardly no time the light went on and I was hauled out of bed and sent outside to pick up cigarette butts in the downpour of rain. I was out there approximately two hours.

I was on the second floor and after breakfast, I was told to climb out and wash the windows. About a half hour later, I heard someone yelling, what are you doing up there?

I said the Sgt. told me to wash the windows. He told me he didn't want me up there and to come down and didn't want to see me up there again. The Sgt. coming out and seeing that I wasn't washing the windows, told me to get back up there and wash the windows, telling me he was the boss. Again shortly after climbing up, I heard the same man yelling, don't you understand English? I told you I didn't want to see you up there. Telling him I had been given orders to wash the windows, the man told me to get the person who told me to wash to windows and bring him out to him. When the Sgt. and I came out and the Sgt. saw who it was he jumped to attention, with me standing there with my hands in my pockets. When the Sgt. saw me just standing there yelled for me to come to attention, when he saw it was the Commanding General. We both got reamed pretty good, and I ended up with Latrine duty and all the rotten jobs that go with it.

We were sent to Camp Forrest, TN. I was assigned to the 905th Field Artillery Battalion B Battery. I was put into the Instrument Section along with some others. We ran surveys to fire 105 Howitzers. I had no idea what they were doing and I kept asking Lt. Art Jarr to put me in the gun section. He told me to keep watching what the others were doing, then one day it all came to me. A short time later, I was promoted to Corporal, and put in charge of the Instrument Section. I carried the Battery Banner whenever we had a parade and soon after I became a Buck Sgt.

Next I was made the recorder, whenever the Battery was firing, I recorded all the commands given by the Officers. Staff Sgt. soon followed, and then I was acting First Sgt.

In October of 1943, we shipped out to Camp Phillips KS, outside of Salina for maneuvers, and approximately a couple weeks later, I had my wife to join me.

In 1943, we were transferred to Arizona to the Gila Valley. We maneuvered in the desert, for what we thought to go to the Japanese Theater. From there we were moved to Camp Kilmer, NJ and trained while there to abandon ship, and waited for our being transported to our destination and what we again speculated on to be the ETO. On July 1, 1944 we boarded the Queen Mary for our trip to Scotland.

My cabin was 10 floors below the main deck. Our whole Division of approximately 15,000 plus a few other troops had boarded for the trip. On the voyage on the way over, the Queen would change course every few minutes to prevent any Sub to set their sights on her. She was supposed to be fast enough to go unescorted. After six days, we landed in Glasgow, Scotland and were put on a train to Winslow, England. Here we again polished our training, preparing for our participation in the war that was raging in France.

After approximately one month in this location, we loaded on trucks to Southampton to board an LST for the crossing of the English Channel and Omaha Beach. Leaving the LST we were marched approximately ten miles inland. While on this march a German Liaison plane flew over and that night the Germans bombed the whole area we were in earlier in the day. Make no bones about it, I was ready to go home.

The following morning we were given ammunition for our small arms, and some of us started to clean up. One of the men went behind some bushes and used his helmet to shave and wash up, when he had finished his helmet was shiny and some of the men thinking it was perhaps a German fires a few rounds at it. Luckily they were bad shots, none of them hitting the helmet. The Captain when he heard the firing came to see what was happening, boy, did we all catch it. This was the beginning of the most terrible months I was to have, but that was the way it was.

Our first encounter came a short time later, near Angers, France. I was told my driver and I was to meet Lt. Edgar Wilson at St. Gemmes/Loire, France, along the Loire River. We stayed in a church steeple and were told no Germans were within miles of us. Across the river from us was an island where the Germans had set up an artillery piece and fired at the church steeple hitting the bell. The explosion, and the round hitting the bell, needless to say we could hear nothing, flying down three flights of steps to the first floor, I don't remember who got there first. Looking at our map cases, we both discovered they were full of holes, but neither of us had a scratch. The Officers from the Battalion came up to see where the firing was coming from, but, when the Germans fired the second shell they took off like a ruptured duck, never to be seen again.

A few days later, I was called to come to Battalion Headquarters, the Colonel told me he was short of a Forward Observer, and wanted me to go to the 2nd Battalion 319th Infantry as their Forward Observer. I stayed as a Forward Observer until the end of the war.

I was promoted to a Tech Sgt. and instead of putting the stripes on my sleeve, I took them off so as not to be identified. The Germans looked for this so they could knock off any Non Com, as they did with the officers when seeing their bars on the shoulder.

Some of my war experience as we moved through France, Luxembourg, Germany and Austria, was as follows: We had captured a small town in Germany that had one street and houses on both sides. There was a barn approximately 100 feet from the end building. We had set up an outpost in this barn, and had settled in the center of the barn. During the night, noises were heard, the Germans were on a patrol, and threw grenades into the barn, following with bursts from their machine guns. We opened fired back with our machine guns, and crawled through the window of the barn and threw hand grenades at them. When daylight came and we looked out, we could see that there was dead and wounded Germans (five total). There were 12 cows, some dead and wounded. The dead cows were bloated almost twice their normal size. As we checked out the open field and looked across, we could see more German soldiers watching us. We decided to make a run for it, one at a time, as the door was opened, and the firing of mortars fell between the barn and the row of houses, the first man made it and approximate one half hour later another man made a dash for it. Shortly after he left, I took a swig of white lightning and made a run for it. Shells were falling all around me.

During another attack, German mortars pinned us down. I received orders to fire a rolling barrage to pin down the enemy. It started great, dropping rounds about one hundred yards ahead of us. The Germans returned our fire with artillery, and with shells falling around our position, infantrymen were falling from such intense fire.

During the Battle of the Bulge, we were pinned down while attacking and I crawled to no-mans-land, ducked into a pillbox and dropped two hand grenades in, firing my machine gun that I had picked up from a dead officer. I received the Bronze Star for this action.

A battalion of the 318th Infantry had been surrounded on Mousson Hill for four days and the 319th was sent to break through to them. (General Searby was KIA on this hill), both the American and German soldiers who were KIA were lying all over the hill. It was a bloody mess. The few men that were left, were seen marching the Germans soldiers down the hill to the POW enclosure.

We were attacking a German city and had reached a plateau just before the city, the ground was muddy and we were sliding all over. While all this sliding was taking place the enemy was firing us on. Shells were landing all around us, including rounds from our own guns. There were six houses on our left on top of the plateau and I made a dash for the first house, just as I got to the door, one of the men called to me, "over here Sarge", I spun around and ran for the location, one of the other men, ran for the house I passed up only for him to be killed as it had been mined and blew up as he entered.

Another time we came to a hedgerow at the end of some woods, I stood up with my field glasses to see what lay ahead of us, suddenly a machine gun started firing, however it hit no one and we kept going.

New recruits came every day, replacing those who were KIA and wounded. They were known as "Reinforcements." It sounded much better than replacements. They were new to war and whenever the Germans fired at us they would run in all directions or start to dig a foxhole. It took effort to calm them down and convince them we had to move forward. The Maginot Line had been built facing Germany, so that we approached it from the rear and in very short time we had passed through it. In WWI the 80th Division Dough Boys fought a battle here at Verdun, France, and the foxholes and shell holes and part of their trenches were still there, and here we were occupying them. History had been repeated. We captured a very large gun in this area, and in order to destroy it, we poured acid down the barrel and then blew it up.

Having been told to report to the Officer who flew the L-4s planes as Liaison, I thought this guy must be crazy. We were partners for the next four weeks. The first day I flew with him, he used hand grenades and German Molotov Cocktails, and flying 20-30 feet above the ground would drop them on the enemy. In the meantime, the enemy was firing at us with their rifles and machine guns, trying to knock us out. We had one occasion when a German Messerschmitt Fighter plane zoomed in on us. We zigged and zagged, twisted and turned and eventually he went away, and that was the last we saw of him. Our landing fields weren't always clear of mines, so we sweat it out each time we landed in a strange field. A few days after I left him, I understand he landed in a field loaded with mines and blew himself up. How lucky can one get!

On another occasion, General Patton and General McBride came into the lines with us. McBride explained we were to take two hills in front of us and we will take those hills and keep going. That day we took six hills.

It seemed we were always on the move with very little rest and on one occasion just outside of Heiderscheid, Luxembourg, we were on the attack for three days. We were very tired and run down, when we were told a new and fresh Infantry would be relieving us, but that I was to stay with the new outfit. I moved into a foxhole that was to be next to the Captain of the new outfit for some rest, they said they would watch out for me. During the night, firing woke me up and it was all around me, I called to the Capt. and there was no answer, thinking he may be wounded or killed, I crawled over to his foxhole only to find him gone. I checked other foxholes and all of them were empty, I was left there all alone, the whole company had pulled out without my knowing. Checking my map, I called back to my Battery, giving commands to fire the artillery, but as I was giving the order I was hit in the back of my head and was knocked out for a while. Coming to, I felt blood running down the back of my neck and passed out again. It was good in a way that I had been hit, as I had not been told that the woods in front of me were their objective. Had I not been hit the mission I had called for was aimed at the woods and I would have had my Battery hitting our own troops. I was wounded at midnight, what a New Year's I had.

Loading me on a jeep, the Medics took me to the first aid station, and was told I was a wheel chair patient, and was transferred to another aid station. While being transported on a litter in an ambulance we were strafed by two German Fighter Planes. Fortunately, they missed, weren't even close.

After being unloaded, I was taken to the operating room, two doctors were to do the surgery, and they gave me a local, stating it would be too much of a shock if they were to use a heavy dose of something else. They started to operate and I was listening to all that was said, and also hearing the scrapping of the instruments as they worked. I was shown the piece of shrapnel they removed, it was 1/4 inches wide and one inch long with a tail on it. I was told by one of the doctors that had the piece of shrapnel had been a touch higher it would have killed me. Again, how lucky can one get?

I was sent to a Replacement Center after my release from the few weeks stay at the hospital and was told to check the bulletin board each day. When my name came up on the board, I learned I had been transferred to the 106th Infantry Division and I should pack my things and be ready to move out. Loading up on trucks we moved out. After driving for a couple hours, we stopped for a rest stop, (remembering what Colonel Browning had told me, if I were ever to be wounded, and taken back to a hospital, I may not be sent back to the 80th Division), instead of my staying with the men and loading on the truck, I took off through the woods and hid in the bushes. When the truck took off, I became scared, as I didn't know where I was, and didn't have any idea what to do. Soon a civilian came through the woods and taking a chance I spoke to him. He answered in broken English. After dark he came back for me and took me to his home where he and his wife fed me. Telling him to watch for any American vehicle for me to get a ride back to my old outfit. After a couple of days, he came running into the house so happy, that he had stopped one of our vehicles. Unfortunately, it was an MP jeep he had stopped. Taking me to their Headquarters, I was told I was a deserter and started the paper work to send me to prison. Telling them what Colonel Browning had told me and after a few phone calls Colonel Browning was contacted and the charges were dropped and I was sent back to the 80th. I can't remember the couple's name, after so many years, I'd love to contact them.

I could go on with many more experiences, but I feel what I have told so far, tells much of what war really is.

Lt. Coward
Company I, 318th Infantry Regiment
Wounded in the Attack of Nomeny

Following, is what I remember about "crouching our way" down that ditch alongside the Nomeny-Raucourt "highway"... where we underwent a furious number of mortar and tree bursts: I believe it was one of those that nailed me just as I had emptied my M1. The "lights went out" amidst a bright/flashing array of splinters and debris.

I felt nothing... put my hand to my left ear, for some reason, and felt a warm, liquid on the entire side of my temple and face. Looking at my palm, it was covered with blood.

My platoon messenger ("runner")... we affectionately dubbed him as "Goforth" was laying on top of me... moaning and grasping for his buttocks. I somehow (?) tore his pants down and noted blood streaming from a jagged flesh wound in his buttock... can't recall if left or right? I instinctively opened up the first aid packet (we all had them on our rifle belts) found the sulfa powder and bandage... sprinkled the powder on his wound while reassuring him... and slapping on the compress bandage. Meanwhile, the tree bursts and direct fire from a nearby Jerry 88 were still dropping all about us. I motioned the men behind me to proceed past our location in the ditch and told one of them to have Sgt. Dooley take over... that I had been wounded.

As I tried to use my left leg to crawl to the rear I noticed complete numbness in the lower extremity... and some pain. I looked at my boot and there was a tear in the leather alongside the outer left side of my left ankle.

Removing my boot, I found the inside slightly bloody where the hole/tear had been noticed. My sock was saturated with blood and removing it I noticed a wound of some kind on the left side of the left ankle... near the left heel. The reader should understand that all of this happened in a very few minutes and it was self-preservation to get out of this hellhole. I did not dress my own wound, but put my boot back on sans sock. Then the pain hit!

I positioned Goforth in front of me and physically pushed and urged him to try to crawl back up the ditch... hopefully, to a medic or someone? Blocking our way was a GI squatting behind a 30 cal. heavy machine gun (water-cooled) and seemingly aiming over our heads toward the fields this side of Nomeny. I shouted for him to permit us to "get by" and he remained motionless. Upon drawing closer I noticed a clean, round hole in the center of his forehead... eyes wide-open, staring over the sights of his machine gun. He was dead.

We pushed by the location and a medic appeared (?) after we had retraced our way up the ditch for some 100 yards or so. He noticed Goforth's problem and assisted both of us further toward the rear... I told him about my heel/ankle, but by that time the whole foot was numb from the high ankle down... not much pain: Said they would look at it at the aid station ...nothing could be done here. I cannot recall how far in distance or time the aid station was located. However, others must have assisted us at some point to see that we reached it. Wounded and confusion was everywhere... I can still hear the 88 firing at "whatever" as I lay in the stretcher at the aid station.

My left boot was removed and the heel/ankle was bandaged. A few hours later I was placed on an ambulance and taken to a "field hospital" located in a power station on the Moselle River. Two, wounded krauts were in the ambulance with me and all they kept murmuring was "Hitler Kaput... Hitler Kaput." I can't recall if I said or "did" anything in their presence? Nothing I can relate, here, at least?

They operated on my wound and I was later told that it was a piece of shrapnel located very close to the Achilles tendon... so close that it was best not to "disturb" the area lest more damage might be done. The wound to my head, it was discovered, was "something" which had pierced my left ear and the medics explained that "ear wounds really do bleed." I "came to" from the anesthesia and looking down noted my left foot elevated and rather heavily bandaged: Of course, I did not know the extent of the wound or the details at that moment. But an orderly was bathing my right foot in warm, soapy water with a sponge. I was also between white sheets and on a stretcher on the concrete floor of this BEAUTIFUL power house." I thought I had died and went to Heaven!" as the saying goes. I then noticed that my feet (...the right one and the toes of the left) were dark brown and that no amount of washing would remove the color. The orderly explained that this was the "usual condition" for infantry who had been on the line for some time... caused by continual moisture staining the skin from the chemicals used in the leather- tanning process.

Then the pain "set-in"... I know they gave me a shot of "something" and it alleviated the hurt somewhat.

After a day or so, I was transferred to Nancy, thence across France to Cherbourg, then Southampton (England)... finally to Wales where I remained until January 1945. The shell fragment had fractured several bones in my ankle and the fragment, itself, is embedded in the Oscalsis of the left heel/ankle where it remains today... next to the Achilles tendon. It has its moments!

Finally, I do not know whatever happened to "Goforth" ...but I am sure that he was well cared for and he's undoubtedly recalling this experience from time-to-time. It's really unfortunate that we do not, for the most part, maintain our links with our fellow GIs "once the battle is over"! Guess that's true for a "Citizen Army"? An old, hand-written list of the names of the men in our weapons platoon (Nov. 44) shows his true name to be "Westover" ...and I believe his home was in Utah or one of the Dakotas? He was/is one of those heroes" you read about from time to time... combat vets of the 80th Infantry Division were ALL HEROES.

BRITISH ISLES

SCOTLAND

IRELAND

ENGLAND

GREENOCK
GLASGOW
FIRTH OF CLYDE

LIVERPOOL
CHESTER
PETTY POOL

MANCHESTER
KNUTSFORD
NORTHWICH
OXFORD

BIRMINGHAM
KIDDERMINSTER
STRATFORD ON AVON
HIGHWORTH
SWINDON
LONDON

SALISBURY
SOUTHAMPTON
BOURNEMOUTH

CHERBOURG

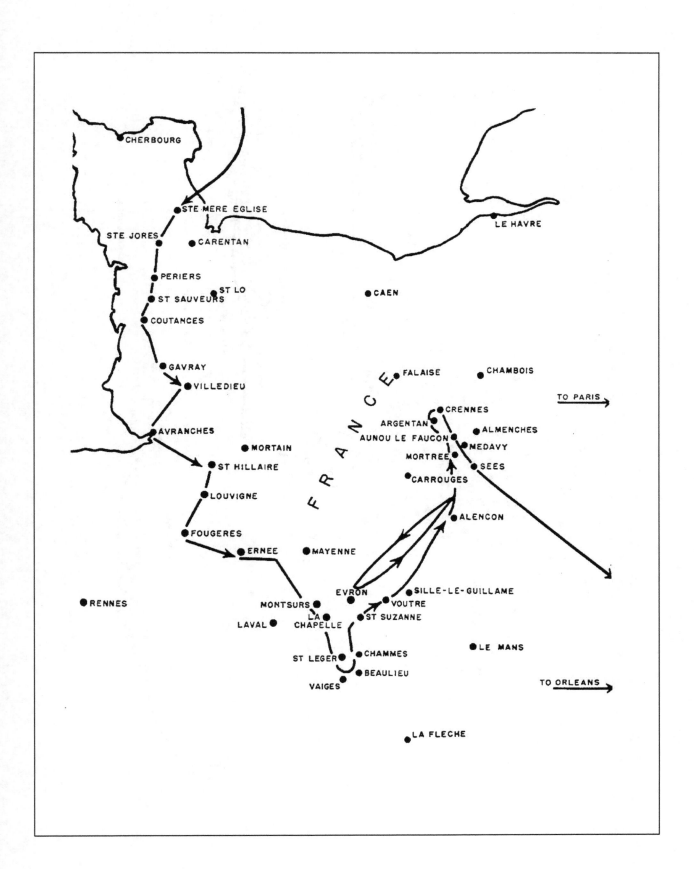

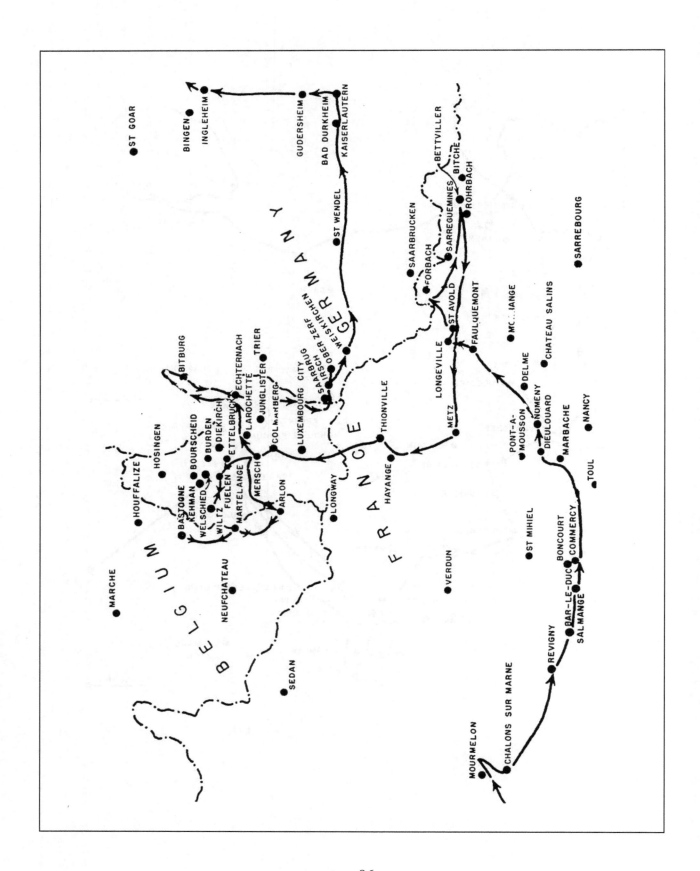

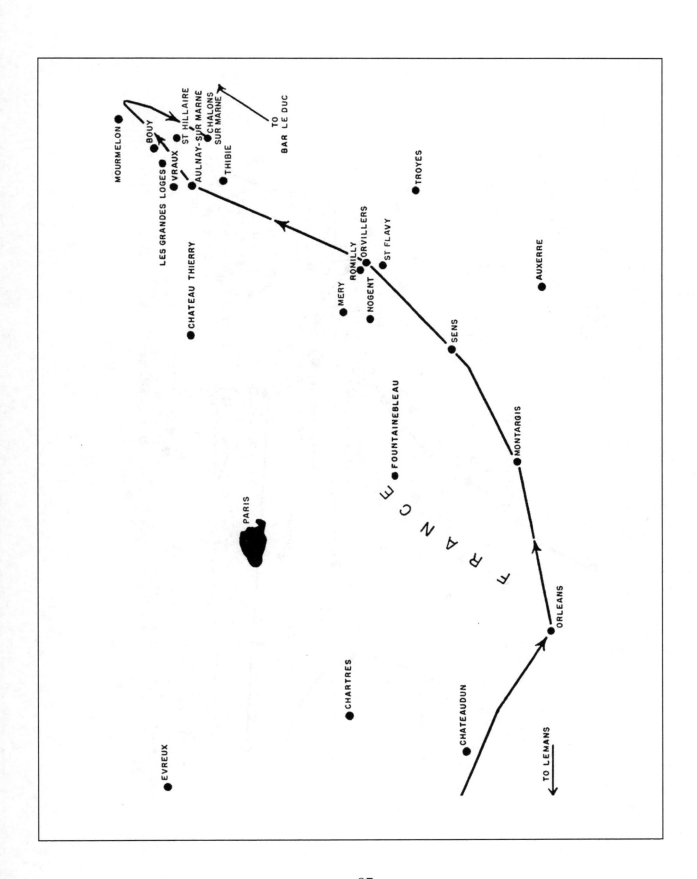

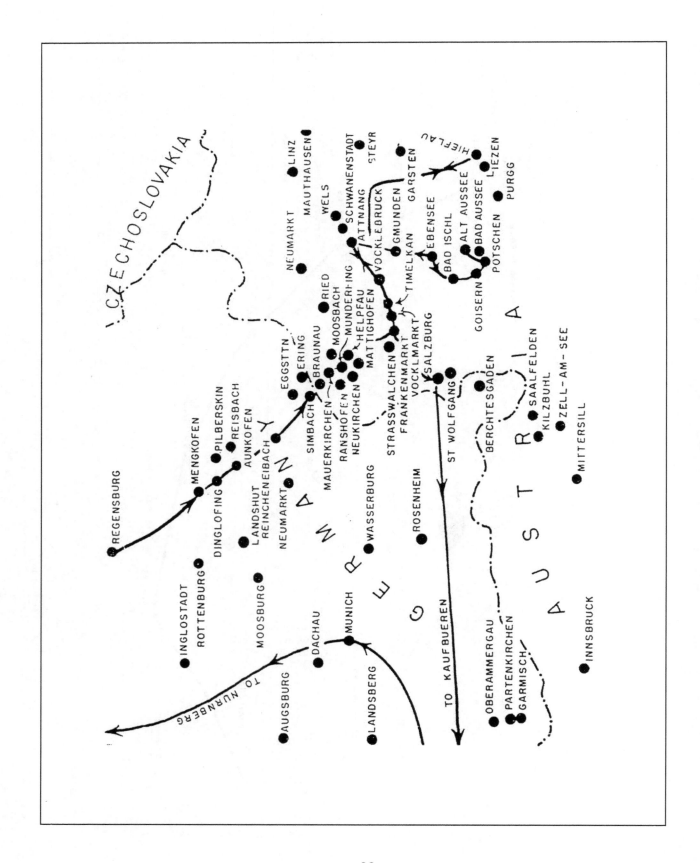

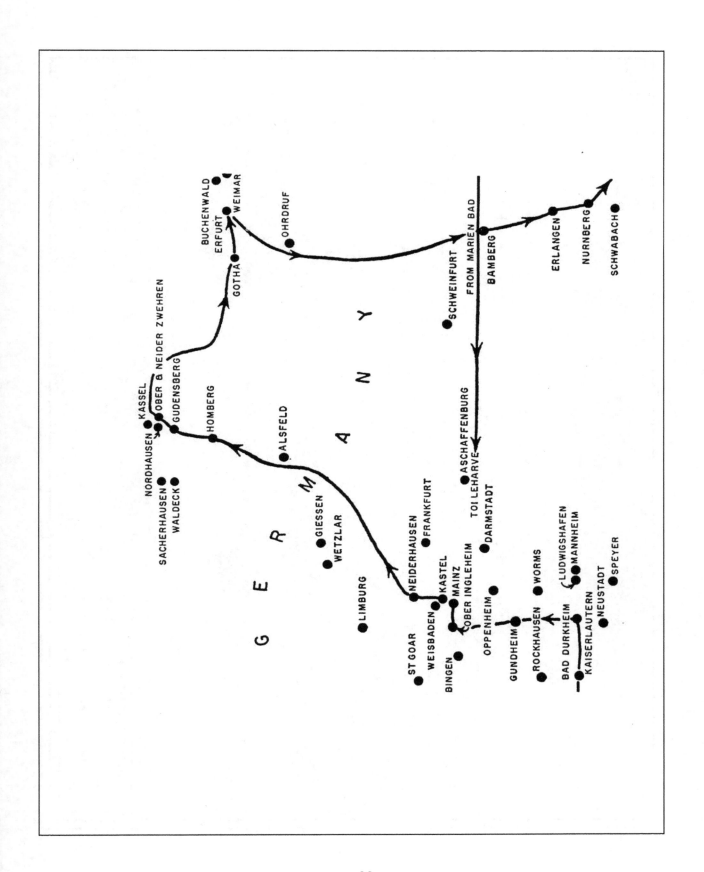

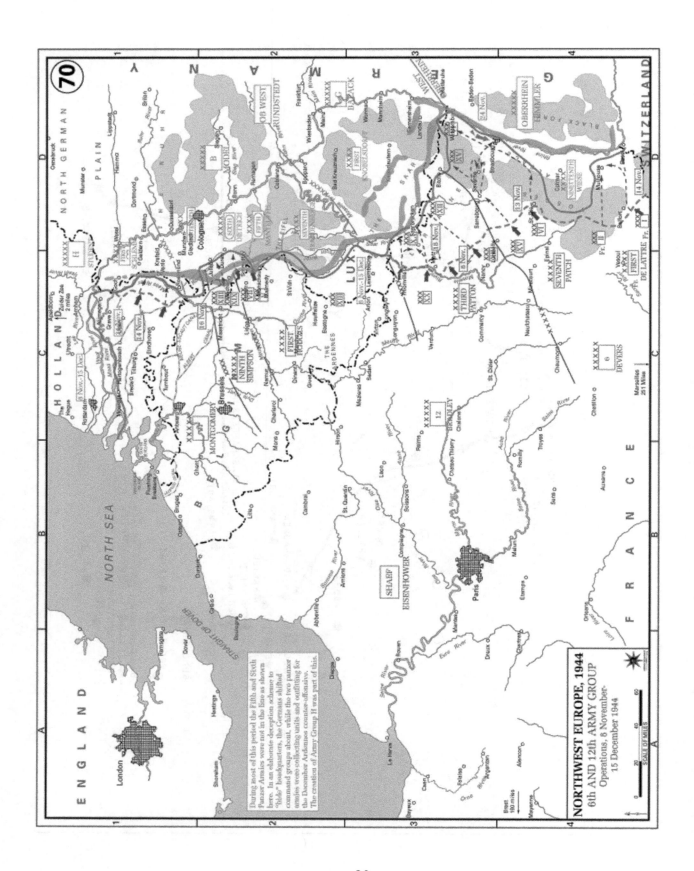

During most of this period the Fifth and Sixth Panzer Armies were not in the line as shown here. In an elaborate deception scheme to "hide" headquarters, the Germans shifted command groups about, while the two panzer armies were collecting units and outfitting for the December Ardennes counter-offensive. The creation of Army Group H was part of this.

NORTHWEST EUROPE, 1944
6th AND 12th ARMY GROUP
Operations, 8 November–
15 December 1944

SCALE OF MILES

Brest
180 miles

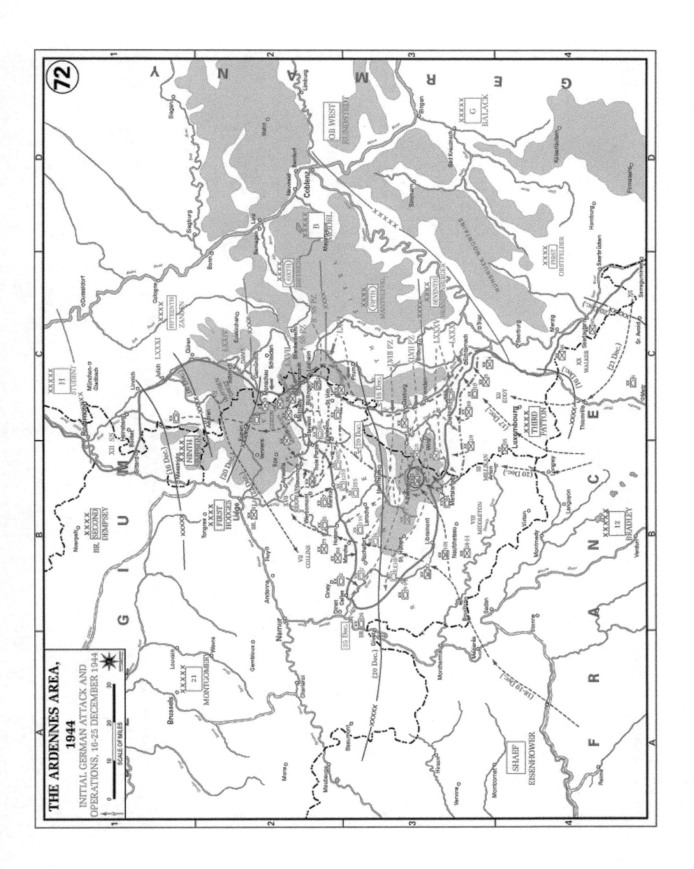

THE ARDENNES AREA, 1944

INITIAL GERMAN ATTACK AND OPERATIONS, 16-25 DECEMBER 1944

SCALE OF MILES

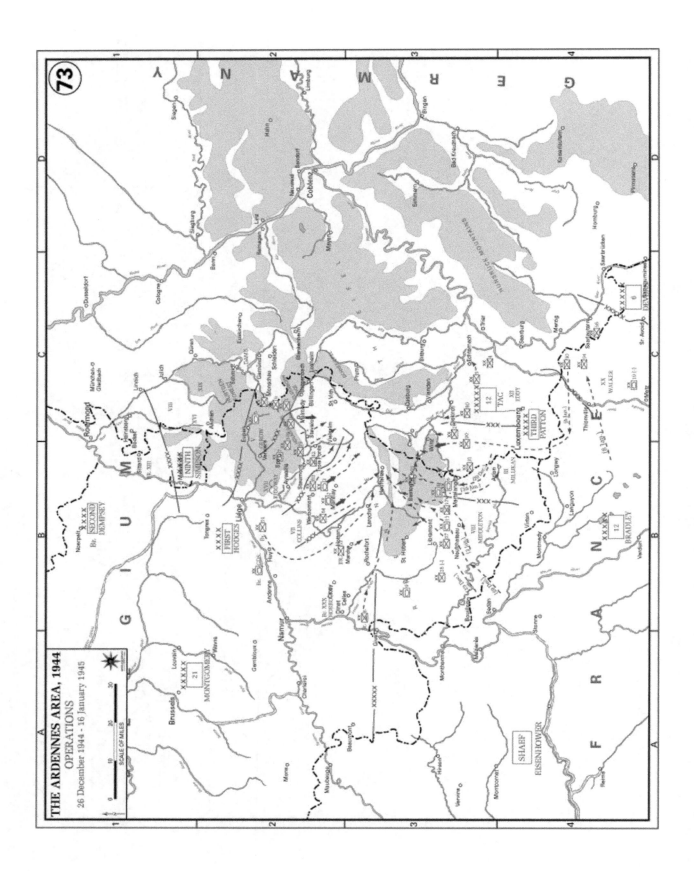

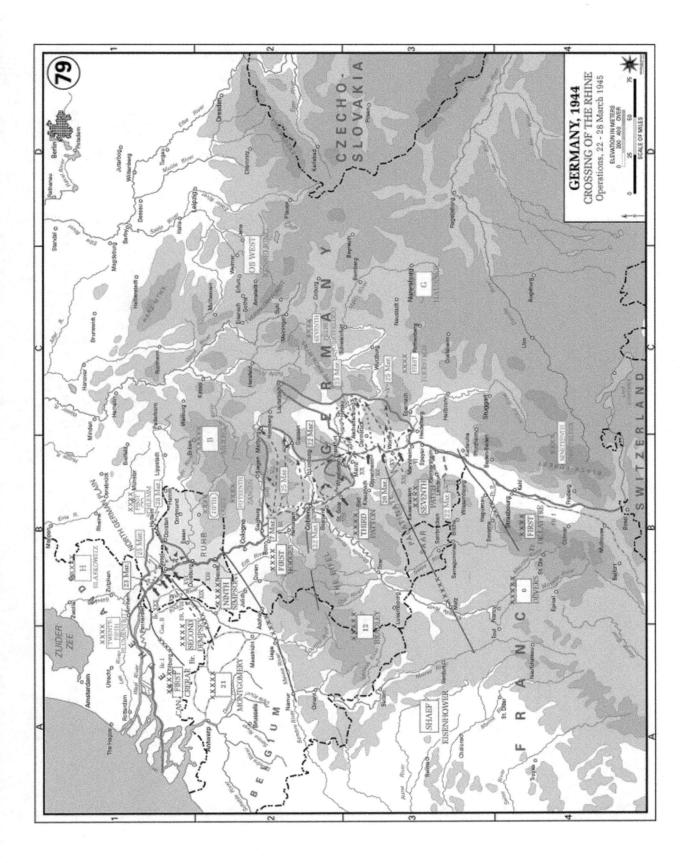

GERMANY, 1944
CROSSING OF THE RHINE
Operations, 22 - 28 March 1945

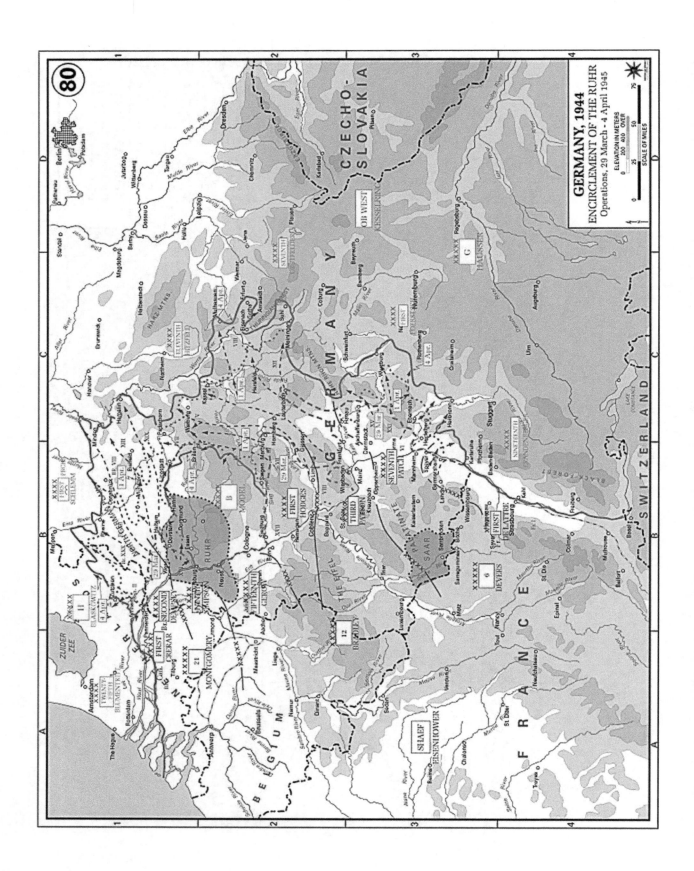

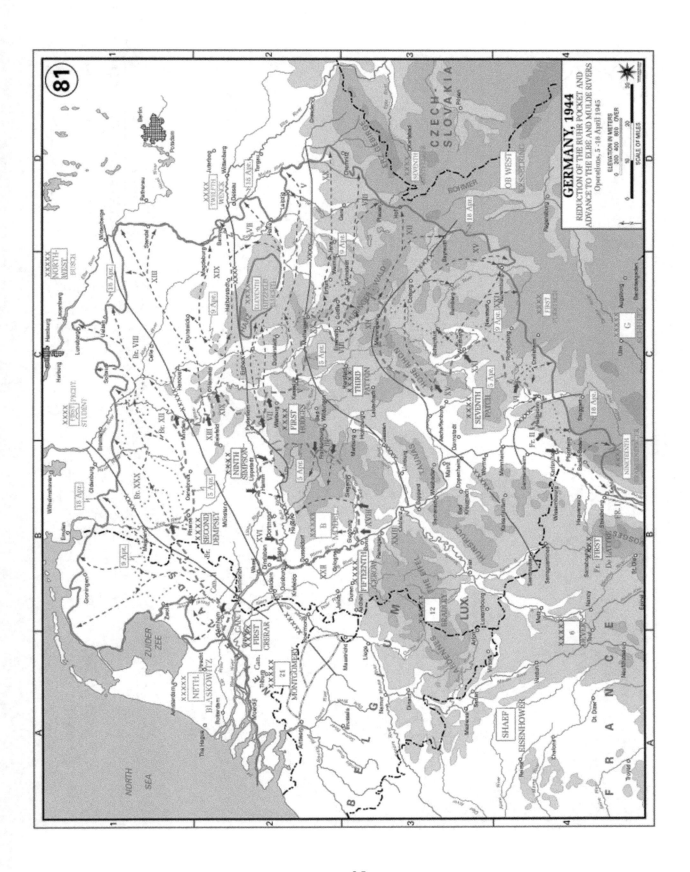

GERMANY, 1944
REDUCTION OF THE RUHR POCKET AND
ADVANCE TO THE ELBE AND MULDE RIVERS
Operations, 5 - 18 April 1945

ELEVATION IN METERS
0   200 400 600 OVER

SCALE OF MILES
0   10   20   30

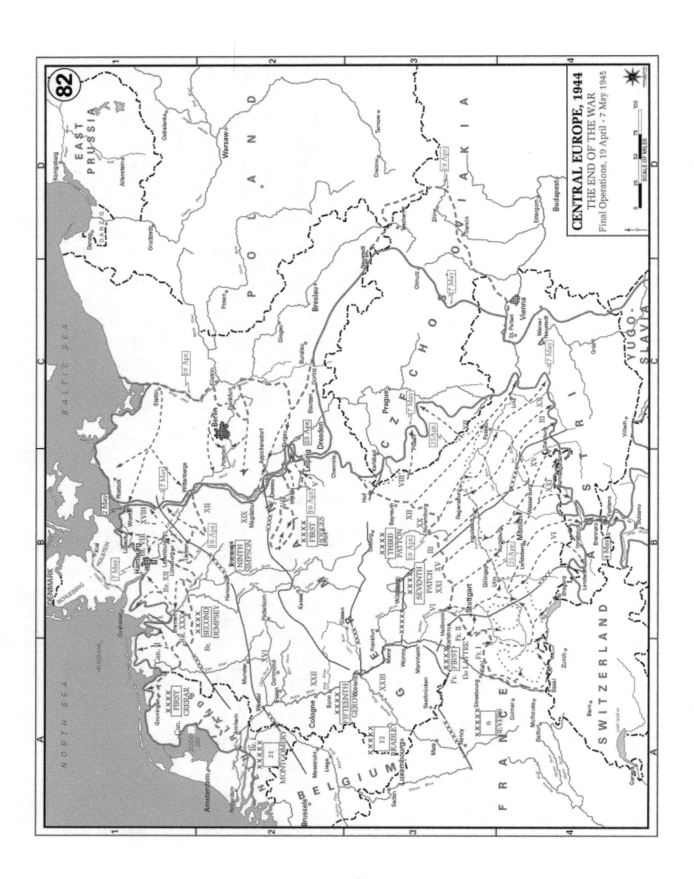

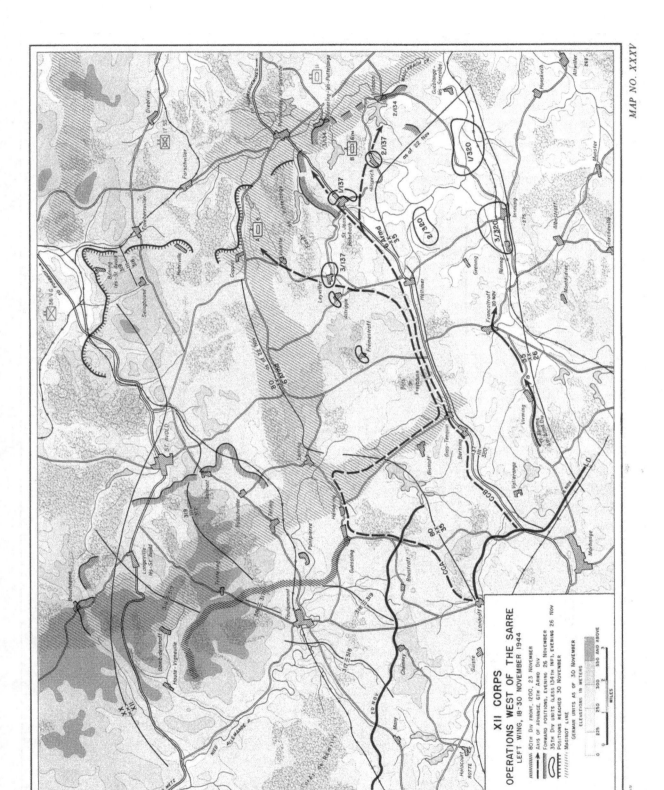

MAP NO. XXXV

XII CORPS
OPERATIONS WEST OF THE SARRE
LEFT WING, 18-30 NOVEMBER 1944

▬▬▬▬ 80TH DIV FRONT, 1200, 23 NOVEMBER
━━━▶ AXIS OF ADVANCE, 6TH ARMD DIV
⟍⟍⟍⟍ FORWARD POSITIONS, EVENING 26 NOVEMBER
- - - - 35TH DIV UNITS (LESS 134TH INF), EVENING 26 NOV
— · — POSITIONS REACHED 30 NOVEMBER
/////// MAGINOT LINE

GERMAN UNITS AS OF 30 NOVEMBER
ELEVATIONS IN METERS

225 250 300 350 AND ABOVE

0   1   2   3
MILES

97

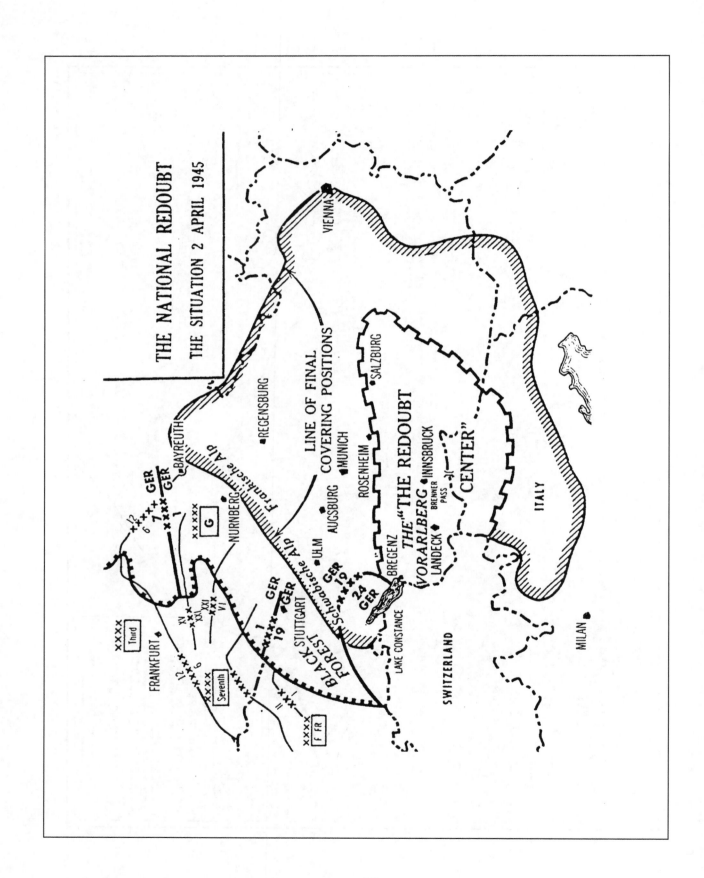

THE NATIONAL REDOUBT
THE SITUATION 2 APRIL 1945

Gene N. Barry
Hqs Company, 3rd Bn, 319th Infantry Regiment
"5 AUGUST 1994"

When I saw this dateline on the newspaper, memories came back of yet another August 5th, this one being August 5, 1944. Fifty years had gone by. When we were very young, 50 years seemed like an eternity away to us; now we are older and it may seem like yesterday.

Celebrations commemorating the fiftieth anniversary of D-Day, the 6th of June had already been held in many places in Europe and there had been numerous television programs about the war in Europe. The magnitude of the D-Day operation was almost beyond anyone's comprehension. So many plans to be made. The vast numbers of men, machines and supplies required. Even with all the preparations, it still was considered a gamble.

In January of 1944 I joined the 80th Infantry Division in Camp Laguna, Arizona and was assigned to Headquarters Company of the 3rd Battalion, 319th Infantry. Because I had telephone field lineman training while in basic training, I was placed in the wire section of the communications platoon.

Camp Laguna was the desert training center for the Army. All troops that were to be sent to fight in Africa were trained there. The 80th was the last unit to be in Camp Laguna, as the African campaign was coming to an end.

The only permanent type buildings in the entire camp were the latrines. Everything else was tents and tents, as far as you could see. Most of the tents were for five men, complete with a small stove and fold-up type canvas cots. In the middle of the tent was a wire from which to hang our blouses, etc. Your rifle had to be stored on the crosspieces under your cot. The tent was without wood flooring. The sand floor was of very soft, fine dry sand. It was impossible to keep your weapon clean.

Almost no one in my company was particularly happy about being in the infantry but we all knew that being in a battalion Headquarters Company was better than being in a line company as they always received the most casualties.

I was 18 years old, would be 19 in March, D-Day was to be the 6th of June and in August the Division was to land in Normandy.

By August 1944 the Normandy beaches were secure, the fighting had moved inland somewhat and troops and materials were pouring on to the beaches as fast as was possible.

Now it was the 80th Division's turn to land in France. After leaving the marshaling area near Salisbury, England we were moved by train to Southampton and there our Battalion boarded a ship for the approximately 80-mile crossing of the English Channel.

While we were waiting on the pier for our turn to board, a group of about 30 English Marines came out of a ship that was tied to the opposite side of our pier. They looked really smart, creamof-the crop type guys, all apparently in excellent physical condition, each one being about the same size as the next, with nice uniforms and black tams. They were armed but without battle gear-packs, grenades, canteens, etc. They lined up rather loosely. Then a young officer came on the pier and stood in front of them. Shortly he gave a command to his men, which was almost inaudible to us, whereupon they snapped to attention and were lined up perfectly. Again, a couple of almost inaudible commands and they faced right and were marching away with that exaggerated arm swing that British troops use when marching. We were all really impressed. Our officers gave commands in a loud, tough sounding voice — supposedly the louder, the better — and this British officer almost whispered his commands. We all looked at each other in amazement, feeling somewhat like a bunch of amateurs compared with these guys. This officer must have given his men a pep talk before they came out. You know, something like: "All right you blokes, there's a bunch of Yanks on the pier. Now is our chance to show them what real soldiers look like."

Shortly afterwards, we boarded our pretty-good-sized ship. We weighed anchor and started the trip across the Channel. We were taken to a large compartment that was empty except for hammocks. Some of the men were trying out the hammocks and lots of them were falling onto the deck, amid a lot of laughing.

Everyone was in a kind of festive mood. We were glad to be away from the intense training and full schedule we had endured during the previous 6 weeks in England.

We got our mess kits and were served a meal of what we first thought was greasy beef stew but later decided it was mutton stew, with some insisting that it was goat.

After several hours of smooth sailing we saw the coast of France. Our ship anchored some distance out to allow us to load in smaller landing craft type boats for the trip to the beach.

So there we were, about to become a part of the invasion of Europe. Many of us were not yet 20 years old, our Non-Coms were a few years older, maybe 22-25 or so, the Battalion Commander was 36, the wire section's two jeep drivers were in their early 40's and were referred to by all as "Pops".

Soon, it was our turn to go over the ship's rail and down a cargo net to a bouncing landing craft. We had practiced going down cargo nets while in the States so it wasn't too difficult, other than that this time we were stepping into a bouncing boat. They cautioned us to hit the boat, because if we missed it and hit the water, it was, "Goodbye." Loaded as we were with equipment, there was no way anyone could be rescued if they went in the "drink."

We huddled in the landing craft as we headed for the beach — like the scenes we had seen in movies. There wasn't any one shooting at us, but even so, it was exciting. I don't think anyone was scared — we were so young. The really scary times were to come later.

When the landing craft grounded, the ramp went down and we waded in water above our knees for the short distance to the beach. From the water to a hill on the far side of the beach was not very far. Ahead was a massive wall of heavy, thick barbed wire, which was strung so close together a rabbit couldn't have found its way through it.

Off to the right was a big concrete gun emplacement, which had been silenced. To the left was a black sign with a white skull with crossed bones and letters painted on it. The letters said: "Achtung, Minen!" A path wide enough for vehicles had been cleared through the barbed wire. We walked in columns of two, up the hill, along this path, and into the war.

After a short distance we were stopped and told that we were to march several miles inland where trucks would pick us up. Before long, we passed a large field hospital. Some of the recuperating wounded came out of their tents and stood by the roadside. Cries of "Get the bastards", "Give 'em hell", etc. were shouted at us.

Sometime after dark we left the road and were told to bed down as the trucks would not pick us up until about 2:00 a.m. It was the first of many, many nights sleeping on the old terra firma in Europe.

I awoke to the sound of lots and lots of motors, as the truck convoy came into our area. It was so dark you literally could not see your hand in front of your face. I was amazed that they found us, as they had to drive without lights.

As I was getting up to gather my gear, a slight cramp gripped my stomach. I knew the symptom of the GIs. I uttered an audible "Oh no, not now!" There was nothing to do but get into a truck. Within minutes the convoy moved out at a very slow pace.

After a short while the cramps became severe. What a terrible place to be at a time like this. Fortunately, the convoy slowed down and then stopped. Some others and I went out the back of the truck. Sounds of the front of the convoy starting to move caused us to some quick action. It was up-with-the-pants and back-on-the-truck. The cramps got worse. Fortunately the convoy stopped again and I got out.

Just then, a Jeep came slowly back from the head of the column. One of the men in it was saying softly: "Snipers ahead! Snipers ahead!" Talk about terror. Here I was sick, with my pants down, the convoy moving out and they tell me, "Snipers Ahead!" No way was I going to be left there alone. I got back in the truck very quickly. Thankfully I did get some relief during another stop. Later I heard that some trucks were not so lucky and had people who couldn't hold it. Those guys were made to sit at the back of the truck on the tailgate. A real mess.

It was still dark when we arrived at the assembly area where we were to get our vehicles, heavy weapons and other equipment. We were put in a large field that was surrounded on all sides by thick hedges and tall trees that were barely discernible in the darkness. This was "Hedgerow Country." There was only one entrance in this big field and that was for the farmer to come in and out of the field to tend to his crops.

Right away, I was put on guard duty. My post was from the gate to the far side of the field. I was to walk to the far side, stop, listen, and then return to the gate, stop, listen, and then do it again. Because I still had stomach cramps, there was sometimes a delay before my return from the far side of the field.

When I was relieved from guard duty I managed to get some sleep before the dawn came rolling in. During the day while we waited for our equipment, I did some exploring, which was kind of dumb, considering the possibility of mines, etc. I went into the hedgerows and saw German foxholes. They were made very precisely, with smooth sides as though made by a sculptor. I found a bloody piece of trouser from an American uniform, letting me know that this wasn't Hollywood. Then I came across a piece of paper with German wording and the swastika on it. I later found out it was a soldier's pass.

After we had our equipment I learned that the 319th was put in Corps reserve. We missed the fighting in the Hedgerows and followed up the advance for days as the breakout from Normandy was made.

Ahead of us was the German Army—the best-equipped and best-trained army in the world, and here we were, young guys who had yet to hear the sound of the cannons.

I sometimes thought that we were like a high school football team that was to be matched against a professional team. We had to learn quickly from our experiences and our mistakes, and we did.

The 80th Division became a very effective fighting unit—always taking their objectives while accepting their casualties. The German Army was still respected, but the American Army was not awed by it.

After several months in the line, the Regiment was put in a rest area near Saarebourg, France, resting and refitting while waiting to attack the Siegfried Line in Germany.

We were there for a week or so when we got the order to move out. I assumed that we were going on a short ride, as we almost always did. Because of that I rolled up my overcoat with my bedroll and put it in our jeep trailer, assuming that I would not need it. The overcoats were cumbersome and it made it more difficult to get in and out of vehicles, which sometimes could mean being in the ranks of the living or the dead. We didn't have enough jeeps in our section to carry all of us, so some of us had to get on the trucks that carried the infantrymen of the line companies. I hopped on a truck with a bunch of riflemen and went on the unexpectedly long, very cold ride to Luxembourg City. I had never before been so cold for so long. We didn't know it, but the Battle of the Bulge had started and we were on our way to help.

Looking out of the back of our truck, we saw vehicles in convoy with their lights on. It seemed there was an endless stream of them. The whole Division was on the move. I stuck my head out and looked to the front of the convoy. It was the same scene — lights as far as you could see. Everyone realized that something "big" had happened or was about to happen, but no one knew what it was.

After driving all night we arrived in Luxembourg City and were billeted in an apartment building. The first thing I remember is being so impressed with the architecture — the magnificent bridges, etc.

When our convoy finally stopped in the City, a young man came out of a house and stood watching. Siegal, one of our radio operators, was sitting next to me and tried to ask him in German if he had a toilet. The man said in perfect English: "What are trying to say?" Siegal said, "Oh, you speak English. Do you have a toilet?" The man said, "Of course we have a toilet, do you want to use it?" Luckily Siegal got back just before the convoy took off again. The next day we were moved forward until we were told to occupy a house on a hillside—what village I don't know, but it wasn't very far from Luxembourg City. Steinsel, maybe.

While there a family of refugees came walking by in front of the house. There was a grandfather and a couple with a small child, maybe 2 or 3 years old. The little boy was crying. When I asked what was wrong, the father said that his feet were hurting him. We asked them to come in the house to get warm. My sergeant immediately offered some of our rations and sent someone to get the Medics so that they could look at the boy's feet. The Medic came and decided that he was hurting because his shoes were too tight and had cut off circulation. I had just received a box of Hershey chocolate bars from a firm I had worked for briefly before going in the Army. I went to our trailer and brought the back a bar and gave it to the boy. His mother took it and gave him a small piece of it and the child stopped crying as the Medic massaged his feet.

We had just been issued a big box 10-in-one rations, which included coffee, cheese, crackers, bacon etc., so we had plenty of food for a meal together.

These people all spoke English, were well dressed, polite and appreciative of everything we tried to do for them. Before they left, the grandfather insisted that each of us have a 100-franc note, which had a picture of their Queen on it. I carried that note throughout the war and kept it until I visited Luxembourg in 1983, when I gave it to Paul Hoffman in Heiderscheid, in appreciation of the hospitality he and his family had shown my wife and I. I have many times wondered about that family—who they were and where they are today.

On the next move forward it was my turn to stay with the rear switchboard. We frequently did that. The advance group would go forward and establish a new wire communication network, while the rear one would remain in place until I was told to close the station and join the advance unit. Sometimes, during a rapid advance the rear unit would leapfrog the advance unit and would become the new advance unit.

While in the rear, I frequently talked to the advance operator. He told me that the Germans were killing our medics, and when I was moved forward we passed two of our medics who were frozen, still bending over the man they were trying to give aid to.

The next time I talked to the forward operator he told me that they were surrounded and that the Germans were running up and down the street. I told him that he must be kidding, whereupon he held his headset out the window so that I could hear the firing. The wire section had set up in the last house of this village. Our section always liked to be as far away from the officers and the rest of the company as possible.

The Germans were unloading from half-tracks right behind the house. Men from the radio section were shooting them from the upstairs windows as they came out of the half-tracks. Two of my friends from the Ammunition and Pioneering Platoon were in the basement where one was shooting through a vent in the potato cellar at the Germans in the street with a .45 caliber burp gun (machine pistol) while his friend reloaded clips for him. They knew there was a full box of .45 ammo in their truck that was close by. When they ran low on ammunition, the man loading the clips ran out to the truck, climbed in, got the box and dashed back into the house. They were firing at him all the way and it was miraculous that he made it. A Panzer Faust set the one tank on fire, but the tank commander stayed on the tank and continued firing his machine gun. The attack was beaten off.

When I passed through the town the next day the German dead were still lying in a field behind the house. All the German wounded had been evacuated. I believe the name of the town was Mertzig or maybe Mersch. A lot of Mirabel and other types of brandy or Schnapps were "liberated" there.

We moved into Heiderscheid and were there for several days. We received intermittent artillery fire while there and two friends of mine were wounded, one of them was killed in a house the next night because he neglected a warning not to sleep in the upstairs of the house. While there, my brother showed up. He was with the First Army Headquarters and had volunteered for a courier run to Third Army. After he made his delivery he came looking for me. During his visit he had me exchange clothes with him. My clothes were very dirty and he said he could get his laundered, while I could not. Brotherly love and affection.

After that, I was in Tadler briefly. Then a few days in a house in Ringel. This house was on the bend of the road at the very top of the town. The land sloped sharply down to the river below and then climbed steeply up on the far side.

Our next move was to Dahl. When we got there, our communications officer told us to get the switchboard in the safest place we could find because they expected a lot of trouble.

DAHL, LUXEMBOURG

For the men of the 319th Regiment, one of the hardest times of the war was during January 1945, in and around the small village of Dahl, Luxembourg. Heiderscheid, Tadler, Ringel and Dahl had been taken and now the German resistance stiffened to protect supply lines to their forces in the Bastogne area.

At that time I was a switchboard operator/field lineman in the Communications Platoon of Hq. Co. 3rd Battalion. We were responsible for laying telephone lines to Companies I, K, L, M and others as needed and keeping them in working order. Dahl was taken and cleared by the time we entered as darkness fell. It was bitter cold, overcast and deep snow was everywhere.

Our Platoon officer told us to find a good, safe place for the switchboards because they expected a lot of trouble. We set up the boards in a small room that was between a house and a barn. The farmer probably used this room for changing clothes. There were two doors in the room, one at the top of a few stairs leading to a kitchen, and another leading to the barn. There was one small window that faced to the north toward the enemy. The wire crews ran the telephone lines to the Companies as quickly as possible. They passed the lines through the small window and then they were attached to the back of the switchboard. The Battalion Headquarters and the Company were notified the line was in and now they were only a phone call away from each other. ...

The linemen were especially glad to get back to the switchboard room this night because of all the artillery and mortar fire the Germans were sending our way. Everyone from the Wire Section stayed in the room where the switchboards were so the crews were always together. If an operator turned the generator crank, and it turned very easily, he knew that the line was broken or open. If it turned very hard and jerky he knew it was shorted.

When a line went out—usually from shellfire but occasionally from getting snagged by a vehicle—a crew went to repair it. The crew might consist of two men on foot for a very short line or one where a vehicle would not be practical. Long lines requiring lots of wire were laid using a Jeep with driver and two or more men. The lines were all in and working and for the moment our job was complete. We had some rations and settled in for the night—17 of us in this small room. Operators worked in shifts of 3 hours on and 6 hours off.

This night my shift started at midnight. At 2:55 I woke my relief operator. About 2 minutes later I heard a single round coming in. A ferocious barrage quickly developed as shells too numerous to count began landing all around. They were hitting on the roof and side of the house, which had very thick stone walls that were holding up despite the hits. A tank pulled up and was putting rounds through the barn—in one wall and out the other. Stones couldn't stop their direct fire. Every line on the boards started ringing as every Company and outpost was calling the Command Post. For the first time ever, my hands shook uncontrollably as I tried to answer all the incoming calls. Now every man in the room was awake. I gladly took my headset off and handed it to the relief operator. Then I sat on the floor with the other men, wondering how long we would have to endure this. The noise became overwhelming as shells continued to hit the walls and roof of the house. Pieces of plaster dropped on us, dust and powder fumes filled the room. It was like being in the middle of a violent thunderstorm and having numerous close lightning strikes. But this wasn't thunder and lightning.

There was a momentary pause in the shelling and the sound of heavy breathing filled the room, as each man gasped for air because of the tension, terror and hopelessness we felt as we lay there taking this punishment. The calm was broken by a really close hit. The force of the blast blew the door to the barn off its hinges and it came crashing in on us. A man jumped up and pushed it back up—a gesture that was little more than symbolic for all the protection that thin wooden door could give us.

The house and barn were taking a lot of hits. Another man leaped to his feet, shouting, "I'm getting out of here!" My Sgt. threw him to the floor. Saying, "You're not going anywhere!" I thought this was like a scene right out of "All Quiet on the Western Front," where a man went mad from the shellfire and ran out of the dugout to be killed. It would have been certain suicide for anyone to go outside. When the shelling finally stopped, the German infantry was very close to us. We heard a German burp gun firing. A Tank Destroyer, which was parked close by, answered the shots with bursts from his .50 caliber machine gun. The attack was beaten back and the noise abated. In the morning, I found a dead German with a burp gun in his hands by a little hedge about

100 yards from the house. He looked to be 16-17 years old. The next day we put the switchboards in the potato cellar, which was off to the side of the short stairway to the house. It was so full of potatoes we had to crawl in. With so little space we had to work lying down. It was close quarters but it gave a feeling of security.

There was a fireplace in the basement that had been used by the farmer for heating wash water. Riflemen who had been spending 2 hours in a foxhole and 2 hours off, around the clock, built a roaring fire in it. They kept it going all day and as the day turned to night the fire was getting bigger and hotter. I was in the kitchen when I noticed smoke coming from a crack in the wall and about that time heard someone shouting, "The house is on fire!"

We went in the potato cellar and frantically cut all the wires and took the switchboards outside. Then we went back in to get our bedrolls, etc. Soon the house was really torching up and the whole area was lit up bright as day. Flames were shooting higher and higher. There were some explosions as grenades and ammunition left in the house started going off; sending up sparks each time. I thought for sure the Germans would really shell us now, but not a single round came in. I was watching the flames when our Sgt. told us we were going to set up in the back room of the church.

By the time I had carried a switchboard there, the room was already being cleared. Furniture, robes— everything was being tossed outside in the snow. This bothered me, but only for a minute—we were desperate. We were lucky to find this room as I don't think there was another place that wasn't occupied or damaged. For what seemed like days and days, it was the heavy shelling early in the morning, followed by an infantry and tank attack that each time was beaten off. Then intermittent shell fire the rest of the day. It was never safe to leave to venture outside. Just going to get chow could be a deadly adventure.

The telephone lines went out repeatedly, mostly from shellfire, and each time they did, a crew had to go fix them, sometimes standing in the spot where the shell landed and seeing the smoke rising from the ground, hoping they wouldn't send another round in. As the days went on, an atmosphere of depression developed and it affected everyone. The crews became more and more reluctant to go out to fix a line. Our Sgt. asked to be relieved. He said that he had more to live for than we did, that he had a wife and child. That was a surprise that didn't go over very well. We were just as worried as he was but we were still hanging in there. He was transferred to comparative safety with Regimental Headquarters Co. I saw him one time but I think he was too embarrassed to talk.

Our switchboard was placed in the closet so that the operator faced outward and their body was inside the closet. This gave a nice feeling of security. Our chief operator was always a quiet man. Now he became even more so. He started wearing his helmet really low on his head so that his forehead was not visible. It was hard to even see his eyebrows when he had his helmet on. He smoked constantly. When he was on the board, all you could see was his helmet, two sad eyes below it and a thin curl of rising smoke from his cigarette. He functioned but seldom had anything to say to anyone and rarely went to chow. Someone must have spoken to our Lieutenant because soon he was evacuated. While on the board I frequently listened to calls from the Companies to Headquarters. More than once I heard officers call in and ask to be relieved, saying that they couldn't take it anymore. If they stuck to their guns and resisted the efforts to talk them out of it, they were told to get their stuff together and come back to Battalion. We never saw them again.

After days of this, I had the feeling that I would give anything to get away from it all even if for just for an hour or two. After being overcast for several days, the weather finally cleared. When we heard the sound of planes we all went outside to see them. Four P-47 Thunderbolt fighter/bombers roared by with a low-level pass in front of us. We all cheered. They then climbed higher and circled us. They were looked magnificent against the blue sky with the sun glistening on them. The planes made another circle and when they were right in front of us the lead plane did a wingover and dove right at us.

There was a half-track parked close by with a .30 caliber machine gun mounted on it. The guy on the half-track put off a very short burst at the plane, changed his mind and leaped off. Seventeen men tried to get through the doorway to the church at the same time. I was the last one in. They were all in a big pile against the thick inside wall. I figured this was it and that it wouldn't do any good to be on top of the pile. I went over in the corner, sat down and waited. The plane's motor roared louder and louder, closer and closer, pulling up with a mighty roar. Then there was a split second of silence before we heard the whistle of the falling bomb. It fell behind the church. The concussion blew out the windows and opened the ceiling trapdoor with a bang. Another bomb had landed in a field off to the right.

Afterwards the planes went to work on the Germans in the next village up—I believe it was Nocher. We watched as eight P-47s lined up in single file, and then the lead plane dove down with guns blazing, disappearing below the horizon, then climbing up above it as tracers from the anti-aircraft guns followed them as they twisted to the right and then to the left. The next plane was already starting his run. As each plane finished his run he turned back to get in line for another run. They continued their runs until there wasn't any more anti-aircraft fire and smoke was rising from the village.

After all this excitement, and being curious as to how big a crater the bombs had made, Murphy and I ran out to see for ourselves. About halfway there, shells started coming in and we thought better of going any further. We started running back to the church, laughing at our stupidity, as the shells were getting closer. Partly from boredom and partly from a feeling of guilt for being able to stay inside while the linemen were repairing lines, I volunteered twice to take the place of a lineman.

One time was to lay a line to Second Battalion. It was a moonlight night. We loaded several spools of wire on the Jeep and took off, pulling the wire from the spool and carrying it a few feet away from the side of the road so that vehicles wouldn't tear it out. When we got to a bend in the road I looked for a place to tie the line so it wouldn't be pulled back on the road. There was nothing but deep, smooth snow. Then I noticed a stake sticking up about an inch above the snow and tied a clove hitch on it. When we got back, our Lt. told us, "Be careful of a minefield on the left side of the road. It is supposed to be one of the most heavily mined fields in Europe. It is marked by stakes." We had just run through it.

The other time I went out with Ted Grom to fix a line but we didn't get far. Without white clothing we stuck out very plainly. A shell dropped 600-700 yards to the right of us. It kicked up a little black frozen dirt and some snow. We didn't pay much attention to it and we continued walking. Another round came in about 200 yards to our right and we suddenly realized that they were registering on us. We started running and now the whole battery took us. Shrapnel sang close and very loud as we dove in a doorway that was to an earth-covered pump house. We didn't know it, but there was a machine gun mounted in the doorway. In our haste to get in, and not knowing the gun was there, we knocked it over. I thought they might give us a bad time about it, but they didn't. Ted and I didn't accomplish much that time but we made the Krauts waste six, or more, artillery shells.

After several more days and several orders to "Move out" being countermanded, we finally did move out and up in preparation for crossing into Germany at Wallendorf. No one was sorry to leave Dahl.

Commander of 2nd Battalion 317th Infantry
As Told to His Son Over the Years Since the War

Many of the things I know about my father's experiences during the war are from conversations with him on various occasions which I wrote notes over the years. There were some things he did not ever speak of in any detail, because they were so unpleasant to think on. My father's memory remained very sharp until his death and he had a keen eye for detail, dates, locations, names, etc. He spoke admiringly of a number of individuals he knew as officers in the army and in the war. He made notes in the margins of various books about events he had personal knowledge of or individuals that were mentioned whom he knew, including the US Army official histories "Breakout and Pursuit" and "The Lorraine Campaign", as well as "The Battle of the Falaise Gap," by Eddy Florentin and Michael Doubler's "Closing with the Enemy." Wes Gallagher of the AP was with the unit for a while, and filed some short pieces, in one he quotes when the battalion took St.-Mihiel, my father was standing in front of the monument to the Americans of WW I who liberated the town. Gallagher also wrote a piece on the Germans murdering a number of civilians in one town, including hospital patients they dragged out into the street. The men seeing this, eliminated all questions about what they were over there fighting for and against, and made them very reluctant to take any SS men prisoner.

Col. Murray had a Lieutenant and a sergeant who were charged with murdering more than a score of German prisoners in a barn. He knew why they had done it, but did not condone it, because he said it would quickly get out of hand if allowed to go unpunished. These Americans had seen men from this same German unit machine gun a number of American wounded in a field along with the medic who was treating them only a few days before.

Col. Murray's main criticism of General McBride was voiced in his view that the General often used the map to make plans and assignments without actually having any first-hand knowledge of the terrain or situation at the front lines. He attributed part of this to the General's background as an artillery officer and felt he did not understand the needs of commanding infantry. A major disagreement he had with the General was over the General's insisting on where he should post his outer perimeter outposts, again based on looking at the map, Col. Murray had pulled the outposts back several hundred meters to the edge of a woods to give the men concealment. The Col. said they had just as good a view of the terrain in front of them and yet were not needlessly exposed, but the General insisted they be placed where he said, which left the men very exposed. Col. Murray said this sort of thing went on all the time. He said they had also argued over the control of the heavy mortars and artillery, General McBride (an artilleryman) wanting to limit the infantry commanders' control over their use.

Col. Murray was quite angry over the initial attempts to cross the Moselle, saying the whole thing was a shambles. He said they had little time to reconnoiter the crossing, it was late at night when they arrived at their positions to prepare for the assault which was to happen within just a couple of hours, and all he'd been told from intelligence was that only light opposition was expected where they were to cross. They did not get artillery support or preparation. After the initial attempts were clobbered, several days later General McBride called for a meeting at regimental headquarters of the regimental and battalion COs. He then took them off a ways into the woods to talk. Gen. McBride was acting totally out of character, very subdued. Finally he said, "Gentlemen, I'm open to suggestions about how to get across the river." The Col. was stunned at first as this was totally out of character for McBride to act this way. One battalion commander refused to make the attempt (for which the Col. voiced the opinion that he felt the man should have been shot). The Col. proposed his battalion lead the assault and how they would do it and what they would need in the way of artillery support, etc., to go across in a narrow front with concentrated and coordinated action to get a bridgehead and then with reinforcements coming over. He said they had attempted to cross on too broad a front with poor planning and little support. McBride was receptive and said, "That's what we'll do", and that was that. Later learning from a friend at XII Corps HQ that orders had already been cut to relieve McBride if they did not get across the Moselle by a deadline Patton had set, and he figured this was what accounted for McBride's demeanor in that meeting.

Again, Col. Murray usually only commented on the men he knew that he felt strong admiration for, but about Gen. McBride he had strong negative feelings. His being relieved from command of the battalion and Col. Cameron's being relieved really rankled him, but given the views he had voiced to McBride at various times he said he was not surprised. He felt that another officer, the assistant division commander (General Searby) would have been an excellent division commander. Of course, he was killed in the fighting in the bridgehead.

Major Karl Neussner who commanded the 3rd Battalion of the 318th was a very good friend, as was his wife was to my mother. I think they shared a duplex with them in the states for a while. Neussner's battalion and the Colonel were cut off and surrounded together for four days not long after the Moselle crossing.

Colonel Murray admired General Eddy as a fine officer as well as the man who replaced him when Eddy was returned to the states with medical problems (General Irwin? replaced Eddy I believe). Col. Murray was a man of very strong opinions who did not mince words. He tended to see things in black and white, without many shades of gray, though sometimes his insights could surprise you. It is certainly possible some of his opinions or views or memories were colored by personal feelings, but he always tried to portray events as honestly as possible at least. Things that he said are sometimes at variance with what others may have said, but generally they ring true. The meeting with Gen. McBride about the Moselle River crossing seemed particularly vivid in his mind, as was his being relieved.

Col. Murray died October 19th, 2000, in Anniston, Alabama. He left the Army after the war, but was called up during Korea to active duty. He ended up stationed in the Canal Zone in Panama. After his discharge he had a life insurance business for some years and dabbled in real estate. He became an agent for the Treasury Department in their Special Investigations unit for a number of years but grew tired of the traveling and being away from home. He returned to Anniston and became chief clerk of the Probate court for some time before retiring. He kept in touch with a few men he knew in the Army and from The Citadel and certainly those were the most enduring relationships of his life.

Captain Charles L. DeuPree
Commander of Company K, 318th Infantry Regiment

"War is Hell"—there is no getting around it. And in combat in WWII in the Infantry, Queen of the Battles, was a classic example. When veterans get in a group and start reminiscing, however, the gory details are rarely brought up, though, they never leave us, and we all know it. Instead, you will hear laughter and moments that helped preserve what balance could be obtained in a world gone berserk. The following is a case in point.

The best way to pass this occurrence is just to quote verbatim from a letter of 22 January 1945. The company was in Welscheid, Luxembourg. I did not realize that security restrictions had long caused the media to refer to the 3rd Battalion, 318th Infantry as the "Ghost Battalion" if they could single us out at all. We usually went "black out".

"As for news around here, I guess I'd better refer you to the papers. Will have lots to tell after this is all over, lots of things you'll laugh at. There's no race quite like the Americans, for instance, can you imagine a bunch that look like something out of Mauldin's characters, footsore, cold, tired, and bearded, finding a sled, patching it up and come tearing down the cobblestone street of a town just captured, laughing, whooping and 'hollering' and turning over, of course! It would have tickled anybody, and you could just feel the tension draining out of your system." Maybe for in the next instance they could be killed.

24 January 1945, Wiltz, Luxembourg: The following is quoted from a letter and illustrates the camaraderie of the people of Luxembourg with the 80th Infantry Division. Somehow some civilians managed to exist in the war zone in spite of the Germans they detested. They braved many things trying to help and befriend the men of the American 80th Infantry Division whom they regarded, and still do, as friends and liberators: I don't see how Europe will ever recover, though. Really, there's so little left halfway intact that you can't realize the situation back home. The Germans seem to live off the country, and the few civilians in the war zone, well, I just don't see how they manage to get by.

"One instance occurred I'd like to tell you of: I was bringing my unit into place and they were very tired and very cold. We found a place that the bottom floor was practically undamaged, just extremely messed up. We started to move in and some civilians who owned the place showed up. They insisted on clearing out the junk, scrubbing the floors, moved in a stove, started a fire and patched up the windows! Of course, the men helped them and everyone talked and laughed and understood little of what was said. But the men were comfortable that night."

Somewhere in Germany, Early 1945

Upon approaching an area where I understood we could receive a visit from General Patton, American soldiers were observed in a hospital outside a well-battered town, with a stream just beyond. Americans? No. suddenly they started firing on us. They were Germans dressed in American uniforms taken from American soldiers killed in battle.

With nothing to rubble around, I dropped to the ground crawling like the proverbial reptile to a cover where I could observe and direct action. Moving flat on the ground, my left hand reaching out felt some strange object.

It turned out to be the only thing not shattered or broken anywhere around. It was a cheaply made small figure of three lop-eared silly looking dogs looking at me. Laughing at the incongruity of the situation, I stuck it in my jacket pocket.

Somehow these funny little dogs were sent home unbroken. On the bottom was stamped "Foreign," not a German word. Where were they made? The U.S.? Regardless, they are placed in a small cabinet hanging by my desk easily seen every time I need a laugh or at least a smile. Even in peace times such occasions do arise! It works ever.

The Longest March Company K 318th Infantry Ever Had, and Didn't Know It.

Close feelings develop in combat. The following illustrates some time during the long coma I was in after being hit, a prolonged continuing dream came into being. The underlying deep concern for the men in K Company took over. Knowing dangers of an uncleared town but having no idea about circumstances after I was hit, I determined to bring the full company back to where I was. The men were my responsibility and should be with me. Somehow, I was realizing that I must be in a safer place than they and that they should be there, too. When doctor's efforts to bring me out of the coma became effective momentarily, the dream was always picked up exactly at the same spot where it was interrupted. This continued for some time, even though transfers in hospitals in France and my waking time became more extended. Finally, one night in what I learned must have been a hospital in Andiel or someplace close to Vittel, I dreamed the company had arrived. Hitting the wall with my right arm I awoke suddenly finally satisfied. That was the last of my dream.

Among the Wounded in a General Hospital
After July 1945

Something of this sort no doubt happened to many of our men wounded in action. Some also missing in action. This is told because it applies to so many, and will give those whom it does not, an idea about what could have been going on with some of their buddies with whom they have lost contact.

After being patched up in several French hospitals, a surgeon finally gave me clearance after V-E Day to return to the States on "The Thistle", a hospital ship. The War Department, trying to be considerate, assigned me to a Texas hospital that must be close to home. It was at El Paso, though, which happens to be on the farthest side away! Chicago was even closer.

Sometime after arriving in July 1945 at William Beaumont Hospital, I was graduated from a wheelchair to crutches and was exploring the grounds on my own. Going over a bridge crossing an arroyo (dry creek) I looked up, aware someone coming from the other side had abruptly stopped. He was a Sgt. in Company K, who had been promoted just before he was declared missing in action. I had gone looking for him, but finally had to give up the search. He was white as a sheet, and I guess I was, too. I was afraid he had been killed, and he knew I had been. It seems he had been captured and put through a series of interrogations. All he would give were his name, rank, and serial number. Trying to pull information they gradually told him bits including his organization, and finally his company. The day came when he was told he might just as well tell all and make things easier, for they had just killed his company commander, whose name was DeuPree. The Sgt. told me they even admitted it was a suicide mission and should be made by a storm trooper.

Like so many of us, recollections of things of 50 odd years ago, especially recollections that were sometimes pushed aside, further complicated at that time by effects of a severe concussion, finally have eluded this sergeants name. If he reads this article or hears about this, or anyone knows anything, please let the editor know.

The "Mascot" .38 Revolver of Company K, 318th Infantry

One of the first questions asked me at the Reunion of the 80th Infantry Division Association held in Louisville, KY 16-20 August 1989, was whether I got my well known hand guns back after I was hit, most thought fatally, by an anti-tank weapon 10 April 1945. Men in K Company 318th Infantry were pretty familiar with them, and told all new men that the .38 revolver was "just like the one Patton carried." It fired German P38 ammunition so there was no shortage there. The handle had a faint glow in the dark and with the gun slung to my back I could be quickly located. This, plus my .41 Derringer, already had quite a history with my family in the earlier days of Texas. Many told me the guns were the reason that men in the 3rd Platoon and then Company K were so successful, each man wanted to be first to get them if ever I got hit!

Yes, I did get them back. Jerry Ray Baxter, a terrific BAR man in the 3rd Platoon, ran to me (learned later) when I was hit in Diedendorf to see if he could help, and he and another put me on a litter. He felt there was no hope. Lt. Col. Paul E. Jacobs, 3rd Battalion Commander, received a wound at the same time while approaching to tell me of the change in orders: Russia was to take Berlin, not us! He got the guns, giving them later to T/Sgt.

Michael Kaminski, who was returning to the States for 30 Days. His sister, June, mailed them to my father from DuPont (Pittston on the envelope), PA on 11 July 1945. Meantime, I spent a year in hospitals before going before a board and being retired for injuries and disabilities. Needless to say I deeply appreciate what each done for me. Such care and thoughtfulness means much. Years later the rare old long barreled nickel-plated pearl-handled revolver was stolen when our home was ransacked during a funeral.

Jose Carrasco
Company E, 318th Infantry Regiment

I joined my outfit, Company E, 318th Infantry, 80th Division on 13 November 1944 after serving in the 601st M.P. Battalion in Sicily. I recall it was very dark and rainy for a few days. We attacked over an open space and it was pure mud everywhere we stepped. We were about half way through when the enemy started to throw some artillery shells at us. We were at a point of no return. I was carrying a 60MM Mortar so you can imagine how it was trying to move with it. One of the times I was lying flat in the mud. I moved the mortar somehow to protect my face and at that moment a piece of shrapnel hit the mortar. Had it not been for me moving the mortar, the shrapnel would have ripped open the right side of my face. So, I believed that I was lucky that the mortar saved me on that first day of combat. So, that's where I got my baptism of fire. So, from then on, we moved up and down the front lines. As of December 16, 1944 I only had about four weeks of battle experience. Then, without our knowledge, they moved us toward Luxembourg. I'm telling you, we had to ride in the freezing cold all night long in the back of trucks. So comes daylight. We didn't know where we were. Someone asked a lady on the sidewalk in French where we were and she answered in English "In Luxembourg." We were really embarrassed. So, from there we found out what was happening and began to move forward. Just then the enemy attacked and I heard someone call my name. It was a buddy that had crossed with me on the H.M.S. Queen Mary. He was in the division we were relieving. He was happy to see me but appeared to be in a state of shock. He had been caught in crossfire by enemy tanks and watched a lot of his buddies die. He was anxious to leave and we said goodbye. I never seen or heard of him again.

In spite of the terrible weather, our morale was good. While we were still in the Bastogne area we made contact with the 101st Airborne Division. Then I got so sick I went to the aid station and the medic told me I had the flu. I was put into an ambulance with three or four wounded American soldiers. They began asking about each other's wounds and there I am with nothing more than the flu. I was in the hospital for a week and away from the division for ten days. But, here I'm getting ahead of myself. While we were still in the area before going into Bastogne, we went into a wooded area. The trees and ground were covered with snow. Visibility was poor. I somehow noticed an enemy machine gun with three German soldiers waiting for us to go by. They were camouflaged very well. We were walking in single file. As I came closer, I ran for about twenty feet and pushed the barrel of the machine gun over knocking it out of place. Then I captured the three German soldiers. Otherwise, they would've shot a lot of our guys in the back. As it got dark that same day, we all got together to talk about what happened since daylight. Most of the homes were burning. I noticed one about sixty feet away not on fire. So I thought, "Better go check this out". As I entered the building I heard voices and much to my surprise they were German soldiers. So, before they saw me I pointed my carbine at them to surrender, which they did. There were about fifteen or twenty enemy soldiers. By that time another American soldier came by and helped me get them out of the building. This all happened the same day we made contact with the 101st Airborne. Eventually we went toward Biesdorf, Germany. Here we went into a building at night. It was very dark when we entered the room. I heard voices out in the hall speaking German. I rushed into the hallway and grabbed the rifle of one of the Germans. We fought for control of it. I pulled the weapon away from him and killed him then wounded the other German soldier. For this I received the Bronze Star.

As we moved from town to town, city to city, we became surrounded. An artillery officer told us all to gather in one room of the house. He then called in the artillery coordinates. The shells started hitting the roof of the house and the Germans took off. It felt pretty weird being shelled by our own artillery.

We were still in the Battle of the Bulge, and, one day about dark I spotted four or five German soldiers going into a broken down house and my friend said "let's go and get them"! I said, "Let's wait until tomorrow morning. They're looking for a place to sleep just like us." So, we waited till next morning and began cautiously approaching them. Much to our surprise, they sat there motionless. They had frozen to death during the night. Then, while still in the Bastogne area, all of a sudden the skies cleared up and what a joy it was to see our planes, C-47 Cargo planes, I think, dropping supplies. Parachutes of all colors. I could even see the GI pushing the supplies out of the planes. Next day, we were side by side with the 101st Airborne.

My company crossed a river, can't remember which one, very early in the morning. It was so dark we kept bumping into each other making all kinds of noise. We were supposed to be as quiet as possible. We got into small boats, five or six guys to a boat and we started to paddle as fast as we could. Then the enemy mortars opened up and done a direct hit on a boat full of GIs. We were able to save a couple of them but the rest just drifted away in the swift current. Once across the river we entered the town. I went into a building that looked like a city hall or something similar. There was a German swastika flag, which I took down and kept. Then the house to house street fighting began. We had to cross a street and our 1st Lieutenant, James H. McFarland yelled to me "Jose, I'm gonna run across the street to the house. When I get there and wave to you, come on across and wave to the other boys to do the same." We waited and waited for the Lieutenant to wave but he never did. One of the guys said to go on across and I told him my orders were to wait until the Lieutenant waved. Eventually, we had to move on without the Lieutenant.

There was no end to the street fighting, from one town to another. In one of those towns I found the safety of the back of the house and dropped to my knees to catch my breath. All of a sudden it sounded like a lion growling very near. It was a German tank. It stopped about thirty feet from where I was. Still on my knees, I thought about throwing a hand grenade into the hatch of the tank but it was closed. All of a sudden I saw the gun move to the left, then to the right of me. I thought "if he points that gun directly at me, he has seen me. But all of a sudden the tank driver threw it in reverse and backed away. I thought, "Thank You, God"! So, we moved on to a few more towns and who do you suppose we found? Nobody else but 1st Lieutenant James H. McFarland. After some back patting, we asked him what happened. He said "well boys, I was captured. When I ran into that house, it was full of German soldiers. They had me before I knew what was happening. After a while, I noticed one of the German soldiers became much more friendly than the others and he ended up helping me to escape. I finally found you guys."

We crossed into Austria and, to my surprise, we were in the city of Braunau. You may recall that is where Hitler was born. Around that area we ran into a lot of people who had been in concentration camps. They were in bad shape, very bad shape! We were not allowed to give them any food due to the fact some of them were too far gone, and by giving them food it would be too much for their parched stomachs and they would die from the food given them. We were told that the Medics would help them. In the meantime, we moved ahead by convoy. You should've seen all the German prisoners coming to the west from the Russian front. By the way, the war in Europe has just ended. The Americans going east could hardly get through the hordes of Germans coming west. If we'd kept going, we'd ended up in Vienna. While we were camped along the bank of a river, some buddies and I were talking in Spanish. A German officer came over, gave us a snappy salute and joined the conversation. He said he had spent some time in Argentina. We had to laugh when he said he thought we would go on in and wipe out the Russians. We told him the war was over and he should go and rejoin his men.

We then went to Kempten, Germany. An officer was giving a speech about us still being at war with the Japanese. He said that some of us would be going stateside and other would be going directly to the Pacific. He said that when we got to Japan, all the Japanese soldiers, civilians and even children would be fighting us. Then we had some maneuvers in the Austrian Alps. Then we got the good news... the Japanese had surrendered. We read in the Stars and Stripes that one bomb destroyed the city of Hiroshima. Of course, we didn't believe it but did when we read a couple days later about another bomb destroying the city of Nagasaki. Thank God, the war was over.

Don Davis
Company K, 319th Infantry Regiment
As a POW

When I left the states as a replacement, I knew there was a possibility of being killed or wounded in combat. I didn't figure, however, on becoming a prisoner of war. Yet that was my status forty-one days after my last view of the Statue of Liberty.

It was only four days after my entry into combat that I received the assignment that caused me to become a guest of the German Government. Our squad was designated to relieve an outpost almost one mile ahead of our lines. After it was dark we advanced in single file to our positions. We moved very cautiously because one never knew when German patrols were in the vicinity. In order to reach our destination we had to pass completely through a French village. We didn't feel at all secure when we saw there were still civilians around, because, although they were friendly to us, they were afraid of Jerry. Half of us stayed on one side of the street that was the approach to a demolished bridge and half went the other side.

The Boche was known to be on the opposite side of the stream. It was our duty to notify battalion headquarters by telephone if we saw enemy movement. The next afternoon we spotted some activity about one thousand yards to our right front. Headquarters did not take us seriously, however. We were ordered to maintain our positions. We weren't seriously alarmed because we were due to be relieved after nightfall. We didn't like it at all, however, when we were informed we had to "sweat out" twenty-four hours more. Shortly before dawn the next morning we heard movement in town. We reported this, but were told that noise was caused by civilians. We knew that the latter did not stir out of their homes after the setting of the sun. However, orders are orders. At dawn we realized our fears, because three krauts came down to inspect the bridge. As we waited for them to approach (they hadn't seen us) we heard a yell. You should have seen those Jerries scatter. You guessed it, one of our French friends had warned the enemy.

We immediately sent a man to warn our buddies on the opposite side of the street. That is the last we ever saw of him. To this day I don't know what happened to him or the other five. I know they weren't captured, and it is doubtful whether they were able to infiltrate back to our lines. About two minutes later, it seemed like eternity, we decided to try to break to safety. I stuck my steel helmet out the doorway on a pole and a machine pistol immediately opened up. The Germans who discovered us obviously returned with reinforcements. When a buddy tested the other exit two automatic weapons commenced firing. Then we knew we were in a trap. We decided to fight it out.

Only one Jerry was foolhardy enough to try to run across the doorway to fling a hand grenade. Instinctively I fired from the hip. No one needs any marksmanship training to make a hit at fifteen yards. Another came at me from around the corner of our position. I don't know who was more surprised, he or I. I was fortunate enough to get the first hasty shot. It was not fatal for him. Regretted this later, because it almost caused my end. In the meantime, my buddies had succeeded in killing and wounding several of the enemy.

About this time the Germans got wise. They realized we had only a small range of vision, so they closed up in the blank arc. Then they began to fire continuously through the doorways and at the walls, thereby pinning us in. When the bullets began to break right through the crumbly mortar walls, and grenades (fragments from one hit me in the arms and legs) began landing close by, we knew it was either "Kamerad" or "kaput" right then. We weren't anxious to be buried in France, so we stepped out with our hands up. We didn't know what to expect because a soldier of any nationality is likely to be trigger-happy when some of his buddies have become casualties. Luckily for us our captors were a regular Wehrmacht unit. However, we hadn't stepped out a minute too soon, because the officer in charge was just preparing to launch a bazooka shell.

They searched us immediately and took away all firearms and ammunition. I had the foresight to hide a Luger in the straw before leaving the barn. Soldiers don't like to find their own weapons in the possession of new captives. I was surprised that they did not take my watch, fountain pen, knife, cigarettes and money. It was at rear echelon stops that I was parted from these personal belongings.

It was good that we had not tried to make a break of it. Their company C.P. was located three hundred yards closer to the American lines on our only route of withdrawal. Gun installations had already been set up. Combat patrols were being sent down the road we had traversed only thirty-six hours previously. This would indeed have been valuable information for our battalion commander.

As we arrived at the C.P., I saw the German whom I had wounded coming out of the first aid station on a stretcher. Unfortunately he also recognized me. He pointed me out to a buddy who was accompanying him. This friend drew a revolver, and then I really began to sweat. I figured my luck had run out, and this was really the end. It is hard to imagine what a helpless feeling one can have at a time like that. Just about that time an officer prevented the soldier to take revenge. I was never so relieved in all my life. About five minutes later we were marched back about two kilometers to regimental headquarters. We were given a bowl of milk a piece of bread and cheese. Thus far we had been treated according to the rules of war.

Late in the morning we rode by truck to division headquarters. It was here we were first interrogated. Like good soldiers we gave only our name, rank and serial number. They found a letter on one of the fellows giving the name of his outfit. I don't think it could have been of military value to Jerry, however. After that they gave us stew, and it was good. In the middle of the afternoon we were drafted for a short spud digging detail. Jerry lives on the fat of the land. The soldiers on the front lines eat better than those in rear echelon areas. About six P.M. we had black bread and some ersatz tea sweetened with saccharine. This black bread was very hard to get used to because of its dryness.

After dark the five of us and six other Americans who had been captured two days previously were transported by truck to army headquarters. We were quartered in a stone building that had formerly been a stable. We got little sleep that night because it was cold and Jerry didn't give us any blankets and there was no place to lie down except on the cold stone floor.

In the morning we were moved to a second floor room of one of the barracks. The latter contained a couple of benches, so we could at least sit down. They gave us a hunk of stale bread, a piece of smelly cheese and a cup of barley coffee. This ersatz brew was a poor substitute for the real article. On this occasion we drank it willingly, because anything hot tasted good. Late in the morning we were searched again. It was here that I lost my money and watch.

At noon we went down to the kitchen. They gave us all the boiled potatoes and gravy that we wanted, so we really gorged ourselves. If we had known what was to come we certainly would have stuffed our pockets too. That evening we were given a small piece of bread and two ounces of sausage a piece. The following day we marched on empty stomachs to Forbach where there was a P.O.W. camp.

It was here our lean days really began. The daily ration amounted to three or four slices of bread and one ounce of sausage. We didn't even get that meager amount the first day because we arrived after ration issue. It was this German hospitality center that I first became acquainted with different species of body lice. The place was filthy. Everyone preferred the hard floor to sleep on even though there were no blankets, because the straw ticks were breeding nests for these bugs, (nevertheless) these friendly companions sought us out and buddied up. We were never able to get rid of them during internment because of adverse living conditions.

There were one hundred forty GIs at Forbach altogether. It was only a transient camp for Americans, so our hosts decided to ship us to Limburg, another temporary camp. On Sunday morning all of us were crowded into three small French boxcars, and then the doors were locked. The allied air corps had wrought such havoc upon the German railroad system that it took two and one-half days to reach our destination less than one hundred miles away. Those sixty hours were bad ones for all of us. The doors opened only three times during the entire journey. A big can was provided for toilet purposes. It was still warm weather in October, so the odor really circulated. There were no benches so everyone had to sit on the damp floor. There was not room for everyone to lie down so at night some stood while others slept. During the whole journey we got only six slices of bread, and a little piece of sausage each.

We arrived in Limburg during an air raid, so our guards were in a surly mood. Several of my companions were beaten up for no apparent reason. We were searched again at the entrance to the Stalag. It was this time that I lost the last remnant of my personals. Late in the afternoon we were deloused for the first time. This process came to be kind of a joke to us. After freeing us from bugs we were always moved into vermin filled buildings. Now I can really sympathize with a scratching dog.

We had to simulate food that day, because we got no rations. Long after dark we were finally moved into the American and British compound. The only available sleeping space I could find was on the cold stone floor. Although I had only one thin, lousy, ragged Jerry blanket, I was successful in catching a few winks. I was so weary after the train ride that the floor actually felt comfortable.

About this time I began to believe the Germans regarded us as cattle. They had crammed 4,500 of us into an area one hundred yards square, containing four barracks. Even the food was a type intended for livestock. Limburg is known throughout the war for cheese of powerful odor. We weren't fortunate enough to sample any of the town's principal product. The daily three slice bread ration is all that tided us over. The rest of our ration consisted solely of grass and cow beet soup. Although everyone was practically starving, much of the latter caused vomiting. We even had to eat this mess by primitive means because only a fortunate few had eating utensils. The majority of us had to use old tin cans and our hands as substitutes.

Sanitation conditions had been good at Forbach in comparison to Limburg. There was only one outhouse type latrine for the entire compound. Offal floated ankle high in and around that building. The stench was unbearable. The filth was naturally tracked into the barracks where everyone had to sleep on the floor because there were no beds. Drinking water was available only three hours a day.

Work details were sent out daily into Limburg to clean up bomb damage. Extra rations were promised, so I volunteered to go the first day. The promise never materialized, so I returned to the Stalag hungrier than if I had not gone at all.

I got one big laugh in the Cheese City, however, across the street from the railroad station was a small park with a statue of a bomb center. An inscription said that Germany would never be bombed. Although the monument itself was unscathed, every building in the vicinity had been devastated. Debris lay all around the base. The memory of this broken prophecy later helped me to face with courage the long months of captivity.

Saturday, October 8th, 1944 was the highlight of my stay at Stalag XIIA. On that day I was officially registered as a Prisoner of War. More important, though, I received one-third of a Red Cross food parcel. Some of the boys killed their share in one sitting. By rationing myself I was able to make mine last until the following Thursday.

Trading over the fence with the Russians in the adjoining compound was forbidden. Nevertheless it was done. If the guards witnessed it, they would shoot the Russians and swear at us. I saw more than one of our Eastern Allies stop a German bullet.

On Wednesday, October 12th, a shipping list was posted. I was very happy to find my name on it. I knew that conditions would probably be better at a permanent Stalag. We left the Stalag Saturday evening without rations.

They didn't give us any Red Cross parcels either, although there were 33,000 on hand. The three and one-half day ride from Limburg to Moosbrugger (home of Stalag VIIIA) was, without doubt, the worst episode of my internment. Fifty of us were herded into each miniature boxcar. Again, there were no benches, so we had to sit on the damp floor. The doors were opened three times during the entire trip. The can furnished for toilet facilities quickly overflowed because many of the boys were suffering from diarrhea and other ailments. The average ration for each day amounted to two slices of bread thinly spread with margarine. Water entered the car only once, and then it was only three gallons. I was in a corner, so I didn't get a drop. By the third day, some of the fellow occupants were in a deplorable condition. It rained that afternoon. Everyone that could cluster beneath a single window to catch raindrops rolling off the dirty roof in spoons, tin cans, etc. Some even licked the damp shirts that had hung outside in order to get a little moisture into their parched throats. The meager quantity thus collected only seemed to increase the thirst. The water I drank at Stalag VIIIA was without doubt the best drink I EVER had.

They crowded all of us into one barracks in the north lager. We were given one old rag (supposedly a blanket) and told to sleep anywhere we found room. I was one of the last ones in so I had to sleep out in the dirt aisle, as all the good spots were already occupied. That evening we were rationed one-fourth loaf of bread and three ounces of bologna. It felt pretty good to be able to loosen the belt on this occasion anyway. Two days later we were deloused and moved into permanent barracks. It was then that I really began the routine of a prisoner of war. Lean times continued until after Christmas, however, due to lack of parcels.

Stalag VIIA was populated by prisoners of all nationalities. At the time of my arrival there were only two to three thousand Americans. Living space was overcrowded at that time. Conditions didn't really begin to get bad, until, they moved in prisoners from evacuated camps as the Allies advanced.

During the first three months of my stay at Moosbrugger I was fortunate to live in a barracks that had electric lights and running water. We slept on three decker bunks, our mattresses were burlap bags filled with excelsior. The latter had more to do with drawing the bugs than any other single factor.

For the first month one hundred-fifty lived in my end of the barracks, an area approximately thirty by seventy-five. At the end of November some of the new captives from Italy were crowded in. During the middle of January one hundred more came in from another compound. Their barracks had been cleared to make room for incoming officers who had been evacuated from a camp near Berlin as the Russians approached. There was no room for bunks, so the newcomers slept on the floor. A week later it was announced that our compound was also going to be used for officers. In the meantime all the British Non-Coms and some of the privates had departed to another Stalag. Nine-tenths of our compound moved into barracks vacated by them. I was among the unfortunate tenth that was compressed into the south lager.

Here there were no electric lights. Illumination for the barracks was furnished by two carbide lamps (equivalent in candlepower to a five-watt bulb.) The fumes from these lamps were very unhealthy. Every morning one's mouth was coated with carbide. Only one water faucet outside provided for 900 men. It was sometimes necessary to wait in line an hour to get a cup of water. I never knew what the term crowded meant until I was quartered here. Only one hundred and fifty of us lived in an area twenty by forty. Ninety percent of the floor space was occupied by bunks. It was necessary to do all our cooking outside.

We moved with no regret to the open compound one-month later. The barracks there were similar to the one I had lived in for the first three months. We had been comfortably settled for just a month when the order came to move again. American forces had captured Nurnberg and twenty thousand evacuated prisoners were to arrive. This time we were quartered in a tent. These further inconveniences were endurable now because we knew that Germany had reached the end of the rope. I was in that same tent on Liberation Day.

Winters were cold in Germany, so naturally there was a fuel problem to contend with. Jerry furnished no fuel whatsoever. However, we always brought wood in from work detail. We were warm enough during the winter months except for a period in December. On that occasion the camp was quarantined for three weeks. The supply on hand was exhausted within a week. After that we simulated heat. The temperature never did drop below freezing, because there were so many of us that the heat from our bodies kept the temperature up somewhat, something like cattle in a barn.

The clothing deal was snafu. We were issued ragged overcoats, two square rags for socks, and two thin, narrow, lousy blankets by Jerry upon our arrival at Stalag VIIA. In December he issued us one pair of patched socks each. That is all the clothing we got from him as prisoners. Uncle Sam issued us clothing through the Red Cross. Due to transportation difficulties it usually arrived too late to do us much good. A few GI blankets were issued in December. The bulk of them were given out in the middle of February when winter was almost over. Comforters were issued ten days before our recapture. I was one of the fortunate few to get a pair of long johns in December. Most of the boys didn't get any until spring when most people discard them. Only one-third of the boys got GI overcoats at the first of March. No one got any socks until the middle of March. Very few got any shirts until February. The comfort parcels were issued five months late. I was one of the lucky few to get a toothbrush. The rest didn't get any until ten days after liberation. Shoes were one item impossible to get when you needed them. Everyone got gloves in January. Up to that time everyone used homemade affairs. However, no ODs were available. After our recapture I broke into a warehouse and completely outfitted myself. Warehouse after warehouse of new clothing was found. All of it stolen loot from former occupied countries.

The food situation, strangely enough, was better at the end than at previous times. This was not due to food Jerry gave us, however. His ration was practically non-existent toward the last. The allied prisoner is indeed thankful to the Red Cross. There was a time of leanness during our captivity when we all tightened up our belts on numerous occasions. From the date of my capture until Christmas, I received the equivalent of less than one parcel for the entire period. These were the toughest days.

Our daily German ration consisted of one pint tea in the morning, one pint soup at noon, and four slices of bread, three or four small potatoes plus an ounce of margarine, cheese or bologna at night. The tea was made from barley. During October, November and December it really refreshed me. After parcels came in regularly containing the genuine product, the taste nauseated me. Thereafter I used that German beverage for shaving, because it was hot. The soup was seldom good. It was usually composed of four parts water and one part old turnip or cabbage. The bread ration is really the only thing that carried us through the trying days. It was very inferior to our bread. The first white bread I sampled after liberation tasted like cake to me. The potatoes were spoiled half the time. I ate them willingly, dirt and all, during the lean days. Later on, however, I was more finicky. The smattering of cheese, margarine or meat that we got was our dessert. The Red Cross food was a godsend. It enabled us to keep our health. The Russians did not get them, as their government did not sign the Geneva Convention. As a result many will carry the marks of malnutrition to the grave. We could sympathize with them because we were in the same boat in the autumn. At that time it wasn't uncommon for us to lick soup cans and raid garbage piles. The heavy smokers didn't hesitate to snip butts one half inch long out of the gutters. Some of them even though they were starving, tightened their belts and sold their bread ration for one cigarette.

Being a private, I was obliged to work. In a way we were better off than the Non-Coms and Officers. For working we got extra food rations. It also provided us with the opportunity to trade. Just before my arrival at Moosbrugger, a twelve-hundred-man work detail had been started at Munich. The very first day I volunteered to go, more to see what it was like than anything else was. We arose at four A.M. the following morning, drank Jerry tea, and marched on empty stomachs to the railroad station. Here we were separated into companies of two hundred men. These companies were sub-divided into groups comprised of fifty men. It took more than four hours to reach Munich thirty-five miles away. This was due to effective allied bombing. We worked until five and then boarded the boxcars. Our return trip was just as slow, so we didn't arrive back at the Stalag until nearly ten P.M. The next day every available man was forced to work. In fact I didn't even see my quarters in daylight for ten days. Transportation continued to be poor. We never returned to our quarters before nine and sometimes not until after midnight.

After five or six days I was pretty fed up with the Munich detail. The Germans had a very effective means of getting the required number of men in the morning, however. They maintained a kennel containing a number of highly trained ferocious dogs. When these pets were in the vicinity it paid to move. You couldn't fight these beasts because the guard accompanying each animal was ordered to shoot if his playmate was harmed. I never waited to find out what would happen, because I knew these bloodhounds were not acquainted with provisions of the Geneva Convention. On one occasion this method backfired on our keepers. Two hounds entered a Russian barracks without escort. About five minutes later the skins and entrails were cast out the door. I understand a few Russians had delicious steaks that night.

After arrival of prisoners from Italy in November we began to get two days off a week. Transportation continued to be bad, however. In January the camp commandant complained. After that we actually began getting back before seven.

We labored, or rather put in our time, all over the city. During the period of my captivity our guards and the civilians we worked under didn't care whether we did work or not, if there weren't any "big shots" or officers in he vicinity. We took them at their word and never lifted a finger unless it was necessary. During the winter of 1944-1945 I must have gone to Munich sixty or seventy times. Only on four or five occasions did I accomplish enough to pay for my transportation or food.

During the first month the entire detail worked on the railroad. Beginning in November some of the companies began to labor elsewhere. At one time or another I was assigned to work at a main Munich hospital, Hitler's bank, the railway offices (heart of the city), Luipold's biggest restaurant in South Germany, the military academy, the police station, the city hall, the museum and various small bakeries and butcher shops. These buildings were, of course, bombed out.

The only incentive for working in town was for trading purposes. Allied prisoners of war kept the Munich black market in operation. We traded five standard articles from our Red Cross parcels, cigarettes, tea, coffee, soap and chocolate. In November when barter was just commencing we gave three to six cigarettes for one kilo of bread, two kilos was standard for a bar of toilet soap, six to nine kilos for a two ounce pack of tea, and six to ten kilos for a D bar. By March GIs had ruined the market. It cost nine to fifteen cigarettes for one kilo of bread, two to three kilos were given for two ounces of tea, three kilos were given for a chocolate bar, and one half to one kilo was tops for soap. All this trading we did was illegal. Fortunately our guards had all gotten the habit of smoking American cigarettes after a successful trade, he generally overlooked it.

However, even after paying this bribe we still had to "sweat out" getting this merchandise into the Stalag where there was a spot check. To eliminate bulges, I had sewn individual pockets around the base of my overcoat. It was possible for me to carry eight loaves of concealed bread at one time. I carried a maximum load successfully into the barracks on more than one occasion. As a result of this trade I never went hungry again after Christmas. After November 1st there was an organized black market dealing with prisoners of war in Munich. There was tremendous profit in it to the operator. One of our guards made enough off the trade to buy a home complete with furniture.

The Germans furnished us with no necessities. The only means we had of bartering our standard of living was by "sleight of hand" methods on work details. Our eating utensils and tools were secured in this way. Food, of course, was the most common thing brought in. Some luxuries were sneaked in. One fellow had a sterling silver tea set. There was even a hidden radio. The latter was concealed during the day. At night it was hooked up, using wire fencing as an Aerial. If the Reichsbahn (railroad) officials had searched, I'll bet they would have found ninety percent of their losses through petty theft in Stalag VIIIA.

In March, a work detail was started at Landshut. This city (population 60,000) was an important railroad junction connecting South Germany with Berlin. The railroad yard had been completely knocked out in a daylight raid by B17s about a week previously. This was an example of excellent bombing. In the yards three hundred yards wide and one mile long there was not a stretch of track ten yards long. Yet, the buildings on either side hadn't been touched. Five thousand laborers worked one month to get two tracks in operation. Less than a day later after an engine chugged over this stretch the air corps came over again—kaput.

With a detail going daily to both Landshut and Munich every available man had to work seven days a week. There were ways to "goof off." I quickly found the answers and applied them. Thus I was able to avoid work even when they "rousted" the barracks with the dogs.

There was no trading in Landshut, so no one cared to go in. I went in two times anyway. It was here that I had my first real contact with the political prisoners. They worked alongside of us, so we were able to talk to them on the sly. They wore black and white striped clothing and wooden shoes. In the winter they didn't even have coats. Every nationality, including German, was represented in their ranks. I even talked to a Canadian and a fellow from Corpus Christi, Texas. A few had been prisoners for nine or ten years. Jerry didn't give them anything, so they had to live by their wits. They would take anything they could lay their hands on. They went in for this on a big scale, too. The second time I was in Landshut, they were stealing flour by the bag. A railroad policeman happened to witness this larceny. He forced three convicts he had caught red handed to carry back the loot. Then ironic isn't it—he shot them. I had secured about thirty-five pounds of the flour from one of the convicts. It felt rather funny eating pancakes, the ingredients of which had cost three men their lives.

I have very few grievances against the German soldier as an individual. Most of them treated me all right. After talking to POWs from other Stalags I consider myself fortunate. However, on one occasion I was mistreated.

It was in November, just after an air raid alert in Munich. Several work groups had occupied the same shelter and were disorganized temporarily. One group had formed and was one man short. A guard from that group thought I was the missing party. There was no interpreter present. At that time I didn't understand German, and he spoke no English. I thought it best to go with him obediently. After I was in the ranks he began to curse me in anger. Then in a fury he began practicing the butt stroke on my back. After three or four blows, I was dazed. He stuck me twenty-five or thirty times before an English lager policeman (Non-Coms who saw that the Geneva Convention was adhered to) was able to stop him. It is amazing that I was able to stay on my feet. Only a jacket and overcoat protected me from more permanent injuries. Even so, I bore bruise marks for weeks afterward. At chow time I received bribes in the form of bread rations and extra soup. This only made me angrier.

A report of this incident was turned over to the International Red Cross. But nothing ever came of it. That guard had beaten other prisoners too. He made the mistake of remaining at the Stalag on Liberation Day. He didn't live long enough to regret his error.

The civilians in Munich didn't seem to give a damn about anything. Even back in October most of them realized that the war was lost. The endless bombing raids knocked out their last bit of initiative and hope. They seemed to be merely waiting for the end.

The Nazi party began to have a bitter taste for both civilians and soldiers. It was difficult to find a Nazi during the last days, and virtually impossible after occupation. This was not because the people's conscience began bothering them concerning the persecuted populations of Europe. No one repented any of the atrocities committed. Everyone blamed the loss of the war on Hitler and the Nazis, but that is the only reason the party fell in disfavor. These now meek people were the same ones that had put Hitler into power and who had cheered him on after the fall of France. If the tables had turned they would have voiced their approval again. In such case our treatment during internment would have been much more brutal.

Munich had been so ruined by bombing that damage inflicted in 1945 didn't cause excitement any more. One civilian told me that 90% of the business district had been damaged and 67% of it completely destroyed. This was not over-exaggeration. Most of the outlying residential areas had been hit. It was foolish folly to repair the railroad, because it was knocked out as fast as it was fixed up. After a big raid in January of 1945, we had to walk four miles to work. In fact the train never was able to go to the heart of the city again.

I sweated several of these raids. I had only one really terrifying experience, however. We were locked in boxcars parked in the marshaling yards when the R.A.F. pulled a surprise raid. Fortunately no missiles fell in the vicinity. The rocking caused by concussion, and the debris hitting the sides instilled fear into everyone's heart.

Surprisingly enough, the German people did not suffer from want, even at last. They had adequate food and their clothing was better than civilians in either France or England. Our work ration had been fair in the autumn. By spring it had diminished to nothing but a bowl of water soup.

On the first of April permanent kommandos were sent to Munich and Landshut. I would have been drafted for the Landshut detail if I had not volunteered for the fifty-man kommando to Freising in the meantime. I guess an act of God saved us from going there at the designated time. For some unexplained reason our journey was delayed one day. In the intervening time the air corps struck. Two thousand people were killed, including the Red Cross representative who had just left the Stalag. The building we were to occupy was completely demolished. For this reason we never did go to Freifing.

The mark declined steadily, and inflation spread gradually in Munich. The real currency in Germany was the ration coupon. The people had more marks than they could spend. That is why the black market flourished. Speakeasies were operating; it cost a good many hundred marks for one night's entertainment. Good watches were worth five to ten thousand marks. American cigarettes sold for fifty marks each. Black market bread rose to fifty marks. The cost with coupons was fifty pfennigs. All other black market prices were in proportion to these.

In the Stalag, money of all countries was valueless. The cigarette was the standard medium of exchange. At one time during my captivity cigarettes were worth ten dollars each. About the only item bought and sold among the Americans was food. Most of the GIs that had watches or rings left at the time of our arrival in Stalag VIIA sold them to French and Poles. The value of anything varied with the number of cigarettes in circulation. Bread sold for six to twelve cigarettes in October and November and December. When officers arrived in January with plenty of cigarettes from personal parcels, the price jumped to over thirty. All other food prices rose proportionately. After April first, very few worked outside of the Stalag. Thus there was very little black market food coming in. This caused the cigarettes to become valueless.

On days off, I always washed up. For the first month and a half I had no soap, and so had to simulate cleanliness. I had only one razor blade when I was captured. It was pretty dull by the time I was able to discard it in December. I had only one outfit of clothing until the last couple months, so I had to wash my clothing in shifts.

Soldiers the world over discuss women as a primary topic in bull sessions. This was untrue in the Stalag. Food was the center of thought and talk most of the time. The YMCA added a lot to easing the monotony of internment. I appreciated the library most. Interest in a book made me forget my surrounding temporarily. In addition this organization had sent athletic equipment. Most of the time we were too weak to expend energy using it. I played some basketball one day. I never realized until then how much physical stamina I had lost.

Musical instruments were also available. The boys of musical aptitude formed bands and entertained us occasionally. Good old American music revived memories and really made us homesick. On more than one occasion the tears came to my eyes. We were especially blue on Christmas, New Years and Easter.

By the middle of April we knew it wouldn't be long. Thousands of prisoners were arriving from evacuated Stalags in the Nurnberg area. Most of the guards had gone to the front. The remaining guards didn't give a damn what we did inside the Stalag. We tore down all the fences between the compounds and used the posts for firewood. We even had exits to the outside.

On Liberation Day I was cooking breakfast when machine guns opened up. There was token resistance by the Germans, but in an hour or so it was all over. It made me feel very proud when I saw the American flag raised at the front gate. I could have hugged that first dust-stained doughboy I saw, he looked so good to me. As far as I am concerned April 29th will always be V.E. Day.

Americans never got along too well with the European nationalities in the Stalag. However, we felt sorry for them. Many of them didn't know whether their families were living or if they had homes to return to. We knew that all of us Americans would find everything at home just about the way we left it. I think it is pretty swell.

You see, I learned something that money or education could never teach me in the United States. I now have a real appreciation for the American way of life.

Don Davis
Letters Written Before His Capture
22nd September, 1944
Somewhere in France

Dear Mom:

As you can see, I am now in a regular outfit. The 80th Division was famous during the last war. The old 80th was made up of boys from Virginia, West Virginia and Kentucky. The insignia stands for the Blue Ridge Mountains bordering those states. The outfit was reactivated about two years ago. This organization is of course, attached to the 3rd Army.

I have one disadvantage here, I have to dig a much larger foxhole than anyone else does. In fact right now I'm sitting listening for phone calls in one. We make regular homes out of these excavations. There is plenty of cut wood lying around to provide roofs. It feels pretty nice being inside if there are any mortar shells lighting in the vicinity.

I'm traveling pretty light now. All I actually carry with me is rifle, ammunition, toilet articles, blanket, stationary, and raincoat. Tonight I am looking forward to a shower. It will be my first in France, incidentally. I never realized how a guy appreciates things like that until I got over here.

We've eaten our last two meals hot, and I don't mind telling you they tasted good after a dose of C and K rations. I guess it is legal now for me to tell you some of the places I've been to or passed through. I have been in England, Scotland, near Paris, Caen, Chartres, Nancy, LeMans, etc. In all the towns I have been in the people seem very happy to be removed from the Nazi yoke. The French, American and British flags are displayed prominently on many of the buildings.

Love, Don

26th September 1944
Somewhere in France

Dear Mother:

This stationary is damp so I guess that accounts for the smudges. I think it will be legible though.

I just finished a meal of hot rations a little bit ago. They taste O.K. warm. I've got a good recipe for making good stew now. Take one can of C ration stew, 4 or 5 ounces of water and one package of bouillon powder from the supper K ration and mix in canteen cup. Heat to desired temperature over fire and then you're all set if you have a nice easy chair to sit down in (am I kidding) and some crackers. It has been raining some lately at night, I've managed to keep my blanket dry on one side, so I've really been O.K. on the sleep situation. By wearing my raincoat I don't get the effects of the water on the ground.

For the last two nights a few of us have had a break. France, as you know, has countless small villages that are really just a collection of farmhouses. We happen to be near one. It's really O.K. sleeping in one of their barns. Straw makes a very comfortable bed incidentally. The civilians are very friendly around here. This morning I had a shot of cognac awaiting me when I woke up. This noon I had a hard-boiled egg to supplement the regular GI K Ration. French cider and wine is usually quite sour. This afternoon I had some that wasn't bad at all.

Keep me posted on all the local news of interest, because, remember, I don't get the Argus over here. The only kind of news we do get is at least two days old. In other words we get the Tuesday edition of Stars and Stripes (printed in Paris) on Thursday. In fact the Stars and Stripes is the only current literature we do see.

I of course, can't tell you where I am. If you read the newspaper reports of the 3rd Army in France, you'll learn more than I can ever tell you.

Two years ago I would not have been able to live this kind of an existence. Now my resistance has built up so that I am able to tolerate (I'll never get used to it) the rigors of an infantry life.

Love, Don

Don was captured early the morning of September 27th 1944

Stars & Stripes 11 December, 1944
Out of the Foxholes - Home for the Holidays

Forty-nine enlisted men and six officers of the 80th Infantry Division leave a collecting point at the front to begin thirty days of furlough in the states. All in the group, headed by Captain Raymond G. Roy of Boston, has been either wounded or decorated twice.

With the Third U.S. Army: The first group of 1300 heroes of the U.S. Third Army leave soon for a thirty day furlough in the States. They assembled today at a replacement center for a late briefing before starting the happiest journey of their lives.

EACH PICKED FOR HEROISM

There are more than 1300 from this Army group alone and each man was selected for his outstanding heroism in battle. All the men have two Purple Hearts or two Combat Medals or a combination of both. These are real front line fighting men who are going home for a well-deserved rest. Some had to be rescued from precarious positions by special patrols, while others were just preparing for a new river crossing when the magic word reached them.

This afternoon there were 170 at the station waiting for the next stop on their unbelievable journey to Paris.

UNSHAVEN AND DIRTY

Unshaven, dirty, wet and mud caked, they stood shoulder to shoulder in a barracks mess hall while Captain Willard Kirby told them about this wonderful thing that was happening. Most of the men had not quite recovered from the shock and just stood as if in a trance. Others had, what seemed to be a perpetual grin on their grimy faces. Some laughed nervously when they were not supposed to and others unconsciously deadpanned the Captain's puns.

They had no inhibitions, no restraints, no rules or regulations. They were free to do as they wished. The world they were fighting for at last lay at their feet. Sudden realization of it, as the Captain talked, brought lumps to the throats of many, and many of the big, strong fighting men laughed heartily to conceal from inquisitive eyes a dampness that had crept into their own. They were going home to be with their families for a month!

"Do you realize" one GI said to his buddy "that I'm going home? It's not a dream... I'm actually going home!

God knows I've dreamed about it long enough, three years to be exact. I'm really going home"!

The captain was still talking, telling the men how they had been chosen from their groups, the most deserving to go home. "We feel proud having you here", the captain said "and we are to give you priority to billets, food and every other facility here. There will be no detail assigned to you... you are free to do as you please."

The GIs had not heard anything like that since being in the Army. It was difficult for them to realize they were being honored, an honor long overdue.

PARIS NEXT STOP

The captain continued "from here you will go to Paris and you will be allowed sufficient time to see the city and see it right. At this point there were cheers and sighs, but one entranced doughboy who looked like a raw boned boy from the Ozarks just stood there with his mouth agape and the fixed expression of wonderment he had when he arrived. To him, it was all just too unreal. "From there," the captain went on. "You will be taken to the next stop over." At that, the Ozark boy turned for the first time and looked at the others as though for confirmation of this miracle about to happen.

BACK TO THE STATES

"And from there, you are going to the states", the captain continued. "I don't know how, but I don't think it makes a hell of a lot of difference. Then you will be free—on your own for a month.

The captain then informed them that they would be supplied with fresh clothes. They would also have hot showers tonight and barbers ready to give the much-desired haircuts. At dinner there would be music by the depot band and movies later in the evening.

"Get yourselves a shave, a haircut and a shower and get your clothes in order, so that when you leave for gay Paree, you can say to yourself, 'I'm all set. Let them do, as they will with me!' Don't goof off get into trouble or go AWOL."

Taken from the 80th Division file of "Dusty" Rhoads

Louis B. Engelke
An MP Officer Recalls the Advance Party to England

1st Lt. Louis B. Engelke remembers many exact details about the Advance Party from the United States to England or about the Advance Party from England to Normandy, although I was the representative of the Division Provost Marshal, Major Donald Hughes, on each of the Advance Parties. We were discouraged from keeping notes or official documents in our little element of the Division; so the only information I can give on the Advance Parties is from information in my head.

The Advance Party to England left Camp Miles Standish, Taunton, MA, for Boston Harbor, departing Boston on 4 June 1944 on one of America's fastest passenger liners which had been converted into a troop ship. It had been the Manhattan renamed the Wakefield. The ship's officers and crewmen were Coast Guardsmen.

Engelke cannot recall any Naval, or Coast Guard Escort for the Wakefield, during the daylight hours, of 4 June 1944, when a Navy or Coast Guard seaplane kept circling overhead the fast, speeding troopship. On the stern end of the boat, Engelke also saw a cannon, which the Coast Guard manned. The ship simply zigzagged its way across the Atlantic to lessen its chances of being torpedoed by German submarines. It went so far north that there was daylight around the clock for a day or two. I believe it was five days at sea when it came southward between Ireland and Scotland to make port at Liverpool, England. My group was lodged at Petty Pool Manor, near Chester, an ancient city not far from Liverpool. The name Chester comes from the Roman word for fortress, Cesta. Having served as a Roman fortress city, Chester still has a Roman wall as a tourist attraction.

In that the Military Police Platoon, of which I was Platoon Leader under the Provost Marshal, was the Discipline, Law and Order element of the division, Col. Max Johnson, Division Chief of staff, and Lt. Col. Leon Clayton, G-1 (Personnel), instructed me, prior to the arrival of the Division in England, to make a survey of all the establishments that served alcoholic beverages in cities and towns in the area that soon would be occupied by the division. I marked the locations of hundreds of pubs and with every community seeming to have at least one Red Lion pub. I had to report back that England certainly was not Tennessee!

During this period, the news media were speculating where General Patton, might be. He had dropped out of sight after the celebrated slapping incident in Sicily. It was not long before we learned the general, whom the media liked to call "Old Blood and Guts", was in a nearby town of Knutsford, England, where the Third U.S. Army was now headquartered after moving from San Antonio, Texas and that we were now in the Third Army. You would hear the question, "Do you know who our Army Commander is?" If the answer was no, and the reply was, "General Patton," the immediate response often was, "I'm glad. I know he is tough, but I don't care how tough he is, or if he slaps us. He knows how to fight, and that's the most important thing."

Engelke went to the Third Army's Provost Marshal's office at Knutsford and secured a number of supply items for the 80th MP Platoon, including hundreds of Main Supply Route (MSR) signs which later would help in the speeding of supplies to the Division's front, also securing a supply of baton flashlights, which were flashlights with an amber extension, which later proved to be excellent for directing Division traffic at night. I did not see General Patton on this visit, but after the Division was committed to action, I chanced to see him almost daily as he checked on the progress of the Division and its regiments.

"I believe General Patton was one of the greatest combat leaders in American history." A superb tactician, he kept his divisions moving, moving, and moving. While this was fatiguing, the surprising of the enemy by Pattonesque sweeps probably saved thousands of American lives in the long run.

The Division Advance Party from England to Normandy traveled by motor column from Chester area through the Shakespeare County avoiding large cities. I remember Brig. Gen. Owen Summers, Assistant Division Commander, and Lieutenant, soon to become Col. August Elgar, the G-3 (Operations), as being the top officers in this group to set up sectors for all the units of the Division which soon would be arriving in the lodgment area just southwest of Utah Beach on the Cotentin Peninsula in the vicinity of St. Jores.

On 1 August 1944 this advance Party left from Southampton to cross the English Channel on a Landing Ship Tank, staffed by a Coast Guard crew. Well known is the fact that someone in an early arriving group of American soldiers (26 Years earlier) in World War I, upon stepping on French soil, shouted "Lafayette, we are here." This was picked up by the news services to be heard around the world.

On 3 August 1944 after our LST carrying some 40 Officers and men, beached itself on Utah Beach and its bow was lowered to serve as a ramp and my driver drove onto the wet French beach sand, I suddenly remembered that three of my grandparents were German-Americans and one grandmother was French-American so I reached down, picked up a handful of the wet sand, and said, "Grandmother, I am here." It was not heard outside my jeep.

The Provost Marshal, upon landing on Omaha Beach, was summoned to the Division CP, (the only other unit beside the MPs ashore) and Major General McBride greeted him with these words. "Hughes, I want you to go to the transit area and get those people up here." The answer was, of course, "Yes Sir." And that is how the most hectic period for a platoon started.

Late in the evening of 3 August 1944, having established liaison with XII Corps representatives charged with clearing the Corps through the transit area, a bivouac was established in the area and the platoon set up for business, total available manpower 2 Officers and 61 EM, amount of transportation, 15 jeeps. Major D.K. Hughes, commanding and 1st Lt. Louis B. Engelke was the only officer present in the platoon.

Guides posted along the beach, for traffic control from the beach to the transit area; inside the transit area; and the transit area to the assembly area. Guides were also posted in the assembly area.

The arrangement worked smoothly. Ships would discharge at the beach, and personnel and vehicle drivers directed to the route and thence to the transit area. Clearance for the convoys of 30 vehicles was obtained for the movement of the convoys to the assembly area from the transit area at 15-minute intervals. By the order of the CG, all trucks were unloaded in the assemble area and returned to the transit. Some were loaded with personnel arriving on foot were taken to the assembly area. Day and night the convoys rolled, each convoy escorted by a lead MP jeep, and followed by another MP jeep to pick up the straggling vehicles. Soon the pressure overtaxed the facilities of the MP Platoon, as business was very good. When the Rcn Troop came ashore they were enthusiastically received, and jeeps and crews were taken over by the MPs as auxiliary MPs and assumed part of the burden of guiding and guarding the convoys. Their help was most gratefully received.

There was no hitch in the plan, just lots of long hours and long labor. Persuading unit COs that they had no responsibility for movements of their units, but that they would best be employed by collecting and organizing their units in the assembly area, in what was perhaps the most difficult task of all.

However in the evening hours of 7 August, the labors were over, and on the 8th, the Division started into action, with the MPs blazing the trail. No vehicles, or men were lost during the movement across the beach and upon completing the mission the Corps representative and the Transit Area CO both acknowledged the excellent and speedy manner in which the Division had crossed the beach, in less than four days, establishing a record for any division size with full equipment, with the possible exception of some D-Day units, whose records were not known. In addition to the duties listed above, all the details of loading, unloading, trans-shipping, formation of convoys and obtaining of clearances was accomplished by the platoon.

The 80th MP platoon was operated under the control, primarily of Provost Marshal Hughes. He maintained liaison with the Commanding General, Major General Horace L. McBride; the Chief of Staff, Colonel Johnson; and the G1, namely G-4 (Supply), Lt. Colonel Sandbag; G-3 (Operations), Colonel Elegiac; G-1 (Personnel), Lt. Colonel Clayton, G-5 (Civil Affairs/Military Government). Lt. Colonel E. Arthur Ball; and G-2 (Intelligence) Lt. Colonel Fleischer.

As the Platoon Leader, I primarily was in charge of keeping Division traffic moving. If the Provost Marshal was not available, I conducted the liaison with the GIs and their top assistants at Division Headquarters and occasionally with the Chief of Staff, if called on to do so, although I was only a First Lieutenant in the four ETO campaigns of the Division.

Getting the 80th Infantry Division, coming into Utah Beach from the Liberty Ships, Landing Ships Tank and Landing Ship Infantry, over the beach and positioned in assembly areas more than 20 miles inland, ready for commitment to combat, in a record time of four days no doubt was the greatest overall achievement of the 80th MP Platoon.

In fact, the MPs were very short on rank in World War II. As I remember, our Table of Organization called for one major, a first lieutenant and a second lieutenant or two. The highest noncommissioned officer was a Staff Sergeant, who handled administrative details for the unit. His name was Warren Pickers, and late in the war he received a well-deserved field commission as a Second Lieutenant.

I recall having about 75 men in the platoon. This was hardly enough to handle traffic control, much less handling prisoners-of-war (over 212,000) on a continuing basis. Since the 80th Division Band had few musical duties in combat, most of the band was attached to the platoon and primarily given guard duties in handling prisoners-of-war brought to the Division POW Enclosure, which often as not would be an open field. Warrant Officer Knapp, who had been a member of the Cincinnati Symphony Orchestra, was the commander of the Band.

After the war, the division MP platoons were replaced by division MP companies, I am told, because a platoon was simply too small for all the duties required. A friend of mine, Brig. General Armin Puck, who was Provost Marshal of the 36th Infantry Division in World War II, told me his platoon was augmented to company size and greater during that war and that practically all other divisions had to beef up their MP units to meet the task.

We were grateful to have the band help us. During the combat period the 80th Division Band played for a ceremony in the Town Square of St. Avold. While the band played for the ceremony in which the top officers of the division performed in prominent roles, the MP Platoon provided extraordinary security. An MP was on the roof of every building surrounding the square and other MPs looked on from windows. We did not want any of our key leaders picked off by a hostile rifleman. The time bombs in St. Avold on 4 December 1944 were bad enough. A time bomb demolished the command post of the antiaircraft battalion supporting the Division. This building was next door to the building occupied by the MP Platoon in the French Artillery School at St. Avold, was believed to be the luckiest day (4 December) in the opinion of the Chief of the platoons Traffic Section Lt. Engelke. When the bomb went off at 2300 hours in the 633rd AAA's Headquarters, I was in my room in the MP Platoon's billet writing on the felt covering of a pair of German Army canteens which I would be sending to two of my wife's teenage cousins back in the states. I could hear two separate heavy explosions in another part of St. Avold. Bomb disposal experts from the 305th Engineer Combat Battalion of the 80th Division were trying to clear all the bombs, but there were too many for them to get to all of them before they exploded.

Specifically, the Historical Narrative of the 633rd AAA AW Battalion noted that the 633rd's Headquarters and Headquarters Battery reported the loss of four officers and 18 enlisted men killed in the time bomb blast, and two additional officers and 18 enlisted men had to be evacuated because of wounds in the explosion.

The only times that I remember any 80th MPs being out of direct Division control was when the 319th Regiment Combat Team was operating on the north bank of the Loire River in the Toul-Nancy area and several jeep loads of MPs again were with the 319th, and also when MP Sgt. Tom Loftus and a jeep or two of the 80th MPs were under control of the 318th Regimental Combat Team and went with the 4th Armored Division to relieve Bastogne in the Battle of the Bulge.

Throughout the campaigns, the 80th MPs maintained traffic control posts at all road junctions within the Division's Zone, from the Light Artillery Line to the Division Rear Echelon. We did something which may not have been done in other infantry divisions when we utilized 24 jeeps of the platoon for round-the-clock traffic control, as well as information service, by putting four trained MPs in each jeep, so there would be an MP on duty at every Traffic Control Point every minute of the day. In 1963, I mentioned this at the Provost Marshal General's School at Fort Gordon, GA., while taking the Advanced MP Officer Course there, and no faculty member had ever heard of such an arrangement. But it was highly successful for the 80th Division.

As the Division moved forward, the rear most team would leapfrog to the hottest forward traffic control point, and so on. The only time I can remember a break in the leapfrog system was when we decided to send a replacement team to the bridge at Heiderscheidergrund, Luxembourg, to give relief to a team that had been under particularly prolonged artillery fire.

Many years after the war, I was happy to read, during a visit to the Adjutant General's office at Fifth Army Headquarters at Fort Sam Houston, TX, that the platoon was awarded the Meritorious Unit Citation in recognition of its service to the Division, which authorized platoon members to wear the rectangular gold-framed decoration over the right breast pocket of the uniform. Quite an honor!

Eight 80th MPs in two jeeps served as a small swat-team type of security guard for General McBride during his daily trips to forward units of the division and observation points.

There does not seem to be any doctrine stating when a Military Policeman may leave his post of duty under enemy attack. I ask about this at the Military Police School at Fort Gordon and told how I and several jeep loads of MPs went to the Sai River bridge site, just south of Argentan, where the Combat Engineers of the Division were putting spans over the river, and the MPs were to establish traffic control as soon as the bridge would become operational. When three German tanks, several hundred yards away descending a gentle slope on the other side of the river, started firing directly at the crossing site, an Engineer officer shouted, "Come on, boys. Let's go!" The Engineers all jumped into their vehicles and roared away. We followed the Engineers in their retreat post haste, to await further instructions. Although promising to do so, after hearing my question on when can MPs pull out without being liable to charges of abandoning their posts, the MP School officer-instructor promised to send me answer after checking with school doctrine, but he never sent it.

We also had IPW (Interrogation of Prisoners of War) teams at the MP Command Post. These teams worked for Division G-2. Most of the personnel in these teams were Jewish men of German birth of draft age who had escaped Nazi Germany. They were very good at getting information out of captured Prisoners of War.

This concludes my recollections, although my memories of my time in the 80th MP Platoon are quite vivid, I do remember our Asst. Division's name was BG Summers. I cannot remember, off hand, all of the first names of the individuals mentioned in this narrative or even if I have spelled the names right. In the last several years I purchased several books containing mentions of the 80th Division, but I have not had time to peruse them sufficiently.

Captain Marion C. "Woody" Chitwood
S-3 318th Infantry Regiment
As I Remember It

Lt. Colonel John B. Snowden commanded the 3rd Battalion before we left the United States. He was a West Pointer, very strict and thorough, but always fair according to the men in Hamper Blue. (Code Name of the 3rd Battalion.) He believed that his staff (S-2 and S-3) should accompany the leading companies in the attack so as to get first-hand information. He always sent Johnny Bier, S-2 with one of the attacking companies and Captain Chitwood, S-3 with the other. However, he would not ask any officer to do anything he would not do himself.

In our first encounter just before Argentan, we were trying to locate a sniper. The Colonel stood erect, without any cover, exposing himself completely. He said the best way to spot this man was to give him a chance to shoot someone. Colonel Snowden was an example of fearlessness throughout the campaign.

Friday 18 August, the objective of the 318th was the road N.158 southeast of Argentan. The 80th was in the battle for the Argentan-Falaise gap. The mission was to close this gap. At 0800 the 2nd Battalion started up the Argentan-Trun road. The 1st Battalion advancing on Argentan had been pinned down by enemy fire. Brig. General E.W. Searby asked Lt. Gallagher Commanding Officer of Company B to take three or four men on a patrol to locate the enemy. The general went along and they located a German tank in a hedgerow to the right of Argentan. When the patrol opened fire the tank withdrew, and two machine guns supporting the tank opened fire on the general, Gallagher and his men. General Searby started toward one of the machine guns. Gallagher prevailed on the general to give him the honor, which he did reluctantly. The men covered Gallagher's advance. Gallagher was lucky and knocked out both machine guns and wounded the tank commander who was visible in the turret. Lt. Gallagher was awarded the BSM (Bronze Star Medal) and is believed to be the first man in the 318th to be decorated. The 2nd Battalion moved up in support of the first. When the fog lifted in the morning the 3rd Battalion was caught suddenly in an open field.

An 88 hit a hay stack killing Lt. Colonel G.A. Lindell, and T. Sgt. James Knight, a platoon Sgt. standing alongside. The 1st Battalion was unsuccessful in the first day of battle. Major Tosi assumed command of the 1st Battalion and was ordered to reorganize and hold the area until the 3rd Battalion could resume the attack the next day.

That night Lt. Colonel Snowden CO of the 3rd Battalion met with Major Tosi and members of the staffs of the two battalions, in a cemetery that was under heavy artillery fire. They made plans to move north which would require crossing two open fields and two blacktop roads. In the middle of the fields we were to cross was harvested grain, when we got this far, the Germans let loose with everything they had. The Anti-tank guns could not get across the river or canal to the rear of us. Therefore was unable to help us. We had crossed a road to the front of us, I was with L Company and John Bier was with K Company as we jumped off, K Company on the left and L Company on the right. After crossing the road there was a grain field extending northward for almost 1/2 mile to a forest line. The first half was slightly down grade, then upward to the woods. When our lead units started up the slope the Germans opened up and the men were caught in the open. Some of the men were lucky enough to find foxholes the Germans had dug, along with some haystacks, however many were caught in the open, and were being picked off one by one. Our radioman that was near me was picked off and his replacement was hit shortly afterward. We heard enemy tanks and saw several coming from behind us accompanied by German infantry, moving out into the fields shooting or capturing our men. I attempted to get the radio but several bullets were hitting around me, so I crawled toward the rear. I ran between two tanks, the turret of the tank on my left was swinging toward me but the road at that point was in a slight cut and I was able to duck down out of his line of fire. I saw a GI with both of his legs blown off, begging for someone to kill him. Col. Snowden advised me that John Bier was with Captain Wilkerson in a shell hole surrounded by Germans. For several hours they were able to hold them off only by calling in artillery on their own positions. (Captain Wilkerson was awarded the Silver Star for this action.) Company M had their mortars set up in a farmyard directly behind the machine guns and us had set up on an embankment overlooking the grain field. A tank coming up on them from the left front on the blacktop road used their machine gun to kill several men of the company, but one of the Sgt.'s fired a grenade into the turret of the tank knocking it out.

A few days before the above action (12 August) we had taken Sillé-Le-Guillaume and this is memorable for me because I was very much in the forefront of the action, but never saw a German nor in fact do I know of anyone who did. We had moved through the center of the town and were moving up a hill to the north when some mines were detected in the road, action was halted until the Engineers could be brought up to clear the road. As we were waiting, an excited Frenchman approached Col. Snowden stating that several Germans were behind his house. Col. Snowden sent a platoon from I believe Company L with me and also sent along a tank to locate the enemy. Behind the Frenchman's house was an orchard overlooking the town of Sillé-Le-Guillaume which we had just passed through, along with other troops attached to us, who were just now passing through the town. I discussed our strategy with the Tank Commander, he was to move counter-clockwise around the orchard, while our platoon would cover the wooded area to the left which would seem a logical avenue of escape for the Germans. I especially impressed on him the need to hold fire until he saw the enemy, thus enabling us to know better where they might be headed. The tank took off pushing down several of the Frenchman's trees and just as he reached the far end of the field, directly above the town, he opened up with his machine guns, we were positive the Germans were going to rush right into our arms, but a few minutes later he pulled up beside us and stuck his head out of the turret, and asked where in the world did they go? I asked, never saw anybody. However, there was a real battle going on back in town. As he fired over the town, our troops moving through knew they were receiving an attack and reacted accordingly. Fortunately (as far as I know) no one was hit, but an awful lot of ammunition was expended. I believe this was our first real firefight or at least thought it was.

A couple days later our orders were to seize our objective in the vicinity of Sees. I don't believe Sees was much more than a crossroads which was actually defended by the enemy, but they were in positions to the north and northeast of Sees. As we approached we came to the east to west road across our front. The road crossed a small stream on our right and on the near side (south) of the road was an orchard. The enemy opened up pinning us down in the orchard and we suffered several casualties. As the Company BAR man ran across the bridge to the right he was KIA by machine fire. Mortar airburst continued to cause casualties and confusion took over. I was with I Company, one of the lead companies and was just as confused and scared as anyone, but something had to be done. I moved to the road and peeped out and saw the body of the BAR man in the middle of the bridge. Crawling up behind his body I reached over and took the BAR and bandoleers of ammo and crawled back behind the 6" curbing on the near side of the bridge. Fire seemed to be coming from a farm house area about 200 yards to the right front. I fired a burst at anything that looked like a likely space where the enemy might be located, not actually seeing the enemy, running out of ammo, I called back across the road for more ammo, shortly after a GI ran across the road and dropped down beside me with several bandoleers of ammo. This turned out to be Bud Campbell a neighbor from our rural section of Bloomington, IN. Neither of us knew the other was in the army. We started firing again and gradually others picked up the firing. A Lt. (I believe Lt. Carter) took a patrol up the ditch along the right side of the road and shortly we saw the Germans taking off uphill back of a farmhouse. The patrol caught several PWs (possibly as many as 12). In the big picture this was insignificant yet hundreds of incidents similar to this when added together make up the big picture. "Allies capture Argentan closing Falaise Gap and capturing thousands of Germans." For us, it changed our lives forever. No more fun & games, no more cocky, overly confident, superman. Now we know what war was really like.

Making slight advances, the 80th and 90th Divisions, occupied Chambois and Croisilles, joining up with the Canadian Army at Chambois thus closing the Gap and a large part of the German Seventh Army was caught.

With CCB 4th Armored Division, the 1st Battalion approached and reconnoitered the Moselle River, south of Metz and north of Dieulouard, for a possible crossing site.

General Patton's old friend General Houdemon, of the French Army who had escaped the Gestapo and returned to his home in Pont a Mousson, advised the Chief of Staff of the 80th Division on 7 September that to bomb the town would kill all the Frenchmen and all the Germans would be safe in bomb shelters. He showed how the hill could be taken by the use of two fords below Pont a Mousson, one above and one below.

The Americans were suspicious and planned to bomb Pont a Mousson. Finally General McBride called General Patton and told him of the Frenchman, claiming to be his friend. Quite 'right,' said Patton, he is my dearest friend: follow his orders as if they were my own.

"During the night he countermanded the attack ordered by General McBride and prepared the attack across the Moselle by ways of the fords."

The Colonel was killed on a hill overlooking the Moselle River, about three days before the crossing was made.

James S. Drylie
Company A, 318th Infantry Regiment
Tells What it is Like to be a New Replacement

I'm sure that my experiences were minor compared with those of you "old-timers" who saw much more combat than I did. However, each combat action affected every individual differently. I went over as a Replacement in January 1945. I was assigned to Co. A, 1st Squad, 1st Platoon, 318th Infantry on Feb. 13, 1945. Forty of us replacements joined Co. A that day, and I was one of 21 who joined the 1st Platoon, after the company had suffered many casualties crossing the Sauer River into Germany several days before. Being a replacement was a very lonely feeling for a 19-year old, or anyone else for that matter. My first foxhole buddy was Will Boyer. Some of my most vivid memories are as follows:

On Feb. 18 I experienced my first attack, which began late at night near Hommerdingen, Germany. Although we didn't meet any German infantry there, I became aware that it was the "real thing" when direct-fire 88s went close over our heads as we walked through a town. Then we were mistakenly fired on by our own tanks. Later, when we became lost, our CO called for an artillery round at a map coordinate to orient our location and the round just missed us.

On Feb. 22 we attacked the town of Mettendorf, which was my first action involving casualties, including the death of my platoon leader, 1st Lt. Nash Santiago. We were pinned down much of the day in a large open area and finally cleared the town at night.

On March 16 while fighting through the Zerf Forest, near Weiskirchen, we encountered heavy fire from the enemy dug in among the rows of tall pines while we crossed one of the firebreak clearings. To this day I hate pine forests! My buddy, Will Boyer, was killed by machine gun fire during that action. Walter E. Snyder became my foxhole buddy after that, but three days later he was killed by an artillery tree burst as we tried to reach our foxhole.

On March 21 we attacked Neustadt by first climbing a very long, high hill, then having to go down the other side through sniper fire, jumping down from about three dozen walled vineyard terraces, each about six feet high (I counted them later). Houses were immediately at the bottom, where we got involved in some house-to-house fighting.

On March 31 I took over as ammo jeep driver, along with Larry Fralick, after the previous driver was wounded by driving over a land mine. During the month of March '45 two Company Commanders of Co. A, 318th were killed: Capt. Gordon Goerke and Capt. Raymond Weiershauser.

During our attack on Kassel April 11, I may have been saved by a heavy streetcar wire hanging down across Frankfurter-strasse. As we were delivering ammo to Co. A, our jeep became entangled in the wire. While removing it a nearby GI told us that we were heading straight for a German roadblock several blocks ahead. I have always been amazed that we didn't get seriously lost in that city without a map.

On Apr. 12 at Erfurt, Larry and I, in our jeep, were fired at and had to take cover in a ditch. I grabbed a Thompson submachine gun that I had found earlier, only to discover that it wouldn't fire. Fortunately, some of our guys took care of the Germans. Time after time I realized how much our lives depended upon actions of our buddies, often unknown to us.

I was, to my recall, the first soldier of the 80th division to enter Weimar on April 12, 1945. I was a BAR man in the 2nd Battalion, 317th, Fox Company, third platoon, third squad. On the morning of April 12, our company was ordered to gather in a large open field just outside of what we knew later as the town of Weimar. There was a jeep parked in the center of the field. A major or Lt. Col., (I do not remember which one) stood up in the jeep and addressing all of us said in a loud voice: "Before you see the town of Weimar. We are going to enter it. We have been given direct orders from Washington to not fire a shot unless we are fired upon. The town has surrendered and we will honor that surrender." He left the jeep with all of us wondering what the Hell was going on. We had not entered any German town for over four months without firing some shots as we entered. There were four Sherman tanks lined up on the road leading to town. Our platoon Lt. told my squad to mount up on the lead tank. I was placed in front with my BAR. The rest of the platoon was mounted on the other three tanks. The tanks were ordered to move out. As we rumbled down the road we passed a large German tank that had been destroyed and was still smoking. I thought that we were lucky to not have met him a little sooner. As we approached the town we passed between three story buildings. We were all very nervous, looking at all the rooftops and windows as we continued down the street. After about fifteen very anxious minutes we arrived at a fountain that looked like the center of town. We got off the tanks and believe that some of our officers went over to meet some of the town officials. Our platoon Lt. told us that the town's people had all been ordered by the mayor to surrender all their weapons to us. We were paired off and told to march up a designated street and the civilians would give us any weapons they had. My buddy and I were ordered up one side street. We had not gone more than a couple of blocks when we approached a large area between buildings that were surrounded on the street side with an eight foot wire. As we approached what looked like a locked gate, a group of very sickly looking men ran to the fence. They all had on striped clothes, like prisoners. One of them in broken English asked us if we were Americans. We said yes and all of a sudden about four of the guys started demanding us to let them out so they could kill Germans. We were confused and did know what to do. I told them in a loud voice that we could not let them out.

They asked us why we would not let them out. We did not know what to do so we just moved on to carry out our orders. About two more blocks from the 'prison' a lady came out of a house and without a word handed me a large, flat wooden box and ran back into the house. The box looked like it was made of cherry wood. I opened it up and was very surprised to see that it was a complete Walther .32 caliber gun. The box was lined with green velvet and there was extra gun parts all nestled in pockets in the velvet. I put the box in my backpack and finding no more houses to march by went back to the center of town. I really cannot remember what happened to the box. I still have flashbacks of those prisoners asking us to let them out to kill Germans.

Regards, Jim

Sgt. Marvin R. Spencer
Hqs Company, 317th Infantry Regiment
How I Saw the War

I am Marvin R. Spencer ASN. 38106930 HQ. Co. 3rd BN - 317 Inf. Reg. 80th Div. In combat I served under General George S. Patton, and his Third Army. I was in the best division and had the best commanding general in the U.S. Army. If a man had any fight in him he would fight for General Patton. I trained in Camp Forrest Tennessee, pulled maneuvers in Tennessee, then moved to Camp Phillips Kansas, and then on to Desert Maneuvers at Camp Laguna, Arizona. (This is where I first met General Patton.) From here we moved to Fort Dix, N.J. and from there to Camp Kilmer, N.J. next on to the Queen Mary (Queen of the fleet) to Jolly Old England. From New York to England in only 5 and a half days. We (80th) camped on King, the 8th racetrack and had advanced battle training. General Eisenhower was "roughin it also" in the King's Palace.

Finally they decided we were ready for combat. I for one was more than ready (had been for a year just tired of "doggin" around). So finally we crossed the English Channel to Utah Beach France. This is where friendship ceased and hell began. I don't recall all the small towns which were many and rough too. I lost many of my good buddies along this route. It seemed like there was always another river or hill where the Krauts were looking down our throats. The Battle of Charlone (?), Metz, Mousson Hill 109, and Mt. St. Jean, where we lost most of our officers and men of the 317th Inf. near where I also was wounded. Argentan was worse of all for me. This was the only hand to hand battle of the war for me. When I went over the hedgerow, there was the biggest German I ever saw waiting for me. He was on his knees, when I hit the ground, he raked me with his bayonet. But he didn't do his job very well, just cut the skin of my stomach for about 6". No intestines came out, just luck. So I did him in. The battle began at 2 minutes till five, the first I noticed my watch it was 10:30.

The battle was over and didn't seem like many men left. You couldn't take three steps in any direction without stepping over a dead or wounded man. It seemed I was in some kind of a daze, you know kind of like the world had come to an end or something. I had not yet, had time to think of me, but when things simmered down a bit, Cpl. Bowman from the 305 Medics came to me and said: Spencer let me check you, seems you are messed up a little. He put a few stitches in my belly and said everything was going to be all right. So he cleaned me up for the next battle. I feel we were fighting for a just cause, I gave it all I had until the medics took my gun away and hauled me out near Mt. St. Jean. There was many more that suffered far more than I did.

On the 19th of September, 317th Infantry soldiers attacked Hill 412. German resistance was great. The enemy did not give up the high ground easily. The hill was very steep, we Headquarters Company of the 3rd Bn. had to push our boxes of grenades up as far as we could and secure them with our trench knife, pull ourselves up and push them up another four feet and secure them again. It was very rough. We finally made it to the top. We took the hill, but were very low on ammo and grenades. The Germans were experts on counter attacks. My commanding officer Captain Martinez told me to take two men, return to our ammo DP and bring more grenades and ammo. I chose PVT Ed Kotch and PFC Carl Rubino and we started out on our mission. We seemed to be doing very well until late in the evening. We came upon about 30 Germans, head-on in the woods. Rubino said, "We are not giving up, right?" I said, "No way!" It seemed we were losing ground fast, when we heard gunfire from the other side of the woods. It was our own Capt. Robert W. Smith of K Co. and 20 or 30 men. He saved our lives. He also told us where a jeep was, that was also a great help.

We went a few miles and found a Chaplain all alone, we gave him a ride and he knew where the ammo DP was. We thought we had it made, but a few more miles and we ran into more Germans. This time over 100 Germans. We were firing at them and all at once they threw down their weapons and gave up. Rubino and the Chaplain could speak German, and well as they could. I told them to tell the Germans to stack all their weapons and rest until we could pick them up. We let four or five hang on the jeep and took them in. First Lt. Turner was at the ammo DP and he took some men and brought in the balance of the German Prisoners. We were so lucky they could have blown us apart; someone above took care of us once again. We left the Chaplain, got our supplies and started out again. This time we felt more confident. We knew where we were supposed to go. We were mechanized too. We were sailing along well until we came to a crossroads about five or six miles of our outfit where we came from. Then more Germans and someone firing a pistol into a treetop; that meant they were in a hole. We got in a ditch and fired a few rounds in their direction, and then a couple of white flags came up. Then went back down. A couple more gunshots came into the treetop. I told Rubino to cover me by firing over my head and I would crawl over their way and feed them a couple of grenades. I gave them a couple of grenades and flags came up again, then disappeared again. I gave them another one and Rubino told them to come out with their hands up. So they came out. There were 23 and we made them lay down on the road and searched them. We got them up to march off. All of a sudden, some of them went forward some back a little. I knew something was wrong. I whirled around and a German shot me in the upper right arm with a .31 caliber rifle. It knocked me to my knees. My rifle butt hit the ground my right arm dangling. The German threw his gun down. I pulled my gun between my knees and fired two shots with my left hand. Rubino emptied his gun on him.

After this people started showing up. Corp. Bowman from the 305 Medics gave me a shot. They cut my clothes off of me and tied my arm on and put a tourniquet on it. Then they were going to put me in a jeep and haul me away, but said I would have to leave my gun. I said, "No. I will not leave my gun." Corp. Bowman said, "Spencer, you need another shot before you go." He gave me another shot and that was all I knew until a Chaplain was talking about writing my wife a letter.

One day in France 1944 Lt. Belloque came to me and said, "Sergeant Spencer, there's a German supply train loaded with airplane parts and all kinds of weapons and ammo. It needs to be blown-up. Destroyed. It's parked about 15 miles in enemy territory. All I have is a hand drawn map and a damn Frenchman who says he can take us to it." I said, "Sir, when do we start?" He said, "Now." Pvt. Kotch, Pfc. Carl Rubino and I had 50 pounds of TNT each which was no safety device, but would blow up a train. I told my men: "Our mission is to find this train and blow it up, not try to kill every German between here and Berlin. We have to get to this train before they can destroy it. We must be alert, but cautious and quiet. When we blow the train, then we will think about coming back here."

Our Frenchman guide knew nothing of safety or taking cover. He just headed straight for the train. Thus we picked up some unnecessary rifle fire on the way. We finally reached the train. It was long and loaded. There was a house near the track. Lt. Belloque told me to try to explain to the people in the house we were going to blow up the train. When I approached the house, a woman came to the door. I tried to explain what was about to happen. She said, "No, don't blow--I get him." She went to the cellar and returned with a P-38 pistol and a German soldier. I kept the gun and gave Lt. Belloque the German prisoner.

There didn't seem to be anyone guarding the train. Later we found there were soldiers on the other side of the train. They were just not expecting company. We started strapping the TNT to the cars and rails. We had used most of the 150 pounds of TNT. Rubino said, "Spencer, that ought to blow up anything." I told him to use all of it. I was tired of carrying it.

There was a large mound of dirt near the track. We brought the primer cord behind it. When I lit the charge, all hell broke loose. The TNT set the ammunition on the train off. Everything was exploding. The dirt mound seemed very small. Pieces of rail—up to 50 feet long—were whirling in the air over our heads. It looked for a while like we might have committed suicide. I was never scared worse during the war. There were 30 or more Germans running across the field while things were blowing up. There were a lot of dead Germans after things quieted down some. They must have been sleeping on the train. After I lit the fuse we never saw our French guide again. He did not stay around for a tip, I suppose he is still running. Our trip back to our company was not too bad, some resistance as usual.

Eric Reilinger
Battalion Hqs, 317th Infantry Regiment
Another POW Story

I was wounded 9 November 1944, the day after the Seille River crossing. I was hit by machine gun fire in the leg. While waiting for the medics to pick me up, I again was wounded by mortar shrapnel and apparently passed out. As I came to, I saw three scrawny Germans poking at me with their rifles, motioning for me to get up. I had crawled into a slit trench that was full of rainwater to get out of the barrage. I motioned back to the trio that I was wounded and couldn't walk. They picked me up and we double-timed across the open field, two of them supporting me while I hopped along on one leg. In a nearby barn was an aid station, where they bandaged my leg, taped up a cut on my forehead and gave me a tetanus shot. All in all I was treated reasonably well, even though their collar insignias indicted that they belonged to the Waffen SS. There were two other wounded GIs in the barn. We were loaded on a motorcycle with a sidecar. The other two GIs in the sidecar, me on the handlebars with an SS guard in back of the driver. Had I been more mobile, this would have been the time to escape. After a rough ride, some of it cross-country, we arrived in a German Field Hospital in Metz. I was separated from the other two GIs and seated on a long bench with a group of lightly wounded German soldiers to await my turn to be treated.

Up until then, I had not been searched or interrogated. I then realized that I carried the battalion's copy of the Division's Signal Operating Instruction (SOI) between my helmet and helmet liner. This highly sensitive document containing all our radio frequencies, call signs, daily passwords, ciphers, etc. I realized that I must somehow get rid of this document. I told the guard who was standing behind me that I needed to go to the toilet. While in that cubicle I was able to flush the (SOI) down the hole in the floor. The guard seemed to realized that he had made a mistake; he tore open the door, dragged me away from the toilet, looked into the hole—too late— the pamphlet was gone. He roughly escorted me back to my seat, where I awaited the medical exam. After the cursory examination, I and five other GIs were loaded in a closed van and driven to another hospital near St. Avold, to be put to bed. So ended my first long day in captivity.

The nurses in this hospital were French Catholic nuns, who noticeable disliked the German patients, probably because of obnoxious behavior in cracking dirty jokes and showing off their pornographic postcards, which they had collected during their occupation of France. This worked to the advantage of the handful of American patients who treated the nuns respectfully. The nuns rewarded us with bigger portions of food and extra desserts.

After a relatively four days in this hospital, I was loaded into a closed van with five other GIs early before breakfast and driven to a temporary Stalag (POW Camp) in the center of Strasbourg, a city on the French side of the Rhine River. Upon arrival we were locked into a room without being fed. They collected all our clothing, which was returned with empty pockets, no belts, no shoelaces.

Mid-morning on the following day, I was brought before a man in a plain brown uniform without any insignias. Judging from the respect the guard accorded him, I assumed that he had considerable authority. He spoke flawless English with a British accent. He started to berate me with statements that German/Americans should not fight against the "fatherland". Although he knew that I spoke German, he conducted his questioning in his salted English. The questions started harmless enough: On what ship did the 80th Division come to England? Who is the 80th Division Commander? Who is the Regimental Commander? And other innocuous questions. I cited my name, rank and serial number after each question. He alternately pleaded softly, shouted, pounded the table, screamed, offered me a cigarette, and I repeated: name, rank and serial number. This went on intermittently for several hours. By the end of the day there were three of us left in the interrogation room. Three others had been excused and fed in clear sight of us. By that time I hadn't eaten for about eight hours. That evening the interrogator made us take our shoes and socks off and stand in adjacent corners on a stone floor of an outside hallway. He instructed a guard not to let us talk to each other, not let us lean against the wall, or go to sleep. Later that evening, the guard, who wanted to get some sleep himself, locked us into a room.

While in the room, we discussed our situation. Of the six from the hospital only three were left. What could we tell them that would be useful to them? I had been away from the 317th about a week. The other two were even longer in the hospital than I. We decided that we answer the questions carefully, and plead ignorance when a critical question is asked. At 6 AM the guard returned and put us into our respective corners. The questioning resumed at 9 AM. This went smoothly for me, until he asked me what our short-term objectives were. I told him, march into Berlin. He got angry, slapped me across the face and said, you're a Sergeant in communications, and you know more than you admit. Eventually, he gave up. That evening we were fed a slice of black bread and a cup of watery cabbage soup, our first meal in 72 hours.

The slice of black bread and the cabbage soup was our daily diet for the next four weeks at Strasbourg, while awaiting transportation to a permanent Stalag. We slept in the basement of the building on a dirt floor with a thin layer of straw. There was a bucket for each of 12 men to serve as a latrine. Each morning the buckets were full to overflowing.

There were 78 Americans, a handful of British POWs and about 8 Frenchmen, who cooked and were KPs. There were 15 German guards, one middle aged Austrian Lieutenant, and an elderly Prussian Colonel in charge. On several occasions we were alerted that we would be moved out during the night just to have it canceled in the morning. One of my details was to clean up the office, where the Austrian Lieutenant worked. He liked to practice his English on me. He confided that he was homesick and wished that the war would end. Periodically, I was detailed to pick up the food in the kitchen. This gave me a chance to talk to the French cooks, who seemed to know what went on, on the outside. I learned that the American 7th Army was advancing rapidly on Strasbourg and that the possibility of us being moved into Germany was remote, because the Rhine River Bridge was clogged with retreating German troops and equipment.

I immediately spoke to the Austrian Lieutenant, explaining that he was left behind, to be taken prisoner when the Allies arrived to set us free. I convinced him that unlike the other guards, he was always kind and upon liberation I would be sure to pass this on to the American authorities. He seemed to appreciate this. That same day I was called to the Commandant's office, and he suggested I put in a good word for him as well. He pleaded that he tried to run a humane camp, but with limited supplies the food may not have been good. I told him to turn the camp over to me and I would see what I could do. To my amazement, he did just that.

There I was a Yank T-4 suddenly in charge of the compound. I let out the POWs and locked up the guards in the basement, and locked the Lieutenant and the Colonel in the interrogation office. The first thing the freed GIs did was head for the supply rooms, gorged themselves with sausages, cheeses and anything else they could get their hands on, and many got violently sick. The situation was difficult to control.

Unfortunately, the American Army didn't show up. The city streets outside our building were swarming with German soldiers. We had a few weapons from the guards, but we were in no position to break out. On the third evening after our take-over, the senior noncom (a Staff Sergeant) and I ventured out through the city heading west. We were undetected when we came to a canal where a thin line of Germans was dug in. The Allies were on the other side. We managed to get across the canal and were picked up by some troops in American uniforms. It was a French armored unit. They treated us like prisoners until after some time, an American liaison officer showed up and I explained our situation to him. He didn't know what he could do for us. He suggested that I go back and try to keep control, the best I could. The Sergeant who came out with me stayed with him, to answer any questions that might come up. By then it started to get light and I needed to get back without being noticed, to await our liberation. At least somebody knew about us.

From our building, we could see the steeple of the City Hall with its German flag. Four days after our takeover, we noted that the Swastika flag came down and a French flag was hoisted. But, no Allied troops ever showed up at our place. As a matter of fact. That same afternoon the French flag came down and the German Swastika flag was back on the city hall flagpole. That evening I lined up the former guards and the ex-POWs, and used the same route though the city, to make it to the Allied lines. We saw no Germans. The French battalion was still dug in along the canal. This time I knew whom to ask for. We turned over the German prisoners. The freed GIs were loaded on 2½-ton trucks, and we were on our way back to a 7th Army replacement depot by December 12, 1944, to be debriefed by SHAEF HQ G-2. On December 16, 1944, I was back in my old outfit, 3rd Bn HQ 317th infantry, somewhere in the Saar Valley just in time to head north for the Battle of the Bulge, a few days later.

Ironically, while being debriefed by SHAEF G-2, I had to swear not to reveal any details of our take-over of the Strasbourg Stalag, only to read a version of it in the Stars and Stripes, several weeks later. So much for keeping it secret.

Herbert Garner
Company D, 317th Infantry Regiment
My Tour of Duty in the Service

On 16 October 1940, I registered for the draft. July 1942 I received Greetings from Uncle Sam. I took my physical on 31 March 1942 and was sworn in on 18 July 1942, and was placed on reserve duty for fourteen days. 1 August 1942, I was inducted into service and was shipped to Camp Robinson, in North Little Rock for five days and then was shipped to Camp Forrest, TN arriving 7 August 1942.

After basic training of 8 weeks, I was put in the kitchen because in basic training, I sprained both of my ankles and due to this I was put in the kitchen. I received a PFC rating on 1 November 1942. I made 2nd Cook on 9 March 1943 and was given a T/5 rating. There were four of us as cooks in the kitchen. I was on a shift for 24 hours then off for 24 hours. Joe Chiara and his crew were on the other shift. Everything was pretty well routine. 10 August 1942, we were up at 0200 for breakfast at 0400, we loaded on the trucks to be on the road by 0600. We rode until 1000, prepared dinner and fed at 1300. Again we were up at 0200 and loaded the trucks and moved out, unloaded and cooked and fed breakfast after riding until 0600. Again loading the trucks and moving only a short way, unloading at 1500, and fed the men at 1900. We then made lunches until 2300. This was the routine we followed for several weeks on what was called a bivouac. The cooks were no exception on going to the rifle range to fire the M-1. I made Marksman on my first try.

Then maneuvers, and bivouac in the hills of Tennessee after we awaited shipping orders. The shipping orders came for us to leave 3 September, for Salina, Kansas. We rode through Tennessee, Kentucky, Indiana, Illinois, and Missouri on a troop train. We arrived in Salina, Kansas on Monday 13 September. This was quite a ride. Upon arriving we were back in the old rut again, after working for a week getting things all cleaned up, and then I was sent to dehydrated food school for a month to six weeks. While there I made T-4 or Sgt. from Salina, Kansas we again boarded a troop train taking several days. We stayed in the Mojave Desert from two to three months on maneuvers in the desert. While here my daughter was born on 21 February 1944. I received a furlough for a five days after she was three weeks old. Red Cross didn't notify me when she was born, but I did receive a furlough.

From Yuma and the desert maneuvers, two other fellows received a furlough along with me. One had an automobile, so I hitched a ride to San Antonio with them, there I caught a train to Little Rock and stayed four days then caught a train back to Yuma and joined my Company. The desert is so hot in the daytime one would nearly burn up and at night water would nearly freeze in the fire buckets. Every morning we'd be covered with sand.

While on maneuvers, one of the officers killed a calf and the whole outfit nearly got in trouble over it until the officers settled with the farmer for it. All we did was cook it. One time on the desert, there came a quick rain. A lot of our equipment was lost as it had been stored in a gully and the rain-washed it away. It only rained for 30 minutes, but the equipment was lost. Another time a group of us got the chance to go to Mexico on a day off and I purchased some silk hose that I sent home to my wife.

It was the last of March 1944, and we had finished our maneuvers in the desert. In fact, when I got back from furlough, my Company was loading up on a troop train. After boarding the train, which zigged and zagged all across the country and not knowing where we were going as no one was talking, or if they knew weren't telling. This I suppose was the reason the information to where we were headed would be leaked to either the Japs or Germans, maybe to both and the train would be sabotaged. (Editor Note: I know we stopped at Raton, CO for exercise. Snow was on the ground.) The train had many, many cars on it, in fact it was so long they had two engines pulling it. Eventually, we arrived at Fort Dix, NJ after 10 days on the train.

After arriving at Fort Dix and getting set up one of the first things we did was ride a miniature train out to the firing range. We were able to get into New York and only about 30 minutes by bus. I went in several times and on one trip I spent the night in a church, with beds in a large room, like a barracks, sort of. We spent the night free of charge. I had the chance to go to Temple, NJ shopping and found a few things for the baby. The next time I was in NY, on 42nd Street and Times Square, there was this huge building lined with telephones, hundreds of phones, I called my wife (Mattie) and I told her I had found a baby buggy for Sandra (our daughter). She asked me where and I said Temple and at that moment I was cut off and never got back to her. Our letters home were censored and any name or location was deleted, especially after we arrived overseas.

While we were at Fort Dix, I was selected to go to North Carolina to train on the 50 Caliber Machine Gun. It was a small camp right on the coast and we shot out over the water where the targets were being pulled by airplanes, the target looked like a bed sheet. After arriving at Dix, I was given a three day pass, I tried to talk the Sgt. into going home, but was turned down as it was good for no more than 100 miles from Camp. We didn't know when we were to be shipped out to Camp Kilmer, before going overseas. So many troops were there and the dining hall was the biggest I had ever seen. I did nothing but steam pork chops and must have seen hundreds of loins. No more passes. It was now time to ship out and on 28 June 1944, we boarded the Queen Mary.

The entire 80th Infantry Division of 15,000 plus Soldiers, 1500 Nurses and 1500 Aviators were on the boat. Of course all the personnel operating the Queen were British and that meant kidney stew, and beans that rattled like rocks in our mess kits. The tables had a 6-inch rim around the edge. The Queen changed course every five to seven minutes to avoid the subs that were looking for her to be able to lay a line and fire on it before she changed course. Most of our troops along with some of the British sailors got seasick. The stateroom I was in normally was for two people, but had been equipped to have 12 bunks, 3 rows, and four high. The first night out, I slept on deck wrapped in a blanket, as I was seasick. I think I must have stayed on deck until we landed in Scotland a week later. Once or twice I thought I would die I was that sick.

We landed at the Firth of Clyde 7th of July 1944 and marched off the Queen with bagpipes playing. We were loaded aboard a train and headed for England, where we were to receive additional training before going into battle. The days were very long, ending about midnight, it seemed it would never get dark. After we had been there about a month, we boarded a truck for

Southampton and all along the way you could see buildings that had been bombed and the ground all torn up where bombs had been dropped. Arriving in the company camping area, we found there was no running water and we had what was called Honey-buckets for commodes. Every morning a horse drawn wagon came and installed a fresh bucket and hauled away the full one. Here we waited for the ships and boats that were to take us across the Channel. We were there for close to 24 hours before we were all loaded and spent the night before leaving for France. Upon reaching the beachhead in France, we went overboard and down a rope ladder into LSTs, which took us close to the shore where they let down the ramp in shallow water and we waded ashore. There were guides on shore to warn us to stay within the ribbons, as there were mines in the area, yet to be cleared. If you had to relieve yourself, a guide was there to show you where to go. Trucks were awaiting us in an open field about 2 miles away and we did double time to the trucks.

The huge field was filled with trucks, jeeps and other vehicles, looking up we saw three planes, German heading toward our group and were strafing as they dove on the trucks, etc., officers were yelling for us to take cover, I along with several others, dove under a truck. Fortunately the truck was not hit, but some of them were. The planes circled for another run and again the officers were yelling for us to get away from the trucks, and to take cover. I headed way down in a potato row with my nose buried in the dirt.

After this attack by the German planes, we found several of our trucks were on fire, and as we were attempting to reboard the trucks, here they came again for another strafing run. One of the men from New York City, saw the plane circle and coming toward us he jumped out of the truck onto the trailer hitch and I had to pull him back into the truck. The AA guns in our convoy knocked one of the planes down.

As we were heading to Avranches, France we had our first casualty, a big sort of a fellow, who was hit and he started to cry and afterward he was sent back to the aid station. Being in the kitchen, my crew and I stayed with the trucks and supplies. We were behind the front line of firing, but yet close enough as was possible, as we had to feed the troops, which we did after dark. We fought through several small towns from Le Mans, and crossed several rivers and then the Moselle River.

Crossing the Moselle River on a pontoon bridge, we were faced for a battle for Pont a Mousson and Mousson Hill, which was a very high hill over Pont a Mousson, and an observation point for the enemy, who was directing the artillery on our positions.

Continuing the fight across France, finding bunkers that had to be taken, the Maginot Line where we found this line turned toward Germany and was not too much help to the enemy, and racing on until we reached Saint Avold, where we surrounded the town.

On one motor movement we were to cross the river of which I have forgotten its name, the bridge had been wiped out and we were to cross on a pontoon bridge. When we arrived at the bridge the guard on duty who was to direct us to the right location, got cold and left his post to get warm, this was after dark and upon locating what we thought to be the right bridge, started onto the bridge but we stopped for some unknown reason and upon investigation we found the bridge was bombed out. We had stopped about a jeep length from where the bridge ended. This then meant, we had to back off the bridge with the trailers. Upon getting off the bridge and a search party sent out to find the right bridge. Thinking back, what would have happened had we not stopped for some unknown reason?

As we moved from town to town in France someone would always have to go forward to locate a place for the kitchen. It became my duty to do so and it was also in one of these little French towns we lost our first cook Benton Kelly. Kelly along with several others was killed when German planes dropped phosphorous bombs on our kitchen. Even though the bomb had hit us, we still had to prepare the meal for the men, I was glad to be alive and cook this meal.

Within two hours of unloading at Saint Avold, we received new orders for us to pack up the trucks and be ready to move within two hours, due to a break though in the north. General Patton had volunteered the 80th Division along with the 35th Infantry and the 4th Armored Division to help relieve the endangered troops in the north. Moving out we traveled in the darkness with headlights on bright. We traveled close to 150 miles and the 80th was in the lines fighting the next morning in Luxembourg. This move was very cold, we were crowded and bunched up in the truck, and huddling in blankets and anything else to try to stay warm. There were no pee stops, so if you had to go, it was, do it over the side, but at the rear of the truck. Upon arrival we found the snow to be close to a foot deep. We used a bulldozer in front of us to park our truck. We set up 1/2 tents to protect the field ranges. Emergency rations were mostly all the men received, and whenever we took food to the men we tried to include fresh socks. To find the men who were in foxholes, we had to kick the snow off the top of the fox hole and part the branches to give their rations, all the while dodging the shells and bullets. There was time when I was lost for three days in the woods, where my jeep was I didn't know. Fagan picked me up after finding me wandering along with other survivors.

The 317th Infantry was awarded the Presidential Unit Citation in the Battle of the Budge. We were in four major battles, I remember hiding behind walls of bombed building in Luxembourg. Behind one of these walls our Battalion Commander a Lt. Col. was leaning against a wall, he had these red spots from head to toe and as I passed him he fell over dead. Flack had got him.

After the Battle of the Bulge we fought through several towns heading to the southern part of Germany, heading for the Rhine River. In crossing the Rhine at Manheim, we entered Germany by the way of a 1900-foot long pontoon bridge under a smoke screen. One way traffic of course, all going to Germany and heading for Wiesbaden. I was in the fifth jeep and after crossing the river we started north chasing the Germans at a fast clip. Bridges had been blown to slow our chase, we forded some river, at times due to the ground starting to thaw, we drove in mud and at times due to this we had to stop and wait for others who were having trouble. It was at these stops the Germans would come out with hands over head and surrender. One walked up behind me and called "Comrade, Comrade". Not knowing if he was alone or maybe a company, I pulled my 45 and passed the word up the column that someone wanted to surrender. A Lt. and Sgt. came back along the line and took the prisoner from me, after they had left, I discovered I had no ammo in my pistol.

We fought our way through several towns, Weimar, Jena, Gera and then was stopped as the word had reached Patton the Russians would be taking the towns we were headed for. We then turned around and headed south to Bamburg, Nurnberg, Regensburg and into Braunau, Austria. War's end 8 May 1945 found us in Liezen, Austria.

At the war's end the German 6th Army commander wanted to surrender his 6th Army to General McBride. He was told all the troops that could get across the Inns River by midnight could be taken prisoner by the Americans, however those who weren't across by midnight would have to surrender to the Russians. With all these POWs pulling guard duty, on all the German prisoners was all we did. I got a three-day pass to go to Paris, and when it came time to go back, I couldn't get a ride back to the company, so I stayed another three days in Paris.

Finally my time came to come home. Leaving the company and going to the Repo Depot we were processed and sent to Marseilles, France, where I boarded a brand new troop transport the SS Breckenridge for the good old USA. Upon arriving at Newport News, VA I was then transported to Saint Louis, MO where I was discharged, given my medals and sent home to Little Rock AR and home.

Dale Anderson
Company E, 317th Infantry Regiment
Tells of Being Taken POW

My Company E, along with the other companies of the 317th Infantry Regiment had taken the northern part of the city of Erfurt and camped overnight. The following day, we captured the town of Jena, which is just east of Erfurt. It was nearing nightfall when the town was secured. My Company E had a section on the east side of Jena, which we were supposed to hold. Outposts were established and my hours were from 0130 to 0330, with a fine fellow infantryman from Chicago. The date was 10 April 1945. Since my squad had a large building to stay in, 14 of us were located there with 2 on guard at the outpost and 2 stationed on guard around the 2 story building with a large courtyard outside of 2 gates.

During my 0130-0330 duty at the outpost, we heard a lot of mechanized vehicles moving about in the distance. We reported this to our squad leader, Sgt. Joe Harlan, who passed it along to our platoon Sgt. and leader. At 0330 my fellow guard went back to bring in our 2 reliefs. It seemed like hours before he arrived, since I was scared being alone. I knew something was going on out there. When our reliefs arrived for their 0330-0530 duty, we both got back to the building for our 0330-0530 guard duty around the building. I don't know the other fellow's name, only that he was from Chicago. After being relieved at 0530, we both hit the sack, being tired, there was no problem getting to sleep. Just before daybreak, everything broke loose. German mortars came flying into the courtyard, blowing out the windows, shades and curtains. This fellow from Texas was in the same room as I was. He jumped up saying, "What shall we do?" I told him to put on his boots and start shooting. The mortar was tearing the roof off and I knew now we had it. We immediately looked out the windows and saw Germans everywhere. I stuck my BAR out the window to use it on the Germans who had their backs to me, and shouting at other GIs. They were about 100 feet away, but my BAR jammed. While I was trying to free it up, a German tank came in between us and started firing. A 30-caliber machine gun was on the windowsill and was knocked to the floor when the fire hit it from the gun. He pumped several hundred rounds at us, but since there was a knoll which was high enough that he couldn't lower his aim. With 5 of us upstairs and nine downstairs, he didn't hit any of us. Only the GI from Chicago got a lot of fragments on his face and eyes. What really saved us was this high knoll, and being flat on the floor we missed the lead. We couldn't move, so we waited. We then heard a GI outside yell at us with his arms raised. "Get rid of all your German souvenirs and get your hands up, come out. They have a tank with an 88 which they will use to blow the building down."

We immediately checked ourselves out for any enemy equipment and filed out single file with hands up. As we left the courtyard, a German SS grabbed me and pointed his Luger at my head and said something in German. I guess we all knew what he meant. I emptied my pockets of K rations, wallet, and flashlight and watch. He didn't want the watch, as it was a cheapie. He wanted us to tear down the fence and use it as a stretcher, which we would need to carry the wounded Germans about a mile back from the front line. There they treated the wounded, along with the GI from Chicago who had an eye injury. We were taken to a German headquarters where we were held for most of the day.

At first I thought we were back in our lines as several of the German officers had pretty blond girls and American Jeeps. There were a lot of Nazi salutes but that ended quickly. A P-51 fighter was flying close overhead and they got scared from maybe a strafing. All the officers took off with the blondes and jeeps, they wasted no time in doing that. A large truck was brought in where they wanted to load 2 large drums of gasoline on first. Since our squad leader, Sgt. Joe Harlan, didn't quite understand, a guard walked around to his back and kicked him hard in the seat. He caught on real quick. We loaded the drums and off we went with 2 guards in the rear of the truck with us. After several miles I noticed signs to Leipzig. All of a sudden shells started bursting all around us. The driver made a hairpin turn and nearly rolled the truck. After we made the turn, I noticed our tank in the distance, with a big white star. Where we were going, I did not know. We stopped near a small town and were lined up against the wall in a sitting positions where we waited for hours, watching the German Army moving east, with thousands of slave labor in stripe uniforms go by. Some couldn't walk, but the German boot prompted them on. We were told to fall in with the rest of the people moving east.

Since one of our GIs was a Greek, he could understand German. The guards would talk to him, and he would relay the message to us. Before we started we were told if anyone would escape, the rest of us would be shot. We all agreed to stay together. It started to get dark and it was then that we had our first bite to eat in nearly 36 hours. Fourteen potatoes were given to us. We shared this with the 14 of us. We marched all night and at daybreak, we marched through a town where the German civilian population would spit on us and say things in German. Only the Greek guy knew what they said. Later we found out what they said. The Greek American GI told us the civilian population thought we were the Air Corp and wanted the SS to take us down in the cellar and shoot all 14 of us. Without the guards, I now believe the civilians would have done us in.

At nightfall, we were led into a large building. Being we didn't know what was there, we held hands tightly as maybe there were holes in the floor and we would fall through. In the total darkness we probed around and found other people there. Everyone was to himself. I found a bunk and crawled in to get some sleep.

Early the next morning, we found we were in a large jail. One DP was up trying to build a fire and cook some potato skins. We didn't let him start a fire.

Shortly afterward the door flew open and a guard gave us a chunk of black bread and a bucket of water to divide among us. Later in the day, the door flew open again. We were all rushed out along with the DPs, or whatever they were, and marched to the mountains nearby. We were in separate groups. They lined us up in a line, and a firing squad was formed. It didn't take us long to figure this was the end of the line. The German SS were ready with rifles in position. They started arguing among themselves. We didn't know what it was all about. They marched us back to the jail and the DPs didn't return with us. From what I could observe, they shot them. The next morning, we noticed no guards, and we decided to make a break for freedom. We tore the door of the jail down, and ran like rabbits across the field, expecting any moment machine gun fire. In the woods we hid and spent the day. Later several tanks came nearby, and we noticed the big white star. We had been liberated, and stayed with this tank force for a couple of days. Later we were sent to our own outfit to find a lot of our fellow GIs hadn't made it.

I should mention that only two infantrymen that I can remember that were captured, along with me were Sgt. Joe Harlan, my squad leader from Arkansas and my assistant BAR man, Gene Manley from Maine.

Thomas R. McMillen
318th Infantry Regiment C.I.C.

When I arrived in the vicinity of the 80th Division Headquarters, they were on maneuvers around Lynchburg, TN. Needing to know where to find them and also wanting a few cigars I went into a Drug Store to see if they could tell me where I would find the headquarters. What should happen while I'm in the drug store but for General McBride to walk in? He asked me what I was doing in the drug store when the troops of the 80th were doing maneuvers and troops were not allowed in any civilian habitation. Telling him I was looking for the headquarters of the 80th, he said to me I am fining you $40.00 under the 104th Article of War; and told me where to report. I had bought five cigars by that time and took them to my assigned area, passing out all but one to my fellow soldiers as "the most expensive cigars I had ever had." After the first meeting I became an admirer of this good and brave man who commanded the 80th throughout the war.

It was not long after arriving at Camp Forrest and being reviewed there by President Roosevelt in his open limo when our division was assigned to the California-Arizona maneuver area. Since I had an automobile and could get gasoline, I invited my mother to go west with me and she rode as far as Phoenix, Arizona where she dropped off to visit one of her cousins. I went on to the maneuver area and enjoyed life on the desert, which, however, turned out very cold and wet. In fact, our clothing never did dry out the six or eight weeks we spent in the area, but we learned quite a bit about desert warfare by engaging in maneuvers against General Terry Allen and his 1st Division which had been pretty well beaten up by Rommel's forces in Egypt.

I had the only private auto in the 80th Division Headquarters and would take 5-6 GIs to various towns as far away as California. We would put one guy on the shelf behind the seat and 3-4 in the trunk and take off for various spots for the evening dinner. I remember one outing from Fort Benning, Georgia to Atlanta where we could only find one hotel room for 6 GIs.

After a cold and wet winter on the desert, our division was sent to Fort Dix for shipment overseas because we were then presumably completely trained for combat. I sold my car to an Air Force Lt. for more than I paid for it. We went by train, probably several trains, with all of our trucks and artillery, and stayed at Fort Dix to wait for shipment overseas. There I met a blind date named Nancy Ford (married her in 1945, in Cleveland) whose sister was married to a friend of mine in the 80th Division Headquarters named Hank Todd. From Fort Dix we went to Scotland on the Queen Mary and then overnight by train and eventually trucks to a larger estate named Pettipool. To move an entire Division and its equipment from the West Coast and then to England was quite a job, but it was facilitated by wartime priorities after Pearl Harbor. Pettipool was a rather pleasant country estate, not far from Liverpool, a major city in England, but having been "fully trained", there was not much for us to do except entertain the local girls who flocked around our bivouac areas. We did go into Liverpool to hear a combo.

Then one day we heard that the invasion of Europe was to begin, and we were sent to bivouac near the White Cliffs of Dover. There we rested for a few weeks and eventually got on a landing craft, which carried several vehicles and at least a platoon of infantrymen to what was known as Omaha Beach. We were unloaded on the beach, not knowing whether we were in combat but finding that the U.S. troops had moved inland into Normandy and we were being slowed down by the hedgerows to which our tanks and troops were unaccustomed.

I remember our first night in Normandy en route to our campsite under blackout conditions with antiaircraft shells bursting overhead along with quite a bit of artillery fire in the distance. We could not use headlights and my driver, Sgt. Raymond, could not see well enough in the dark to drive so I took over and our contingent eventually ended in an open area and pitched our tents in the dark. The whole procedure was rather scary, but actually all of the hard work was being done by the divisions, which had arrived in Normandy before us. Thinking back on it, it is amazing that our landing in France went rather smoothly.

Our first combat was against the German 7th Army at what was known as the Falaise Pocket in Normandy near Argentan, France. We surrounded and defeated the Germans, and thereby opened up a good bit of France without much enemy opposition between there and the Moselle River.

At the Falaise Pocket our artillery moved in 155 mm cannons to fire artillery shells into the middle of the forest. I learned this by waking up in the morning and finding one of the "Long Toms" pointed over my tent which apparently had been from there most of the night. Later that day after the German 7th Army had retreated, we went down into the valley where the woods were located and found a terrible mess of war materials, dead horses and complete chaos which had been vacated by the German Army. When I learned that the German Army had fled, I went around the Falaise Pocket looking for enemy documents and encountered some British soldiers in a jeep coming from the other side. I guess we were the first ones to go around this Pocket. At that time we were attached to the British 1st Army under General Montgomery because General Patton was in Scotland somewhere to decoy the Germans.

From the Falaise Pocket, we advanced through France until we reached the Moselle River. Our main deterrent was the French First Army, which had to stop at each little town and celebrate. General Patton ran out of gasoline because his supply lines could not keep up with us. We spent the winter on the west bank of the Moselle River above Dieulouard, France. I was the first American to enter Dieulouard. Trees felled by the Germans had blocked the road, and General McBride thought the town was inaccessible. Soon thereafter a couple of my agents spent most of the winter in a small inn there, but the rest of us spent the night in sleeping bags. The only enemy contact was a dumb German who did not know the password and was shot and killed not too far from my tent. I did not know about this until the next morning.

One of our missions in the Counter Intelligence Corps was to locate and search German Headquarters, which had been vacated to see if we could find any maps or other intelligence materials. We were supposed to get into these headquarters as soon as possible after they had been vacated. I remember going up to one our battalion headquarters and on the way back in the evening I saw tracer bullets from a German machine gun flying over my head. Naturally, I kept the jeep going as fast as I could, and reported this event to headquarters, and not too long thereafter one of our officers was ambushed and killed, apparently on the same road on which I had used to return from the battalion headquarters. As usual, the Germans left no documents behind for us to find.

I did obtain a very good map from a French forester, which I gave to our artillery commander. The general said that the map was probably worth a couple artillery divisions because it was so much better than any we had. I had promised to give it back to the forester after we had left the area and I did so, actually a month or so after we had crossed the river. He seemed to be surprised that I returned it.

After we crossed the Moselle, I went into a suburb of the city of Nancy named Jarville to the house where I had stayed with the Karcher family in 1937. They had fled to southern part of France when the German troops had come in, but I got their address from one of the local residents of Jarville and wrote them a letter with my APO number on it. Surprisingly enough, I received a letter from M. Karcher a month or so after I had written to him, and several years later he and Mme. Karcher came to the United States and Winnetka on their 50th Wedding Anniversary trip. Their son, Fernand has been here two or three more times and has retired as an apparently wealthy vinegar merchant. He and his wife Madeline take one or two overseas trips a year, usually with the French company known as Club Med., and we met them once in Grindelwald, Switzerland.

The next event, which I recall, was when the 80th Division took the town of St. Avold, France. It took us two or three days of blockading the town before the Germans finally pulled out. About that time one of my agents picked up an Alsatian line crosser with a radio transmitter. We ask him what his mission was and he said that he was to report back to the Germans about the effect of the seven bombs, which they left behind in St. Avold. We of course did not know of these but instituted a search and found most of them. One exploded that night in an anti-aircraft battalion quarters and killed almost all the men in it, probably because they had not been told by our division about these time bombs. Another one went off in a building, which we were going to occupy the next day as our C.I.C. headquarters. When we went back to the house, there was nothing there except a pile of wood and debris in the basement where the house had been.

However, nobody in our division suffered any casualties from these bombs, although a few caught cold by moving up to the caves with the locals. The agent whom we had arrested was sent back to the 3rd Army Headquarters where we understood that he became a "double agent." In other words, he would send messages on his radio to the Germans as though he were still a Nazi, but the messages actually originated in one of our intelligence headquarters. I do not know whether he got any messages of value back.

A couple of incidents occurred to me as happening after we left St. Avold in Germany. One was my "capture" of a hand full of German soldiers with a lighted match. We were up in some small German town, and I was searching a house, which I thought might be a deserted German headquarters. I went down into the basement without a flashlight and was groping around by lighting matches to see if I could find any papers or other worthwhile items when one of the matches shown up the faces of German soldiers huddled in the back of the basement. I was alone and pretty well frightened and ran out of the basement into the area where troops were standing. One of my friends who was an Infantry Officer shouted to the men to come out, which they did. We searched them and found very little of value, but I confiscated a handgun from one of the soldiers. I later gave this gun to a friend of mine who said he had no chance to get revolvers or hand guns in the rear echelon where he was stationed. This was the only weapon I personally captured and rather reluctantly gave it to him, although in fact I could get German handguns quite easily when they were discarded or collected by our troops.

For example, I got two very nice German 12-gauge shotguns from a stack of weapons, which the local citizens had been ordered to be deposited in the Town Square. These were brought back home for me by my father who visited the troops after the war in Europe was over, when he made the mistake of asking if there was anything he could bring back for me. I still have these guns and use one of them regularly for hunting dove and pheasants. It is a 1928 FN (Belgian) manufacturer and quite a good shotgun. The other gun is hanging on the wall in our house at the farm and is unusual because it has a third chamber and barrel for a rifle shell about the size of a .30 caliber.

Another incident was when Sgt. Raymond and I decided to go up to a "liberated" town on the other side of a small river and see if we could find a German Headquarters. The Germans had supposedly vacated this town, but actually on the way there we passed a number of our infantrymen in foxholes that were not too happy to see us driving around and drawing German fire. Actually, when we approached the river we did get fired upon by the German 88 artillery piece which came close enough to throw up pieces of debris at us, so Raymond and I did not cross the river and fled back to safer areas. It was not particularly pleasant to have a German 88 shooting at us from about a half mile away, and I can see why the GIs were not too happy with this particular trip which we had made.

Another amusing incident had occurred in Northern France or Belgium. We had a call from headquarters to come up and act as an interpreter for some unidentified enemy troops whom our GIs had locked up in a barn. I sent Klimek up to see who the people were, because the GIs thought they were German. Actually they were Walloonese. They were harmless French or Belgium citizens, and they were so gratified to be released by Klimek that they gave him a live goose. He took it back, gave it to Gen. McBride and they enjoyed a goose dinner cooked by his Chinese chef. At Weimar, the former capital of Germany we overran a factory, which was making 35 mm Leica cameras and also some very good field glasses. My German agents picked up a couple of Leicas which they said had been assembled for them after the city had fallen into American hands, but they did not get any for the rest of their friends in the C.I.C. I did get a binocular which I later gave to the brigadier general who was at that time commanding our artillery battalion. The binoculars were probably better than any we could manufacture in the United States, as were the cameras, but they were too large to be of any value except in the field with troops.

Looting of German homes or possessions was a serious offense according to the Articles of War, but as a practical matter the provision was very seldom invoked against American soldiers. I did defend one or two looting cases successfully, but never took any loot myself and never found any of our C.I.C. men who actually took anything from the Germans. One of my special agents, Motel, did take possession of a Mercedes German touring sedan, which he locked up in a garage. I asked him why he did this, and he said he was going to return after the war and retrieve the automobile. I myself had liberated a German sedan, which I took with me when I was transferred to head up the XII Corps C.I.C. I was then stationed in Marienbad, Czechoslovakia and soon sent back to the states, so I gave this car to one of the Red Cross girls from St. Louis whom I had met named Franny Rayburn. Several years later she showed up in Winnetka to say hello. We had so many civilian cars in our division, all painted with the drab green of a military vehicle, that Gen. McBride finally prohibited the acquisition of any additional civilian vehicles.

At the Western edge of Alsace Lorraine we came up against the Siegfried Line that the Germans had constructed facing the Maginot Line. We were about to attempt to breach the southern end of this fortification which ran almost the entire length of the western boundary of Germany when we were ordered to go to Luxembourg, on 19 December 1944. We traveled by jeep almost continuously for about 36 hours under black out conditions and entered Luxembourg shortly after. There we penetrated the southern edge of the German Special Forces, which had overrun our divisions in Northern France and Belgium. I learned the value of air power because several days of overcast grounded our planes. When the skies opened up we had great support from our fighters and bombers and stopped the German "bulge."

When our 318th regiment relieved the road center of Bastogne, it had been occupied by the 101st Airborne Division, which had come in overland but had then been surrounded by the Germans. That conquest just about ended the Battle of the Bulge, and we then turned east again and crossed the Rhine River at Wiesbaden. This city was accessible by a pontoon bridge, which had been built under gunfire by engineers of the United States Army. That city became the first place where we were able to obtain civilian housing and electrical systems. Wiesbaden had not been involved in any serious bombing or fighting, but as we left there we did encounter several cities which had been heavily bombed by the American and British air forces—Kassel, Nuremberg, Weimar, etc. The Division made a map of our route for the entire war, which I have framed and is better than my memory.

We crossed all the way through Germany, ending almost at Chemnitz, which was then near the German border with Russia. As a matter of fact, the Germans were running away from the Russian troops and surrendering to us in such numbers that we could do nothing but send them back to our rear echelons in the interior of Germany.

At that time, Roosevelt, Churchill and Stalin made an agreement at a meeting in Yalta to divide Germany and Berlin into three sectors, and we had to pull back from Chemnitz all the way to the Rhine and south into Bavaria in order to accommodate the Yalta agreement. Very frustrating and hard on the Germans who traded our occupation for Russian.

By that time the German Army was pretty much in disarray. I recall as we went southerly from town to town, our German speaking agents would telephone ahead to the next town to find out if the German troops were still there. We really had some serious opposition going south into Bavaria and the war ended when we were somewhere around Vocklabruck. We sent a truck with a loud speaker on it to tell the local residents that the war in Europe was kaput.

When we ceased the invasion of Bavaria, headquarters asked us to send a Hungarian speaking agent down to the border to help with the surrender of the Hungarian Army. Sgt. DeHuzar, who had worked for Dovemuhl and Ted Buenger in Chicago, went down and encountered the remnants of the Hungarian Army, headed by a General and in possession of the Hungarian treasury of gold. The general had with him also an attractive young lady, which apparently was common practice among the European generals. DeHuzar took their surrender and turned the gold over to the 3rd Army.

In the same area, one of our agents participated in the discovery of many works of art in a salt mine, which apparently had been collected to be turned over to Goering after the war. Craig Smythe, a classmate from Hotchkiss and Princeton, was one of the principal officers in charge of restoring these works of art to their proper places, either museums or personal owners, but he actually did not come to the salt mine or the area where we were stationed. He said he knew a Lt. Foley who was from the 80th Division, but I was never able to ascertain it was anyone that I knew. In fact, I did not know Craig Smythe's participation with the liberated artwork until I discussed this with him at my 60th reunion at Hotchkiss.

From Mariebad, I was sent back to the United States due to my accumulation of "points" based upon the length of service. We traveled in 40 and 8 boxcars for three days, all the way across France to Le Havre where we boarded the Queen Mary once again and returned to Camp Kilmer in New Jersey. From there I went to Washington where my father and mother were living, reunited with Nancy Ford, went to the Army-Navy football game and eventually visited her family in Cleveland where we became engaged to be married.

In retrospect, it seems to be a waste of manpower and money to try to settle disputes by major wars, or even smaller ones. All the events which I have written about here involved chaotic and dangerous times which accomplished little of lasting benefits to other nations, although my own military experience was of great value to me once I had lived through it. As I write, both of the candidates for president of the United States are campaigning on improving our military strength, for what purpose? T.R. M 10/15/2000

Bill Petrollini
Company I, 317th Infantry Regiment

St. Julien, France, 3 September 1944. As Platoon Sgt. of Company I, 317th Infantry, my platoon was chosen for the point in an attack. I had placed two scouts out in front, with the 2nd scout back about one hundred feet, I was following with the rest of the platoon following about one hundred feet behind the 2nd scout.

We had been pursuing the Germans all day and well into the night, without any food and an occasional ten minute break. The enemy had dug in on the west bank of the Moselle River and was waiting for us. They let the first scout go by, but then wounded the 2nd scout. Time was 0500 and we had been pinned down with our Company Commander by heavy machine gun and rifle fire.

I was laying on my back watching machine gun tracer bullets zing by approximately two feet over my head, I rolled across the road to the other side, which was about five feet lower than the side I came from. Crawling forward I saw two armored vehicles with one looking like a half-track.

I called for my bazooka team, and while waiting for them, I spotted a plum tree nearby and I proceeded to eat a few, I was starved. The plums were only half-ripe, but me being hungry I ate them anyway.

When my bazooka team came forward we got off a shot, hitting the half-track. That gave our position away, and we were then under more intense fire than before, they really laid in on us. The first mortar shell they fired landed right on target wounding me and four other members of my platoon. I yelled for everyone to get out of the area and to scatter. Later I learned there was an observer hidden in a monument halfway up the hill, and he had watched our every move.

I was patched up my the platoon medic and I worked my way back and reported to Captain Carlson our company commander, what we had encountered. He told me to go down the road and wait for an ambulance to pick me up. After a while when no ambulance came along, I spotted a bike abandoned by a German, and I went flying down the hill on that bike. After pedaling for a while I heard a vehicle behind me and thinking it may be German, I jumped off the bike while it was still moving and into a ditch.

Looking up from the ditch I saw it was one our jeeps going back for ammo. I jumped into the middle of the road and flagged him down. He would not stop, but he yelled for me to jump on the trailer. I ran alongside of the trailer and gave a flying leap and landed on the rear end of the trailer. I nearly missed.

He dropped me off at the Battalion Aid Station, and from there I was sent to a Field Hospital and continued on to a General Hospital on the English Channel. When I told my company about my experience they had a very big laugh about it, but to me it wasn't that funny.

James Swindell
Joins the 80th

I joined the 80th Infantry Division and Company K 317th Infantry, somewhere around Bastogne in January 1945, and continued with them as a scout until the deactivation in 1946. However, I did not get to come home. At 18 years of age, I did not have enough points. I had no family and only twelve weeks of training. I have often given it thought as to the men who were left over there. I was one of the oldest, but not in age, but time in combat of the men in my company. But, still I had to stay. My wartime with the 80th was the Ardennes, and Rhineland battles.

I remember the day I left, it was very emotional. My buddies lined up to say goodbye to me all through the tent that housed us on out to the truck that was to take me away.

The war was not over for me, as about 3-4 hours of riding we were stopped at American roadblock and checkpoint. I was there for approximately 24 hours. I don't know the location or the name of the outfit. Just beyond this American checkpoint was the Russian checkpoint. Approximately 1800-2000 the Russians decided to have a war of their own and started firing on our group. The first volley of rifle fire, killed the Sergeant in charge of our group, and wounded another. Taking cover we returned the fire, I think they may have been drunk on Vodka and got a little careless. When morning came it seemed that only five of the Russians were alive in their camp.

When morning came and replacements were sent and they found what had happened, I was put in a jeep and was sent back to Headquarters and told to report to a Captain whose name escapes my memory. On the way back reality set in and the thought that we had killed our own allies, and there may be a Court Martial, and a possibility of my going to jail, thinking I'll never get home. After reporting to the Captain he got up from his desk, came around to the front facing me, he handed me a carton of cigarettes and some papers, at the same time telling me to get my gear and be in front of the building in ten minutes. Not one word was said about what had happened at the checkpoint.

I was sent by jeep to Nurnberg, Germany arriving at 1000 hours. I was given a new uniform, along with boots, white helmet, a rifle, an MP Arm Band, and was taken to a large fenced in brick house. I was told that Supreme Court Justice Robert Jackson lived there, and I was not to let anyone in but him. Mr. Jackson was our U.S. Representative to the War Crimes Trial.

Later around 1800 hours, a big black car came down the road toward me and turned into the driveway. He didn't stop to be identified, and I made a split second decision to fire two shots over the top of the car, instead into it, and perhaps killing who ever may be in the car. The driver slammed on the brakes, throwing Mr. Jackson on the floor. The driver was begging for his life, and please don't shoot Mr. Jackson, it is my fault.

Asking the driver for some ID, he handed me both his and Mr. Jackson's ID, with this I told them to pass on. As they moved on Mr. Jackson had rolled down his window and as they moved past me he shook my hand and said, "I wish to commend you Son, you did the right thing.

The unit I was with at this time was the Big Red One, the 1st Infantry Division. I learned we had a German prisoner that could speak English, and having a German Light Meter, I ask him to translate the instruction on how to use the meter. I paid him with American cigarettes. His name I shall never forget was Wernher von Braun.

He never stood trial and was given amnesty and came to the USA to live and later headed up our space program. I was still at Nurnberg when General Patton died and was sent to Luxembourg to be part of the Honor Guard at his funeral. My post was approximately 25 feet from the Grave Site.

I returned to the USA on my 20th birthday, 6/26/46. Looking much older and very tired, than before I left from home.

Harry A. Wolfe
Company G, 318th Infantry Regiment
Misses the Hot Chow

One day, perhaps on or about 1 November 1944, near towns of Nomeny and Rouves, France, we were having noontime hot chow for a welcome change, which consisted of hot "C" rations rather than the usual cold ones. Hot chow was served from a large garbage can which did not add to its appeal. I had just filled my mess kit and was seeking a place to sit when sounds of approaching planes were heard. Two fighter planes, in the lead was a German being chased by an American. They came roaring through at a low level. Just as they were passing over, one of them released a small bomb. Of course, everyone scattered for safety under or behind whatever would provide protection. I chose to dive under an old farm wagon. In the panic of the moment, I spilled all of the contents of my mess kit. After a few calming moments of swearing and sweating, I recovered enough composure to return to the chow line for a refill. About the time I got near enough to get my refill, the garbage can was empty, so back to another period of cold rations. I'm sure the swearing and cursing of the war and all participants continued for quite a long time. It was just another episode of disappointment and bitterness, which we all endured many times.

Harry A. Wolfe — G Company, 318th Infantry Regiment, 80th Division.

Norman Brunner
Company B, 318th Infantry Regiment
One Lucky Man
Submitted by Granddaughter Joyce Miller

Dear Dad,

You wanted to know how it was the hun got close enough to get my razor and not me. Well you asked for it. Here it is. A long time ago at Argentan I led the platoon onto the field. It was a trap. We were sky lined. They surrounded us on three sides with tanks and MGs and opened up. I hit the ground and crawled 10 yds. in the furrow of a potato field. How I love that plant now. I shot a Machine Gunner and hit the dirt. They opened everything on me but the good old potato hill was there. Thank God!

They held me there with small arms fire for 3 hrs. My pack was showing above the plant. They are afraid of the M-1 so didn't get too close.

Then they began to search with 88s. That story about firing above man ain't any Bull so I decided to move.

I crawled within 30 yds of a hedgerow and found myself in the hands of 5 German privates. Well immediately I was relieved of all weapons and equipment. There went my razor. They missed a hand grenade in my belt. They motioned for me to empty my pockets. Then one of our machine guns started up some 100 yards away. That was my chance. I pulled the pin and dropped the grenade in their laps. They forgot me and hit the ground. That gave me about 4 seconds in which I hauled ass over that hedge fence head first and dropped in a ditch on the other side darn near breaking my neck. But that's what saved my hide. The grenade went off and I came out shooting an M-1 I got off a dead GI in the ditch. I don't know whether the 5 were dead or alive. Didn't stop to ask just tactfully withdrew but rapidly.

For Now

Love "Bud"

Harry Nutting
Company I, 317th Infantry Regiment
Hiding Under a Kitchen Cabinet for Four Days

I joined Company I, 317th Regiment, 80th Infantry Division during the last week of October 1944. With the exception of a few small firefights and holding actions, I hadn't seen a great deal of action until November 28, 1944 when we were ordered to attack the small village of Farbersviller, France. My experiences during the attack on Farbersviller remain to this day my most unforgettable memory of my time spent as an American Infantryman.

We entered the village in force about 1030 hours and succeeded in driving the Germans out of the village by dark. I was posted in a house on the outskirts of the village with three other men whom I did not know when the Germans counterattacked. The German counterattack was heavy and our position was in danger of being overrun. As the Germans attacked my position with hand grenades and small arms fire, I fired my BAR at the Germans wounding at least two. Looking around, I noticed that two of the men posted with me had already left the house. By then, the house was surrounded by the enemy who were throwing hand grenades through the doorway. One of the grenades killed the other American soldier and I was wounded in the left arm, side, and left leg by grenade shrapnel.

I then ran further into the house and hid under a sink in the entryway. Hiding under the sink was in itself no small feat considering the difficulty of trying to fit a 6'4" frame into such a small space. The Germans entered the house looking for Americans but did not find me. They were so close to me at times that I could have reached out with my hand and tripped them. After searching the house and coming to the conclusion that the dead GI was the only one in the house, the Germans left.

After spending most of the night there, I left my hiding spot and made my way to the basement of the house where I discovered several old French civilians who gave me some food. Not knowing exactly what to do or where to go, I decided to leave the building and try to make my way back to the American lines. This decision would ultimately get me in even more trouble.

I left the building and went across the back yard. At that point, I heard voices, which I thought, were that of my own comrades having a "bull" session. I ran into another building where the voices were coming from and much to my surprise discovered the voices belonged to about a dozen German soldiers, who had thoughtfully left their weapons stacked against a wall. I guess they were as surprised as I was for they didn't react for several moments, most likely thinking that I had a squad of men outside with me. I made a quick exit and ran down the street with bullets flying all around me. Thankfully, their aim was poor and by the time they came out onto the street, I had ducked into another house. I climbed down a ladder in the house to the stable area in the cellar. The Germans made a search of the house but never looked in the cellar where I was.

To my great surprise, I found another American GI also hiding in the cellar. I don't remember his name but I do recall that he was a cook transferred to the Infantry and that his home was on Long Island, NY.

167

After spending five days in hiding, and being hungry, we decided on the morning of December 3 to leave the village. We were able to find our way back to the American lines by listening for and following the sound of the artillery shells coming in.

After reporting to my outfit and Intelligence headquarters at St. Avold, I was sent to the hospital for treatment of my wounds and trench foot. Upon recovery from my wounds, I rejoined my outfit in February 1945. Later, 88 shell fragments fired from a German Tiger tank seriously wounded me. I was hospitalized in Luxembourg and England and eventually evacuated to the U.S. for further treatment. I was discharged from the hospital at Buzzard's Bay, MA in November 1945.

Because of the five days that I spent in the village of Farbersviller, I have been christened the "mayor" of Farbersviller by PNC E.E. Bredbenner. A report of my experiences in Farbersviller was sent to the present day Mayor, Laurent Kleinhentz. On January 5, 1995, I received a letter from Mayor Kleinhentz which read as follows:

"Owing to your outstanding acts of heroism during the battle of Farbersviller in December 1944, I and my town council would like to appoint you honorary mayor of Farbersviller." In addition to the letter and proclamation from Mayor Kleinhentz, Mayor Kleinhentz presented me the Gold Medal of Honor and the Gold Certificate of Honor for the liberation of Farbersviller at the 1995 80th Division reunion in Charlotte, NC.

C. Robert Harmon
Anti-tank, 319th Infantry Regiment
A Personal Story

I was drafted into the Army of the United States on 12 July 1943, and reported to Fort Lewis, Washington, for active duty on 2 August 1943. I was 18 years age and experiencing what most of the males in the high-school graduating class of 1943 found awaiting them as they received their diplomas, I estimate that 90% of my own local class was in uniform by autumn of 1943.

As with so many of us, I had considered various options for service. I am a "Puget Sounder" and grew up around the freight dock, which my father managed in the Port Town of Olympia, Washington. When I was 17, dad and I visited the recruiting offices for the U. S. Merchant Marine Academy and, at the same time, I spoke with an U.S. Marine Corps Recruiter in Seattle.

However, I entered the Army as one of several thousand men who had been accepted for engineering training in a program termed The Army Specialized Training Program. The ASTP, as it was called, had several goals. One was training professional Engineers in a thorough, accelerated course. Another was keeping Colleges and Universities alive during the wartime shortage of students. As with several other Government actions between 1941 and 1944, ASTP testified to the concern that World War Two could last a while, perhaps as much as five to eight years. Given the sweep of Japanese control from the north Pacific to Java and Burma, this was not an unreasonable estimate.

I went through a good basic Infantry training in a Regiment of ASTP men at Fort Benning, GA. (A location termed by its Cadre, but, not by us, as the "Paradise of the Infantryman"). The cadre was excellent and this was against their standards that I measured the Officers and NCOs I met in the 80th Division. I am happy to say that I felt almost all of the men under whom I served were excellent and that several were outstanding.

After Benning, I studied a general Engineering curriculum at (then) tiny Arkansas State College, in Jonesboro, AR. The faculty did their best and the local townspeople were superb in their hospitality to all of us. But, Math has always been a weakness for me and I fell behind the rapid pace of studies in Physics and Chemistry. When I realized what was happening (that is, that I was about to be busted out of school), I sent a personal letter to the Commandant of the jump school at Fort Benning, inviting him to avail himself of my services in the immediate future. Naive? Yes! Extremely! At the first Academic Board of Review I faced, "Army Channels" (of all communication) were brought to my astonished attention, and, shortly after, I and several other academic misfits found ourselves in the 80th Division in the Desert Training Grounds in AZ. So far as I know, by the way, all of the ASTP who went to the 80th survived the war. Lucky!

Certainly the assignment to the 80th and to the Antitank Company of the 319th Infantry Regiment was lucky for me. Just how lucky, I began to appreciate after watching rifle and heavy weapons folks in action during our four European Campaigns.

169

My squad, platoon, and company had some Eastern City men and a sprinkling of Mid-Westerners, but most of the troops were from eastern coal and steel towns and from the Blue Ridge area and they were, in general, a delight to know and to learn from. The Division was in the Desert during the winter of 1943 and that was a splendid introduction to the unit training and to the tracks of life in the field.

I came into the company on a Sunday evening, reported to the Charge-of-Quarters, was welcomed nicely, introduced to a young Lieutenant from Aberdeen, Washington, who did his best to make me feel welcome, and, finally, taken to see one of the most important men in any company, the Mess Sergeant, Sgt. Shepherd. It was long after suppertime, But Sgt. "Shep" personally saw to it that I was fed. And, that's my firm impression of the way in which he tried his best to serve us in action with the Third Army.

When one considers the rigors experienced by replacements that suffer through the "Repldepples" in the states and in Europe, one can understand how grateful I am for joining the 80th in the desert.

I was lucky to come to the 80th and lucky to come through. In the summer of '45, I was a clerk/typist in the Regimental Headquarters Company of the Antitank Company records. It is my impression that only seventeen men from the company (of whom I was one) went all the way from Normandy, through Lorraine, and the "Battle of the Bulge" and the Siegfried Line, the Rhine River crossing, Germany and Austria without getting WIA, or sick enough to be pulled off the line.

We lost one man because of Trench Foot and another because of Tuberculosis, and another one from Battle Fatigue. I could have been one of the latter: During the fight across the River Our, and into the West wall ("Siegfried Line") I told my Lieutenant (one of those steady Southerners, name Ellers) that I didn't want to go up front anymore. He just said, OK, and told me to get some sleep. Early the next morning, he said "its time to go." And, we went. Great psychology! Great Leadership! I had some hard moments after that, but never again thought about refusing duty. I'll always be grateful to Lt. Ellers for his smooth handling of my resignation from the Army!

The Antitank Company was broken up just before the "Bulge" and most of the men went to the line companies. My luck held, and I was one of the three 57mm gun crews assigned to guard Regimental Headquarters, and to run occasional patrols out in front of our lines, The patrols led to some interesting adventures, such as one day in central Germany where some of us captured some Hitler Youth in the morning and, then that afternoon, a warehouse containing about 90 German men in their late 30s and early 50s who had just been mustered into the "after women and children" defense forces of the Reich. I was one of the men "riding shotgun" for Colonel Costello, C.O. of the 319th Infantry Regiment, when he talked to the Garrison at the lovely old German City of Weimar into simply abandoning the place without a fight. We rolled into town, shortly before noon, and we met a grateful Burgermeister and a large group of appreciative citizens of the ancient center of German Culture.

Another fantastic experience was being assigned as one of about fifty men to guard (in May of '45) the ancient Salt Mines at Alt Aussee, Austria. We were up there for almost a month, pulling guard duty over almost 10,000 art objects, including 5,700 important paintings by such artists as Rembrandt; just being there was an education.

Finally my post-war life as a University Professor of History has taken me back to Europe from time to time and I have been fortunate to be in touch with Europeans who are extremely grateful to the Americans for liberating them from the German occupation and the despicable policies and practices of Nazism.

General Roland Mentre, French Air Force (Retired) was a fifteen year old boy (and, the oldest male left in the village) when we liberated Nomeny, in the Province of Lorraine, in the autumn of 1944. Fifty years later, he set up a reception at the Maire (City Hall) honoring America and the U.S. Army when I returned to Nomeny with some of my family in 1994. The people of Luxembourg have two special organizations devoted to the study of their Liberation in September of 1944, and, again in the "Battle of the Ardennes" in 1944-1945. They extend an extravagant, heartfelt welcome to any and all ex GIs who return for their commemorative ceremonies in June of each year. I have had Belgians and even Germans walk up to me when I was wearing my 80th Division Jacket, and thank me for their liberation. The city of Weimar celebrates its liberation around 12 April of each year and many 80th Veterans have attended and been impressed with the gratitude made so evident there.

It was a privilege for me, a very young Westerner, to serve with the 80th and to survive it all. I shall always remember the words of one of the 319th riflemen who had gone all the way through from Normandy:

"We were Lucky: There was a lot that didn't make it."

Casualty List Totals
August 3, 1944-May 8, 1945

Unit	KIA	DOW	DOI	SWA	SIA	LWA	LIA	CAP	MIA	OFF	EM
Dv Hq	1/0	0/0	0/0	2/0	0/0	0/0	0/0	0/0	0/0	3	0
Sp Trs	0/0	0/0	0/0	0/0	0/0	0/0	0/0	0/0	0/0	0	0
HQ	0/0	0/0	0/0	0/0	0/0	0/0	0/0	0/0	0/0	0	0
Hq Co	0/0	0/0	0/0	0/1	0/0	0/1	0/0	0/0	0/0	0	1
MP Plat	0/0	0/0	0/0	0/1	0/0	0/0	0/0	0/0	0/0	0	1
Ord Co	0/0	0/0	0/0	0/1	0/0	0/0	0/1	0/0	0/1	0	0
QM	1/2	0/0	0/0	0/2	0/0	0/3	0/1	0/0	0/1	1	8
Sig Co	1/1	0/0	0/0	0/0	0/0	0/0	0/1	0/0	0/0	1	3
Med Det	0/0	0/0	0/0	0/0	0/1	0/0	0/1	0/0	0/0	0	2
Band	0/0	0/0	0/0	0/0	0/0	0/0	0/0	0/0	0/0	0	0
317th Inf	44/1007	16/140	0/2	42/660	3/21	120/2579	47/1136	0/2	43/1845	312	7392
318th Inf	42/1067	6/117	0/0	60/1273	3/61	91/2079	8/580	0/15	30/873	238	6065
319th Inf	35/621	7/85	0/0	24/630	3/21	58/1745	8/300	0/0	13/447	148	3847
Hq Arty	1/1	0/0	0/0	0/1	0/1	0/0	0/0	0/0	0/0	1	4
Hq Btry	0/0	0/0	0/0	0/0	0/0	0/0	0/1	0/0	0/0	0	1
313th FA	4/16	1/5	0/0	5/33	0/2	10/41	1/8	0/0	3/2	24	107
314th FA	6/13	0/3	0/1	5/16	0/2	6/25	2/10	0/0	0/4	22	74
315th FA	0/5	1/0	0/0	3/1	0/2	4/15	2/11	0/0	0/3	10	37
905th FA	2/4	0/4	0/0	2/13	0/1	2/27	0/10	0/0	0/1	6	60
80th Rcn Tr	0/10	0/0	0/1	0/2	0/2	1/21	0/9	0/0	0/10	2	55
305th Eng Bn	1/30	1/2	0/0	5/40	0/0	2/74	1/8	0/0	1/13	11	167
305th Med Bn	0/8	0/0	0/0	0/6	0/1	0/11	1/5	0/0	1/0	2	31
Grand Totals	139/2785	32/356	0/4	148/2679	9/115	297/6622	67/2080	0/17	89/3199	781	17857

KIA-Killed in Action...DOW-Died of Wounds...DOI-Died of Injuries
SWA-Seriously Wounded in Action...SIA-Serious Injured in Action
LWA-Lightly Wounded in Action... CAP-Captured...MIA-Missing in Action
OFF-Officers...EM-Enlisted Men

Of the above 89/3199 MIA's, all but 12 returned to duty.
Of the MIA's captured, Morning Reports show 1077 captured with 1069 later returning to Military control. The Records I worked from show 2924 KIA, 114 less than other Records later found.

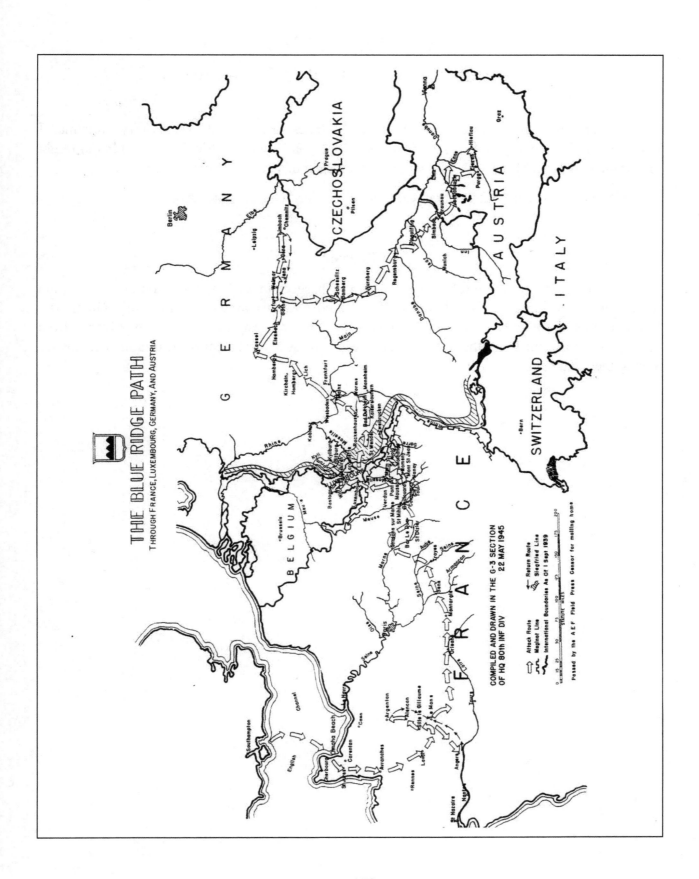

173

Christmas... 1944
Headquarters Third United States Army

To each officer and soldier in the Third United States Army, I wish you a Merry Christmas. I have full confidence in your courage, devotion to duty, and skill in battle. We march in our might to complete victory. May God's blessing rest upon each of you this Christmas Day.

G. S. Patton, Lieutenant General, Commanding Third United States Army

Prayer

Almighty and most merciful Father, we humbly beseech thee of thy great goodness to restrain these immoderate rains with which we have to contend. Grant us fair weather for Battle. Graciously hearken to us as soldiers, who call upon thee that armed with thy power, we may advance from victory to victory, and crush the oppression and wickedness of our enemies and establish thy justice among men and nations. Amen

About the Author

Robert T. Murrell served as Secretary of the 80th Division Veterans Association for 16 years. In that capacity, he edited and published the quarterly news magazine of the Association, THE BLUE RIDGE. His writing skills have resulted in the publication along with co-editor Edgar Bredbenner, who helped to write the first ever 80TH INFANTRY DIVISION HISTORY. Also, several books about the infantries of the 80 Division during WW II, as well as a compilation of individual stories of men who served in the various companies of the Division. He long had the desire to write the history of the entire 80th Division for the period 1942-1945, and at the age of 91, began the task of doing just that. In 2007, he was appointed as the Association's Historian and acquired the documentation that had been held by his predecessor, enabling him to chronicle the day-to-day activities of the 80th Infantry Division, E.T.O. Mr. Murrell has visited the battlefields four times, gathering writing material on each visit.

Mr. Murrell was born on May 19, 1916, in Louisville, KY, the son of Emmett and Annie Murrell. His father was a ready-to-wear salesman and his mother a housewife. At the outbreak of the war in Europe (after serving in the Army Air Corp Reserve, and being discharged in 1941), he enlisted in the Army and received basic training at Camp Forrest, TN with other members of the 80th Division. He was assigned to Company M 318th Infantry. While serving in that unit as a Heavy Machine Gun Section Sergeant, he was awarded the Silver Star, Bronze Star with "V" Clasp and two Oak Leaf Clusters, American Defense, American Campaign, Good Conduct, ETO, Armed Forces, Army of Occupation Medals, Combat Infantry, and Expert Infantry Badges. He also wears the Expert Pistol, Rifle, and Machine Guns Badges.

On April 16 1942, he married Doris (Bell) Murrell and they are the parents of Robert J. and Gayle C. Murrell. He retired in 1972, after being employed in the Rotogravure Printing Field as Plant Superintendent.

Mr. Murrell is a life member of the VFW, Church Member, and The Elks Organization.

Also available by this author are:

- 317th Infantry Regiment History
- 318th Infantry Regiment History
- 319th Infantry Regiment History
- 80th Division Operational History
- The Stories of the Men of the 80th
- The Blue Ridge Division Answers the Call

CPSIA information can be obtained
at www.ICGtesting.com
Printed in the USA
LVHW01s1435201217
560369LV00013B/635/P

9 781516 978205